21世纪高职高专规划教材

高等职业教育规划教材编委会专家审定

# 电子技术专业英语

主　编　周国娟　金红莉
副主编　苏福根　吕殿基

北京邮电大学出版社
www.buptpress.com

## 内 容 简 介

本书涉及电子元器件、仪器仪表、集成电路、数据手册、电子应用、EDA 软件、3G 通信和微机等专业英语资料。书中还介绍了专业英语的基础知识、翻译技巧、应用文体等内容，为读者系统了解、掌握并熟练运用专业英语奠定基础。在书的后面附有译文、电子类专业词汇、EDA 软件菜单的中英文对照、参考答案和专业词汇索引，便于读者查阅。

本书可作为各类高等职业院校电子信息技术专业及相关专业的英语教材，也可供相关技术人员参考。

## 图书在版编目(CIP)数据

电子技术专业英语 / 周国娟,金红莉主编. --北京：北京邮电大学出版社，2012.8(2022.12 重印)
ISBN 978-7-5635-3131-8

Ⅰ.①电… Ⅱ.①周…②金… Ⅲ.①电子技术—英语—高等职业教育—教材 Ⅳ.①H31

中国版本图书馆 CIP 数据核字(2012)第 156403 号

| | |
|---|---|
| 书　　　名：| 电子技术专业英语 |
| 主　　编：| 周国娟　金红莉 |
| 责任编辑：| 王晓丹　马晓仟 |
| 出版发行：| 北京邮电大学出版社 |
| 社　　　址：| 北京市海淀区西土城路 10 号(邮编：100876) |
| 发 行 部：| 电话：010-62282185　传真：010-62283578 |
| E-mail：| publish@bupt.edu.cn |
| 经　　销：| 各地新华书店 |
| 印　　刷：| 北京九州迅驰传媒文化有限公司 |
| 开　　本：| 787 mm×1 092 mm　1/16 |
| 印　　张：| 12.5 |
| 字　　数：| 311 千字 |
| 版　　次：| 2012 年 8 月第 1 版　2022 年 12 月第 6 次印刷 |

ISBN 978-7-5635-3131-8　　　　　　　　　　　　　　　定　价：26.00 元

·如有印装质量问题,请与北京邮电大学出版社发行部联系·

# 前　言

　　电子信息技术已渗透到人们工作和生活的各个方面。社会对专业人才的英语水平要求也越来越高，电子信息英语也随之独立成为一门专业外语，并在电子信息技术应用中发挥巨大的交流作用。一个电子信息方面的人才除了要掌握电子信息科学的基本理论和技能外，更重要的是具备快速获取新的信息科学方面知识的能力。而电子信息英语（尤其是阅读能力）则是体现这种能力的一个重要方面。

　　本着使学生在学完基础英语之后能掌握本专业相关的科技英语词汇，掌握科技英语的构词法、句法特点及翻译、理解技巧，提高阅读、翻译和理解专业英语资料的能力的宗旨，本书在结构、内容安排等方面，吸收了电子信息行业部分工程人员的工作经验和编者在教学改革、教材建设等方面的经验，结合电子技术专业知识和科技英语基本翻译、阅读方法，力求体现高等职业教育的实用性特点，内容选取与新技术紧密结合，满足当前教学改革的需要。

　　本教材内容共包含10个单元，每一个单元为一个学习情境，按照难易程度依次递进的思路设计的。并结合专业、实际的器件、仪器、电路、应用来进行组织。让学生在专业英文资料的阅读中去了解器件特点、仪器使用、电路设计和实际应用；在应用中来加强对专业词汇的掌握、英文资料的翻译和理解能力。通过对不用的学习情境的学习，反复训练，培养学生阅读并理解简单专业英语资料的能力；培养简单的专业英语交流的能力；能借助词典阅读中等难度的英文专业资料，并正确理解和翻译；拓展学生运用英语进行交际的范围和继续学习的能力。

　　在教学过程中，我们了解到学生在学完"大学英语"课程后，虽然已具有一定的英语阅读能力，但在阅读专业英语时还会遇到不少困难。主要原因有：对专业英语词汇不熟悉，专业资料接触太少，不熟悉英语科技文章的结构和体裁。针对学生遇到的这些困难，我们在编写过程中力求体现下列特点。

　　（1）易读性：本书的取材多选自专业资料，语句原味，不仅表达简练、顺畅、纯正，而且具有一定的趣味性，有较强的可读性和易读性。

　　（2）目标明确：在每单元课文之前，确定了本单元的知识目标和能力目标，提供了与课文内容相关的讨论问题，以使学生对课文知识有所了解，更主要的是给学生更多的发挥想象的空间，并营造以学生为主体的教学环境，促进学生的自主学习。

　　（3）图文并茂：本书加入了大量的真实的照片，来加深学生对实际的器件、仪器、设备、产品、软件等的感性认识，加深理解。

　　（4）教学做一体：根据高职的教育目标和高职学生特点，本着实用的原则，本教材针对实际的器件、仪器、设备、产品、软件等而设计的，在教学过程中可结合实物来实施教学，边讲解、边操作、边学习、边理解，来实现教学做一体，以适应教学改革的需要，提高教学效果。

（5）注重应用：以电子技术专业英语的应用为主线，每个单元均针对本单元的英语资料设计了"具体应用"来进行实际操作，使学生在阅读完专业英语资料后能根据所得信息进行应用，让学生实际动手去做，在做中学。大大地提高了学生的学习兴趣。使学生在学习过程中不会感到枯燥、乏味。

本书内容共分 10 个单元，每个单元包括课文、专业词汇、阅读材料、翻译知识、应用能力和拓展练习。在书的最后附有译文、电子类词汇、EDA 软件菜单中英文对照、课后练习参考答案，便于学生学习巩固。考虑到具体的教学安排和教学对象，教师可根据需要对教材内容进行取舍。

本书主编周国娟、金红莉，副主编苏福根、吕殿基，参编吴新杰、熊国灿。审稿付丽琴教授、吕殿基副教授。

限于编者的学识水平与实践经验，书中不足之处在所难免，恳请广大读者批评指正。主编邮箱：zhouguojuan2004@163.com。

编 者

# Contents

Unit 1  Introduction ·················································································· 1
  1.1  Text ······························································································ 1
    1.1.1  History about Electronics ·············································· 1
    1.1.2  Electronic Major ························································· 2
    1.1.3  Introduction to Some Courses ········································ 3
  1.2  Reading Materials ········································································ 5
  1.3  Knowledge(专业英语特点) ····························································· 6
  1.4  Exercises ····················································································· 7

Unit 2  Components ················································································· 9
  2.1  Text ······························································································ 9
    2.1.1  Resistors ······································································· 9
    2.1.2  Capacitors ··································································· 11
    2.1.3  Inductors ····································································· 13
    2.1.4  Semiconductor Diode ··················································· 13
    2.1.5  NPN Bipolar Transistor ··············································· 15
  2.2  Reading Materials ······································································ 18
    2.2.1  Nonlinear Resistors ····················································· 18
    2.2.2  The Transistor as a Switch ·········································· 19
  2.3  Application ················································································ 21
  2.4  Knowledge(专业词汇) ·································································· 21
  2.5  Exercises ··················································································· 23

Unit 3  Instruments ················································································ 24
  3.1  Text ···························································································· 24
    3.1.1  Multimeters ································································· 24
    3.1.2  The Digital Oscilloscope ·············································· 25
  3.2  Reading Materials ······································································ 30

3.2.1　Analog Oscilloscope …………………………………………………… 30
　　3.2.2　Signal Generator ………………………………………………………… 32
　3.3　Application ………………………………………………………………………… 32
　3.4　Knowledge(词义) ………………………………………………………………… 33
　3.5　Exercises …………………………………………………………………………… 34

Unit 4　Integrated Circuit ……………………………………………………………… 36
　4.1　Text ………………………………………………………………………………… 36
　　4.1.1　Information on Integrated Circuits ……………………………………… 36
　　4.1.2　Bipolar Integrated Circuits & MOS Integrated Circuits …………… 38
　　4.1.3　The Process of IC Design ……………………………………………… 38
　4.2　Reading Materials ………………………………………………………………… 39
　4.3　Application ………………………………………………………………………… 40
　4.4　Knowledge(翻译技巧1——被动语态) ………………………………………… 41
　4.5　Exercises …………………………………………………………………………… 42

Unit 5　Datasheet ………………………………………………………………………… 44
　5.1　Text ………………………………………………………………………………… 44
　　5.1.1　DM74LS194A Datasheet ………………………………………………… 44
　　5.1.2　NE555 Datasheet ………………………………………………………… 47
　5.2　Reading Materials ………………………………………………………………… 49
　5.3　Application ………………………………………………………………………… 50
　5.4　Knowledge(翻译技巧2——长句翻译) ………………………………………… 51
　5.5　Exercises …………………………………………………………………………… 51

Unit 6　User Manual …………………………………………………………………… 53
　6.1　Text ………………………………………………………………………………… 53
　　6.1.1　Introduction to iPhone 4 ………………………………………………… 53
　　6.1.2　iPhone User Guide ……………………………………………………… 54
　6.2　Reading Materials ………………………………………………………………… 58
　6.3　Knowledge(用户使用说明书) …………………………………………………… 60
　6.4　Exercises …………………………………………………………………………… 61

Unit 7　Appliances ……………………………………………………………………… 63
　7.1　Text ………………………………………………………………………………… 63
　　7.1.1　Television ………………………………………………………………… 63
　　7.1.2　Refrigerator ……………………………………………………………… 66

7.2　Reading Materials ……………………………………………………………………… 68
   7.2.1　Digital TV …………………………………………………………………… 68
   7.2.2　The Microwave Oven ………………………………………………………… 69
7.3　Application ………………………………………………………………………… 70
7.4　Knowledge(求职信) ………………………………………………………………… 71
7.5　Exercises …………………………………………………………………………… 74

**Unit 8　EDA Software** …………………………………………………………………… 76

8.1　Text ………………………………………………………………………………… 76
   8.1.1　Quartus II …………………………………………………………………… 76
   8.1.2　Protel ………………………………………………………………………… 80
8.2　Reading Materials ………………………………………………………………… 84
8.3　Application ………………………………………………………………………… 86
8.4　Knowledge(求学信) ………………………………………………………………… 87
8.5　Exercises …………………………………………………………………………… 87

**Unit 9　3G** ………………………………………………………………………………… 89

9.1　Text ………………………………………………………………………………… 89
9.2　Reading Materials ………………………………………………………………… 91
   9.2.1　The Cell Approach …………………………………………………………… 91
   9.2.2　The Phone's Internal Structure ……………………………………………… 92
9.3　Knowledge(摘要) …………………………………………………………………… 93
9.4　Exercises …………………………………………………………………………… 95

**Unit 10　Microcomputers** ……………………………………………………………… 97

10.1　Text ………………………………………………………………………………… 97
   10.1.1　Basic Computer …………………………………………………………… 97
   10.1.2　The Motherboard …………………………………………………………… 98
   10.1.3　The System Bus …………………………………………………………… 98
   10.1.4　Main Memory ……………………………………………………………… 99
   10.1.5　BIOS (Basic Input/Output System) ……………………………………… 99
10.2　Reading Materials ………………………………………………………………… 101
10.3　Application ………………………………………………………………………… 104
10.4　Knowledge(科技论文写作知识) …………………………………………………… 105
10.5　Exercises …………………………………………………………………………… 107

**Appendix 1　译文** ………………………………………………………………………… 109

UNIT 1　电子技术简介 ……………………………………………………………………… 109

1.1 文章 ………………………………………………………………………………… 109
　1.1.1 电子技术的历史 …………………………………………………………… 109
　1.1.2 电子专业介绍 ……………………………………………………………… 109
　1.1.3 课程介绍 …………………………………………………………………… 110
1.2 阅读材料 ……………………………………………………………………… 111

UNIT 2　元件 ………………………………………………………………………… 111
2.1 文章 …………………………………………………………………………… 111
　2.1.1 电阻器 ……………………………………………………………………… 111
　2.1.2 电容器 ……………………………………………………………………… 112
　2.1.3 电感器 ……………………………………………………………………… 112
　2.1.4 半导体二极管 ……………………………………………………………… 113
　2.1.5 NPN双极型晶体管 ………………………………………………………… 113
2.2 阅读材料 ……………………………………………………………………… 114
　2.2.1 非线性电阻器 ……………………………………………………………… 114
　2.2.2 三极管用作开关 …………………………………………………………… 114

UNIT 3　仪器仪表 …………………………………………………………………… 115
3.1 文章 …………………………………………………………………………… 115
　3.1.1 万用表 ……………………………………………………………………… 115
　3.1.2 数字示波器 ………………………………………………………………… 116
3.2 阅读材料 ……………………………………………………………………… 119
　3.2.1 模拟示波器 ………………………………………………………………… 119
　3.2.2 信号发生器 ………………………………………………………………… 119

UNIT 4　集成电路 …………………………………………………………………… 120
4.1 文章 …………………………………………………………………………… 120
　4.1.1 关于集成电路 ……………………………………………………………… 120
　4.1.2 双极型(晶体管)集成电路和MOS集成电路 …………………………… 121
　4.1.3 集成电路的设计过程 ……………………………………………………… 121
4.2 阅读材料 ……………………………………………………………………… 121

UNIT 5　数据手册 …………………………………………………………………… 122
5.1 文章 …………………………………………………………………………… 122
　5.1.1 DM74LS194A数据手册 …………………………………………………… 122
　5.1.2 NE555数据手册 …………………………………………………………… 123
5.2 阅读材料 ……………………………………………………………………… 124

UNIT 6　用户使用手册 ……………………………………………………………… 125
6.1 文章 …………………………………………………………………………… 125
　6.1.1 iPhone 4介绍 ……………………………………………………………… 125
　6.1.2 iPhone用户使用手册 ……………………………………………………… 126

6.2　阅读材料 ……………………………………………………………………………… 127
UNIT 7　应用 …………………………………………………………………………………… 128
　7.1　文章 …………………………………………………………………………………… 128
　　7.1.1　电视 ……………………………………………………………………………… 128
　　7.1.2　关于冰箱 ………………………………………………………………………… 130
　7.2　阅读材料 ……………………………………………………………………………… 131
　　7.2.1　数字电视 ………………………………………………………………………… 131
　　7.2.2　微波炉 …………………………………………………………………………… 131
UNIT 8　EDA 软件 ……………………………………………………………………………… 132
　8.1　文章 …………………………………………………………………………………… 132
　　8.1.1　Quartus II ………………………………………………………………………… 132
　　8.1.2　Protel ……………………………………………………………………………… 134
　8.2　阅读材料 ……………………………………………………………………………… 135
UNIT 9　3G ……………………………………………………………………………………… 135
　9.1　文章 …………………………………………………………………………………… 135
　9.2　阅读材料 ……………………………………………………………………………… 137
　　9.2.1　手机(蜂窝)技术 ………………………………………………………………… 137
　　9.2.2　手机的内部结构 ………………………………………………………………… 137
UNIT 10　微机 ………………………………………………………………………………… 138
　10.1　文章 ………………………………………………………………………………… 138
　　10.1.1　基本型计算机 …………………………………………………………………… 138
　　10.1.2　主板 ……………………………………………………………………………… 138
　　10.1.3　系统总线 ………………………………………………………………………… 139
　　10.1.4　主存(内存) ……………………………………………………………………… 139
　　10.1.5　BIOS(基本输入/输出系统) ……………………………………………………… 140
　10.2　阅读材料 …………………………………………………………………………… 140

**Appendix 2**　电子类专业英语词汇 …………………………………………………………… 143
**Appendix 3**　Quartus II Menu 中英文对照 ……………………………………………………… 159
**Appendix 4**　Protel 部分分立元件名称及菜单中英文对照 …………………………………… 165
**Appendix 5**　参考答案 ………………………………………………………………………… 173
**Appendix 6**　技术词汇索引 …………………………………………………………………… 181
**参考文献** ……………………………………………………………………………………………… 190

# Unit 1  Introduction

 Knowledge aims:

1. Technology English characteristics.
2. Translation skills.
3. Understand the electronic technology.

 Ability aims:

Can translate the professional literature.

 Pre-reading

Read the following passage, paying attention to the questions.
1. Who invented the transistor?
2. What courses should a student majoring in electronics study?
3. What career will a student majoring in electronic technology follow?

## 1.1  Text

### 1.1.1  History about Electronics

Fifties and sixties in the 20th century, the most representative of the advanced electronic technology is wireless technology, including radio broadcasting, radio, wireless communications (telegraph), amateur radio, radio positioning, navigation and other telemetry, remote control, remote technology. Early that these electronic technology led many young people into the wonderful digital world, radio technology showed a wonderful life, the prospects for science and technology. Electronics began to form a new discipline. Radio electronics, wireless communications began e-world journey.

The early radio technology promotes the development of electronic technology, foremost of which is from electronic vacuum tube technology to semiconductor electronic technology. Semiconductor electronics technology enables active devices to micro-miniaturization and low cost radio technology with greater popularity and innovation, and greatly broadened the field of non-radio control.

At the time of the invention of the transistor in 1947 by John Bardeen, Walter

Brattain, and William Shockley, the only way to assemble multiple transistors into a single circuit was to buy separate discrete transistors and wire them together. In 1959, Jack Kilby and Robert Noyce independently invented a means of fabricating multiple transistors on a single slab of semiconductor material. Their invention would come to be known as the integrated circuit, or IC, which is the foundation of our modern computerized world. An IC is so called because it integrates multiple transistors and diodes onto the same small semiconductor chip. Instead of having to solder individual wires between discrete components, an IC contains many small components that are already wired together in the desired topology to form a circuit. A large number of digital logic circuits, such as gates, counters, timers, shift registers, and analog switches, comparators, etc. provide excellent conditions for the electronic digital control, transforming the traditional mechanical control to electronic control.

70 years into the 20th century, large scale integrated circuit appeared to promote the conventional electronic circuit unit to specific electronic systems development. Many dedicated electronic system units into the integrated devices such as radios, electronic clocks, calculators. The work of electronic engineers in these areas is changed from the circuit, the system designed to debug into the device selection, peripheral device adapter. Electronic technology and electronic products enabled electronic engineers to reduce the difficulty.

### 1.1.2 Electronic Major

The training objective of electron techology major: the major trains the students who will adapt to a twenty-first century developing need, have improvement in terms of moral, intellectual and fitness level as well as appreciation of aesthetics. Get to know theoretical foundations of electron science and technology, signal analysis and processing and auto-control, etc. Based on circuit analysis and synthesis design capabilities and microprocessor (monolithic machine, programming controller PLC, embedded system, etc.), students will be more proficient in the use of EDA technology and modern computer electronics design and production technology, and can be engaged in a variety of practical electronic devices or products, development, and design. Cultivate the high-tech application professionals with strong innovative ability and practical ability.

Major courses: Engineering Drawing and CAD, Protel Technology, Computer System and Application, C Language Programming, Electrical and Electronic Technology, Circuit Synthesize Design, Radio Circuit, Microcontroller Theory and Applications, Embedded Systems, EDA Technology, Microprocessor Application Development and Production, Principles of Automatic Control, PLC Technology and Applications, Signal Analysis and Processing, Power Electronics, Household Electrical and Electronic Equipment and Maintenance, Modern Communications Technology, Professional English, etc.

Graduates of this major can gain the following knowledge and ability.

(1) Have theories, professional knowledge and basic skills of applying electron technology.

(2) Have the analysis ability, developing, keeping the electron product and the electronic equipment in repair, stronger computer application ability. Know how to monitor instrument performance in the commercial run, and develop, design and repair domestic appliances and master EDA technology.

(3) Master the document retrieval, inquiring method, have the certain English document reading ability, and have certain special field capability of sustainable development.

### 1.1.3 Introduction to Some Courses

As a student majoring in electronic technology, you will study many courses such as,

**1. Direct Current (DC) Circuits & Alternating Current (AC) Circuits**

This course covers the fundamental theory of passive devices (resistor, capacitor and inductor) and electrical networks supplied by a DC source, and then an introduction to the effects of alternating voltage and current in passive electrical circuits is given. This module also covers DC machines, three phase circuits and transformers.

**2. Analog Electronics**

This module introduces the characteristics of semiconductor devices in a range of linear applications and electronic circuits consisting of these devices (Fig 1.1). The following specific topics are covered.

Fig 1.1  Electronic circuits

- Semiconductor diodes: PN junction diodes, special purpose diodes
- Transistors: field effect and bipolar transistors
- Signal amplifiers: practical amplifiers, biasing circuits, operational amplifiers circuit
- Other circuits: rectification, regulation and DC power supplies

**3. Digital Electronics**

In this unit, the following topics are covered.

- basic concepts about logic circuits
- number representations
- combinatorial logic circuits

- sequential logic circuits
- CMOS digital circuits
- logic operations theorems and Boolean algebra
- number operations (binary, hex and integers)
- combinatorial logic analysis and synthesis
- sequential logic analysis and synthesis
- registers
- counters
- bus systems
- CAD tools for logic design

**4. Microcontroller Systems**

The use of computers and microcontrollers is now found in every field of the electronic industry. This use will continue to grow at a rapid pace as computers become more complex and powerful. The ability to program these devices will make a student an invaluable talent to the growing electronic industry. This module enables the students to program a simple microcontroller to perform typical industrial tasks. Assembler and C are used to program the MPU (Microprocessor Unit). The students will set up the internal devices such as RS232 port, timer, interrupts, counters, I/O ports, ADC etc. The program will then use these devices for control operations.

**5. Computer Programming for Engineering Applications**

It is a continuation of more advanced programming techniques. The language of C will be used for teaching purposes. Emphasis is towards the use of programming for engineering applications and problem solving. The electronic technology will provide a sound educational foundation to enable graduates to follow a career in electrical engineering, power and control engineering, electronic technology computer engineering, telecommunications engineering etc.

# Technical Words and Phrases

| | | | |
|---|---|---|---|
| electronics | [ilek'trɔniks] | n. | 电子学 |
| representative | [repri'zentətiv] | adj. | 代表性的,典型的 |
| telegraph | ['teligrɑf] | n. | 电报,电信 |
| telemetry | [ti'lemitri] | n. | 遥测技术,测距术 |
| digital | ['didʒitəl] | adj. | 数字的 |
| vacuum | ['vækjuəm] | n. | 真空 |
| tube | [tju:b] | n. | 管 |
| semiconductor | [ˌsemikən'dʌktə] | n. | 半导体 |
| miniaturization | [ˌminiətʃərai'zeiʃən] | n. | 小型化;微型化 |
| innovation | [inəu'veiʃən] | n. | 革新,改革,创新 |

| | | | |
|---|---|---|---|
| assemble | [əˈsembl] | vt. | 集合,召集,聚集;配装,装 |
| circuit | [ˈsəːkit] | n. | 电路;回路;线路图 |
| slab | [slæb] | n. | 厚板,平板;厚片 |
| solder | [ˈsɔldə] | vt. | 焊接 |
| topology | [təuˈpɔlədʒi] | n. | 拓扑数学 |
| analog | [ˈænəlɔːg] | n. | 模拟 |
| sensor | [ˈsensə] | n. | 传感器 |
| servo | [ˈsəːvəu] | n. | 伺服电动机 |
| scale | [skeil] | n. | 比率;缩尺 |
| adapter | [əˈdæptə] | n. | 接合器;转接器 |
| communication | [kəˌmjuːniˈkeiʃən] | n. | 讯息;通信 |
| promote | [prəˈməut] | vt. | 促进;发扬;引起 |
| major | [ˈmeidʒə] | adj. | 主要的 |
| | | n. | 主修科目,专业 |
| microprocessor | [maikrəuˈprəusesə] | n. | 微处理机 |
| dyadic | [daiˈædik] | adj. | 二价的;双值的;双积的;二数的 |
| pragmatism | [ˈprægmətizəm] | n. | 实用主义;实际观察 |
| innovative | [ˈinəuveitiv] | adj. | 创新的 |
| comparatively | [kəmˈpærətivli] | adv. | 对比地;比较地 |
| synthesize | [ˈsinθisaiz] | vt. | 综合;合成;(使)合成 |
| monolithic | [mɔnəˈliθik] | adj. | 整体的;庞大的 |
| instrument | [ˈinstrumənt] | n. | 仪器;器具 |
| commercial | [kəˈməːʃəl] | adj. | 商业的,商务的 |
| retrieval | [riˈtriːvəl] | n. | 纠正;补偿 |

## 1.2 Reading Materials

### Do You Know These Electronic Systems

Some electronic systems are familiar from everyday life. For example, we encounter radios, televisions, telephones, and computers on a daily basis. Other electronic systems are present in daily life, but are less obvious. Electronic systems are used in automobiles to control fuel mixture and ignition timing to maximize performance and minimize undesirable emissions from automobile engines. Electronics in weather satellites (Fig 1.2) provide us with a continuous detailed picture of our planet.

Other systems are even less familiar. For example, a system of satellites known as the Global Positioning System (GPS) has been developed to provide three-dimensional information for ships, aircrafts and cars anywhere on the earth. This is possible because signals emitted by several satellites can be received by the vehicle, by comparing the time of arrival of the signals and by using certain information contained in the received signals concerning the orbits of the satellites, the position of the vehicle can be determined.

Fig 1.2 Weather satellites

Other electronic systems include the air-traffic control system, various radars, compact-disc (CD) recording equipment and players, manufacturing control systems, and navigation systems.

## 1.3 Knowledge(专业英语特点)

**一、专业英语与基础英语不同**

专业英语专业性极强,这种专业性是一种综合能力的体现,绝非"普通英语知识加专业词汇"那么简单。翻译专业英语时只有把英语知识、专业知识、汉语运用能力及英汉两种语言的异同结合起来统筹考虑才能得到较为准确的翻译结果。

Eg:The thermistor is a ceramic semiconductor bead, rod or disk.

普通英语翻译:热敏电阻是一种陶瓷半导体圆珠、圆棒或圆片。

专业英语翻译:热敏电子是一种陶瓷半导体器件,它(一般)被做成圆珠形、圆棒形或圆片形。

按普通英语翻译时这句话把热敏电阻翻译成了圆珠、圆棒或圆片,而不是半导体器件。显然从专业角度来讲,其逻辑上是错误的。

专业英语至少应包括以下四个方面的能力要求。

**1. 懂英语**

即要求具备相当的英语知识与能力,包括词法、语法、文法等以及基本的英语背景知识。

**2. 具备必要的、准确的、较全面的专业知识**

既要求在汉语环境下具备正确、丰富的专业知识及一定的专业技能,同时又具有相关的专业英语词汇、句型、方法等。

**3. 娴熟的汉语表达能力**

即要求运用汉语的能力要熟练、流畅、准确。

**4．英语、汉语两种语言间的融通能力**

即要求对两种语言间的差异与共性有必备的了解,进而能够自如、准确、流畅地进行语言转换。

"专业英语"就是这四项能力的综合运用。

二、专业英语特点

**1．语言表达的规范性和逻辑性**

在专业英语的运用中,尽量保持书面专业英语中的完整、严谨等特点,采用近似于书面表述的口语表达方式,很少采用日常口语中的非正式用语。

**2．专业英语所使用的词汇具有统一性与稳定性**

(1) 纯专业性词汇都是随科技发展而新创建出来的,多见于新的学科中,词义单一。如diode(二极管),radar(雷达),laser(激光),ohm(欧姆)等。

(2) 纯科技性符号、公式等,一般只用在专业文章中。

(3) 专业上专用的一些缩略语,如PC(个人计算机),IC(集成电路),AC(交流电路),AM(调幅),CAD(计算机辅助设计),EDA(电子设计自动化),PCB(印制电路板)等。

**3．专业英语表达上的客观性**

专业英语中论述者在意思表达上努力避免出现基于主观性或个人行为的表述形式,尽量采用一种非个人化的表述方式,目的是力求体现出科技知识的客观性与科学性。实现这一表述方式的具体方法除了尽量采用仪器仪表读数、有依据的数字等来表述外,语言结构上还经常采用"被动语态"、"祈使句"等句子结构。

**4．专业英语论述的严谨性与逻辑性**

严谨性与逻辑性是专业英语的核心。

# 1.4 Exercises

Ⅰ．**Translate the following phrases and expressions**

1. 电子技术
2. 无线通信
3. 计算机工程
4. 组合逻辑电路
5. DC source
6. signal amplifier
7. integrated circuit
8. sequential logic circuits
9. radio technology computer engineering
10. alternating current circuits

Ⅱ．**Translate the following sentences into Chinese**

1. Would you go to a pop concert that had no amplifiers, large screens or lighting effects?

2. The credit goes to the British engineer John Logic Baird who followed the footprints of Marconi and tried to send the images in the same way as the speech.

3. The real electronics what it is called today actually started after the discovery of the transistor effect.

4. Surprisingly his ideas worked and gave birth to the integrated circuit industries.

5. This module introduces the characteristics of semiconductor devices in a range of linear applications.

6. The use of computers and microcontrollers is now found in every field of the electronics industry.

7. This module enables the students to program a simple microcontroller to perform typical industrial tasks.

8. The program will then use these devices for control operations.

9. Emphasis is towards the use of programming for engineering applications and problem solving.

10. The electronic technology will provide a sound educational foundation to enable graduates to follow a career in electrical engineering.

# Unit 2　Components

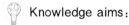  Knowledge aims:

1. Professional glossary.
2. Components datasheet.
3. Glossary.

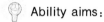  Ability aims:

Can read components materials.

  Pre-reading

Read the following passage, paying attention to the questions.
1. What is a resistor?
2. What is Ohm Law?
3. What is a capacitor and what is an inductor?
4. What is a semiconductor diode?

## 2.1　Text

### 2.1.1　Resistors

A resistor is an electrical component that resists the flow of electrical current. The amount of current ($I$) flowing in a circuit is directly proportional to the voltage across it and inversely proportional to the resistance of the circuit. This is Ohm Law and can be expressed as a formula: $I = \dfrac{U_R}{R}$. The resistor is generally a linear device and its characteristics form a straight line when plotted on a graph.

Resistors are used to limit current flowing to a device, thereby preventing it from burning out, as voltage dividers to reduce voltage for other circuits, such as transistor biasing circuits, and to serve as circuit loads.

Generally, resistors (Fig 2.1) consist of carbon composition, wire-wound, and metal film. The size of resistors depends on power ratings. Larger sizes are referred to as power resistors. Variable resistors are adjustable: rheostats, potentiometers, and trimmer pots.

Precision resistors have a tolerance of 1% or less.

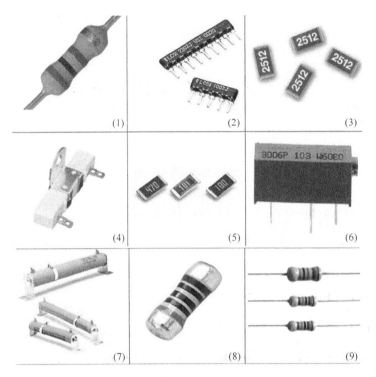

Fig 2.1  Fixed and variable resistors

If you are a bit serious about the electronic technology, I recommend learning the "Color Code". It makes a lot easier. The same color code is used for everything else, like coils, capacitors etc. Again, just a color code associated with a number, like: black=0, brown=1, red=2, etc.

The resistor in Fig 2.2 is a 4-band resistor. The first band is the tens values; the second band gives the units; the third band is a multiplying factor, the factor being 10's band value; the fourth band gives the tolerance of the resistor. No the fourth band implies a tolerance of ±20%, a silver band means the resistor has a tolerance of ±10% and a gold band has the closest tolerance of ±5%.

For a 5-band resistor, the first band is the hundreds values (Fig 2.2), the second band gives the tens, the third band gives units, and the forth band is a multiplying factor, the factor being 10's band value. The colors brown (1%), red (2%), green (0.5%), blue (0.25%), and violet (0.1%) are used as tolerance codes on 5-band resistors only. All 5-band resistors use a colored tolerance band.

Can you "create" your own resistors? Of course and not difficult. Here is how to do it. Draw a line on a piece of paper with a soft pencil (HB or 2HB will be better). Make the line thick and about 2 inches (5 cm) long. With your multimeter, measure the ohm's value of this line by putting a probe on each side of the line; make sure the probes are touching the carbon from the pencil. The value would probably be around 800 kΩ to 1.5 MΩ depending on the thickness line. The resistance will drop considerably, if you erase some of it (length-wise obviously!). You can also use carbon with silicon glue and when it dries, measure the resistance, etc.

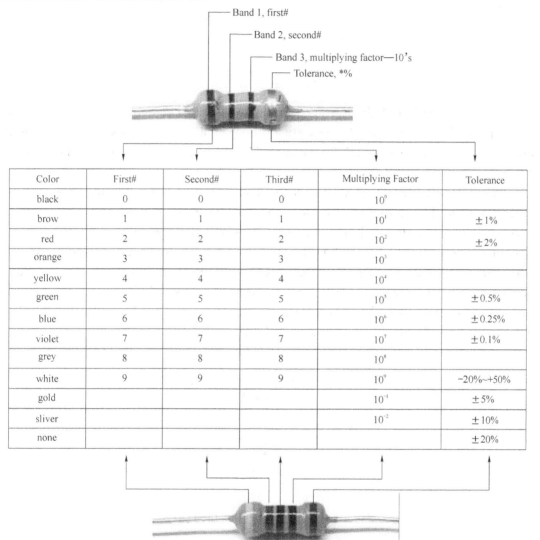

| Color | First# | Second# | Third# | Multiplying Factor | Tolerance |
|---|---|---|---|---|---|
| black | 0 | 0 | 0 | $10^0$ | |
| brow | 1 | 1 | 1 | $10^1$ | ±1% |
| red | 2 | 2 | 2 | $10^2$ | ±2% |
| orange | 3 | 3 | 3 | $10^3$ | |
| yellow | 4 | 4 | 4 | $10^4$ | |
| green | 5 | 5 | 5 | $10^5$ | ±0.5% |
| blue | 6 | 6 | 6 | $10^6$ | ±0.25% |
| violet | 7 | 7 | 7 | $10^7$ | ±0.1% |
| grey | 8 | 8 | 8 | $10^8$ | |
| white | 9 | 9 | 9 | $10^9$ | −20%~+50% |
| gold | | | | $10^{-1}$ | ±5% |
| sliver | | | | $10^{-2}$ | ±10% |
| none | | | | | ±20% |

Fig 2.2  An example of resistor color code

### 2.1.2 Capacitors

A capacitor is an electrical device that can temporarily store electrical energy. Basically, a capacitor consists of two conductors (metal plates) separated by a dielectric insulating material (Fig 2.3(a)), which increases the ability to store a charge. The dielectric can be paper, plastic film, mica, ceramic, air or vacuum. The plates can be aluminum discs, aluminum foil or a thin film of metal applied to opposite sides of a solid dielectric. The conductor-dielectric-conductor sandwich can be rolled into a cylinder or left flat. The symbols of capacitor are shown in Fig 2.3(b).

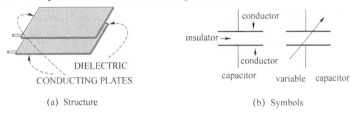

(a) Structure  (b) Symbols

Fig 2.3  Capacitor structure symbols

A capacitor will block DC current, but appears to pass AC current by charging and discharging. It develops an AC resistance, known as capacitive reactance, which is affected by the capacitance and AC frequency. The formula for capacitive reactance is $X_C = 1/(2(f_C C))$, with units of ohms.

Capacitors are available in various shapes and sizes (Fig 2.4). Usually, the value of capacitance and the working DC voltage are marked on them, but some types use a color code similar to resistors. Small-value capacitors of mica and ceramic dielectrics are indicated in pico farads ($10^{-12}$ F), but only the significant digits are shown on the package, for example, 105(Fig 2.4(7)) means $10 \times 10^5$ pF$=1$ $\mu$F. Tuning capacitors (such as used in radio) use air as a dielectric, with one set of plates, which can be rotated in and out of a set of stationary plates. Trimmer capacitors are used for fine adjustment with a screw, and have air, mica and ceramic as dielectrics.

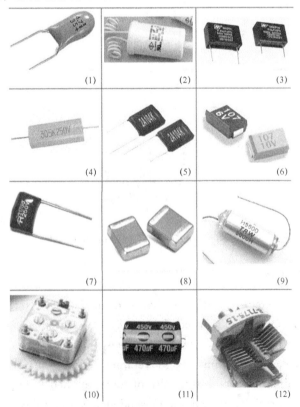

Fig 2.4  Capacitors

## 2.1.3 Inductors

An inductor is an electrical device, which can temporarily store electromagnetic energy in the field about it as long as current is flowing through it. The inductor is a coil of wire that may have an air core or an iron core to increase its inductance. A powered iron core in the shape of a cylinder may be adjusted in and out of the core.

An inductor tends to oppose a change in electrical current; it has no resistance to DC but has an AC resistance to AC, known as inductive reactance, which is affected by inductance and the AC frequency and is given by the formula $X_L=1/(2\pi f_L L)$, with units of ohms. Inductors are used for filtering AC current, increasing the output of the RF (radio frequency) amplifier.

Inductors are available in variety of shapes (Fig 2.5): air core, iron core (which may look like a transformer, but has only two leads), toroidal (doughnut shaped), small tubular with epoxy, RF choke with separate coils on a cylinder, and tunable RF coil with a screwdriver adjustment.

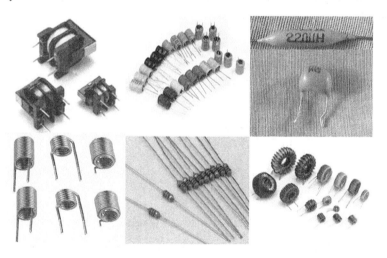

Fig 2.5　Various inductors

## 2.1.4 Semiconductor Diode

A semiconductor diode (refers to diode in short) is the simplest possible semiconductor device. A diode consists of a PN junction made of semiconductor material. The P-type material is called the anode, while the N-type material is called the cathode (Fig 2.6).

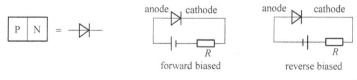

Fig 2.6　Diode

A diode is forward biased when the anode is more positive than the cathode (greater than the turn-on voltage, which is approximately 0.3 V for germanium and 0.7 V for silicon). In this condition, the internal resistance of the diode is low and a large current will flow through the diode (depending on the external circuit resistance).

The diode is reverse biased when the anode is less positive than the cathode. In this case, the internal resistance is extremely high, so perfect diodes can block current in one direction while letting current flow in another direction.

Diodes can be used in a number of ways. For example, a device that uses batteries often contains a diode that protects the device if you insert the batteries backward. The diode simply blocks any current from leaving the battery if it is reversed, which protects the sensitive electronics in the device.

A diode's behavior is not perfect, as shown in Fig 2.7. When reverse-biased, an ideal diode would block all current. A real diode lets perhaps 10 μA through—not a lot, but still not perfect. And if you apply enough reverse voltage (V), the junction breaks down and lets current go through. Usually, the breakdown voltage is a lot more voltage than the circuit will ever see, so it is irrelevant.

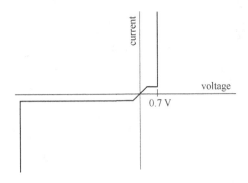

Fig 2.7  A diode's behavior

When forward-biased, there is a small amount of voltage necessary to get the diode going. In silicon, this voltage is about 0.7 V. Though a large forward current can flow through the diode, too much current through the diode in either direction will destroy it.

Some pictures of diodes are given in Fig 2.8.

Fig 2.8  Various diodes

## 2.1.5 NPN Bipolar Transistor

There are two types of standard bipolar transistors, NPN and PNP, with different circuit symbols (Fig 2.9). The letters refer to the layers of semiconductor material used to make the transistor. Most transistors used today are NPN because this is the easiest type to make from silicon.

The NPN bipolar transistor consists of an N-type emitter (E), P-type base (B), and N-type collector (C).

An amplifier can be built with a transistor. Fig 2.10 shows the two current paths through a transistor. You can build this circuit with two standard 5 mm red LEDs and any general purpose low power NPN transistor.

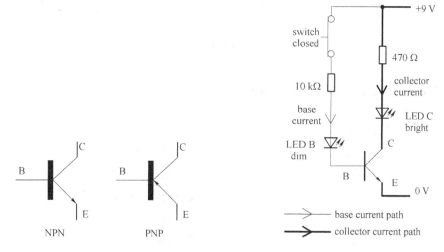

Fig 2.9  Transistor circuit symbols

Fig 2.10  The small current controls the larger current

When the switch is closed, a small current flows into the base (B) of the transistor. It is just enough to make LED B glow dimly. The transistor amplifies this small current to allow a larger current to flow through from its collector (C) to its emitter (E). This collector current is large enough to make LED C light brightly.

The amount of collector current ($I_C$) is directly proportional to the amount of base current ($I_B$) and the collector current ($I_C$) will be less than the emitter current ($I_E$), since a small base current ($I_B$) must flow to turn on the transistor. The relationship of the currents is $I_E = I_C + I_B$. The ratio of $I_C$ to $I_B$ is called the current gain of the transistor and indicates its ability to amplify. This current gain is called beta($\beta$) and is expressed as $\beta = \Delta I_C / \Delta I_B$, when the voltage from C to E ($U_{CE}$) is held constant.

To turn on an NPN bipolar transistor, the base must be more positive than the emitter (about +0.6 V for silicon). When the transistor is turned on hard (in saturation), this voltage is about +0.7 V and the resistance from C to E is low and may even appear almost as a short.

When the switch (Fig 2.10) is open, no base current flows, so the transistor switches off the collector current and both LEDs are off. The resistance from C to E now is high and may appear as an open. Actually a transistor's behavior is not such perfect, a small leakage current ($I_{CBO}$) from C to B is always present and may cause stability problems for a transistor circuit.

Fig 2.11 displays various bipolar transistors.

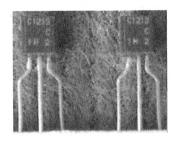

Fig 2.11  Various bipolar transistors

## Technical Words and Phrases

| | | | |
|---|---|---|---|
| reactance | [ri'æktəns] | n. | 电抗 |
| resistance | [ri'zistəns] | n. | [电]电阻值,电阻 |
| resistor | [ri'zistə(r)] | n. | [电]电阻器,电阻 |
| linear | ['liniə] | adj. | 直线的,线状的,线性的 |
| plotted | ['plɔtid] | adj. | 标绘的 |
| carbon | ['kɑ:bən] | adj. | 碳的,碳处理的 |
| | | n. | [化学]碳 |
| precision | [pri'siʒən] | n. | 精度 |
| | | adj. | 精密的,精确的 |
| tolerance | ['tɔlərəns] | n. | 公差 |
| recommend | [rekə'mend] | vt. | 推荐 |
| | | vi. | 推荐;建议 |
| capacitance | [kə'pæsitəns] | n. | 电容量 |
| capacitor | [kə'pæsitə(r)] | n. | (=capacitator)电容器 |
| multimeter | [mʌl'timitə] | n. | [电]万用表 |
| probe | [prəub] | n. | 探针 |
| silicon | ['silikən] | n. | [化学]硅;硅元素 |
| dielectric | [daii'lektrik] | n. | 电介质;绝缘体 |
| mica | ['maikə] | n. | [矿物]云母 |
| ceramic | [si'ræmik] | n. | 陶瓷;陶瓷制品 |
| aluminum | [ə'lju:minəm] | n. | 铝 |

| cylinder | [ˈsilində] | n. | 圆筒；[数]柱面；圆柱状物 |
| screw | [skruː] | n. | 螺旋；螺丝 |
| inductor | [inˈdʌktə] | n. | 感应器；互感，自感 |
| coil | [kɔil] | n. | 线圈；卷 |
| anode | [ˈænəud] | n. | [电]阳极，正极 |
| biased | [ˈbaiəst] | adj. | 偏压的，偏置的 |
| bipolar | [baiˈpəulə(r)] | adj. | 有两极的，双极性的 |
| cathode | [ˈkæθəud] | n. | 负极，阴极 |
| inverter | [inˈvəːtə(r)] | n. | 反相器 |
| leakage | [liːˈkidʒ] | n. | 漏，泄漏，渗漏 |
| polysilicon | [pəliˈsilikən] | n. | 多晶硅 |
| amplifier | [ˈæmplifaiə] | n. | [电子]放大器；扩音器 |
| approximately | [əˈprɔksimitli] | adv. | 大约，近似地；近于 |
| germanium | [dʒəːˈmeiniəm] | n. | [化学]锗(32号元素，符号 Ge) |
| transistor | [trænˈsistə] | n. | 晶体管，三极管 |
| emitter | [iˈmitə] | n. | 发射极，发射体 |
| base | [beis] | n. | 基极 |
| saturation | [sætʃəˈreiʃən] | n. | 饱和；饱和状态 |

| be inversely proportional to | 与……成反比 |
| be affected by… | 受……影响 |
| be available | 是可利用的，可用的 |
| be directly proportional to | 与……成正比 |
| be expressed as a formula | 用公式表示成…… |
| be proportional to | 与……成比例 |
| be used to… | 被用于…… |
| doughnut shaped | 环状的 |
| in various shapes and sizes | 各种形状和尺寸 |
| to serve as | 用作…… |
| be assumed to | 被假设成…… |
| be labeled | 被分类为……，被标志为……，被标注为…… |
| break down | 毁掉，制伏，压倒，停顿(此处指二极管烧坏) |
| current operated device | 电流控制器件 |
| forward/reverse biased | 正偏置/反偏置 |
| internal resistance | 内阻 |

## 2.2 Reading Materials

### 2.2.1 Nonlinear Resistors

Standard-type resistors usually maintain their value regardless of external conditions, such as voltage, temperature, and light. These types of resistors are referred to as linear resistors. There are other types of resistors referred to as nonlinear, whose resistance varies with temperature (thermistor), voltage (varistor) and light (photoresistor).

The thermistor (Fig 2.12) is made from metal oxides, such as manganese, nickel, copper, or iron. Usually, a thermistor has a negative temperature coefficient, where an increase in temperature causes a decrease in its resistance. The typical resistance change is about $-5\%/℃$ with a range of from $1\ \Omega$ to more than $50\ M\Omega$.

A thermistor might be used to control the stability of a transistor by being part of the biasing network. The thermistor is mounted close to the transistor. When the temperature increases, its resistance decreases. This results in less forward bias voltage from emitter to base; the current through the transistor decreases; and the circuit becomes more stable. When the temperature decreases, the thermistor resumes its initial value and the normal bias voltage is again present.

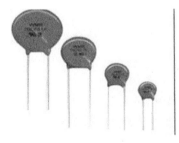

Fig 2.12  Thermistors

Varistors are similar in appearance to thermistors, but their resistance decreases with an increase in voltage. The current that flows in a varistor varies exponentially ($U^n$) with the applied voltage and may increase as much as 64 times for a given varistor. Most often, varistors are used as protection devices for other circuits, such as being placed in parallel across switch contacts to prevent sparking and in inductive circuits to prevent voltage surges.

A photoresistor (Fig 2.13) is made of a high resistance semiconductor. If light falling on the device

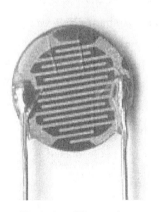

Fig 2.13  Photoresistor

is of high enough frequency, photons absorbed by the semiconductor give bound electrons enough energy to jump into the conduction band. The resulting free electron (and its hole partner) conduct electricity, thereby lowering resistance.

### 2.2.2  The Transistor as a Switch

Because a transistor's collector current is proportionally limited by its base current, it can be used as a sort of current-controlled switch. A relatively small flow of electrons sent through the base of the transistor has the ability to exert control over a much larger flow of electrons through the collector.

For the sake of illustration, let's insert a transistor in place of the switch to show how it can control the flow of electrons through the lamp (Fig 2.14). Remember that the controlled current through a transistor must go between collector and emitter. Since it's the current through the lamp that we want to control, we must position the collector and emitter of our transistor where the two contacts of the switch are now. We must also make sure that the lamp's current will move in the direction of the emitter arrow symbol to ensure that the transistor's junction bias will be correct.

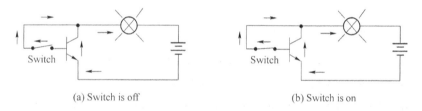

(a) Switch is off            (b) Switch is on

Fig 2.14  The transistor as a switch

In this example, an NPN transistor is chosen.

We are faced with the need to add something more so that we can have base current. Without a connection to the base wire of the transistor, base current will be zero, and the transistor cannot turn on, resulting in a lamp that is always off.

If the switch is open, the base wire of the transistor will be left "floating" (not connected to anything) and there will be no current through it (Fig 2.14(a)). In this state, the transistor is said to be cutoff. If the switch is closed (Fig 2.14(b)), however, electrons will be able to flow from the emitter to the base of the transistor, through the switch and up to the left side of the lamp, back to the positive side of the battery. This base current will enable a much larger flow of electrons from the emitter to the collector, thus lighting up the lamp. In this state of maximum circuit current, the transistor is said to be saturated.

Of course, it may seem pointless to use a transistor in this capacity to control the lamp. After all, we're still using a switch in the circuit. If we're still using a switch to control the lamp—if only indirectly—then what's the point of having a transistor to control the current? Why not just use the switch directly to control the lamp current?

There are a couple of points to be made here, actually. First is the fact that when used in this manner, the switch contacts need only handle what little base current is necessary to turn the transistor on, while the transistor itself handles the majority of the lamp's current. This may be an important advantage if the switch has a low current rating: a small switch may be used to control a relatively high-current load. Perhaps what is more important, though, is the fact that the current-controlling behavior of the transistor enables us to use something completely different to turn the lamp on or off.

Consider this example (Fig 2.15 (a)), where a solar cell is used to control the transistor, which in turn controls the lamp.

Or, we could use a thermocouple (Fig 2.15 (b)) to provide the necessary base current to turn the transistor on.

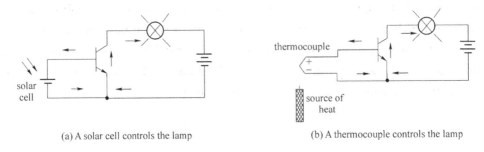

(a) A solar cell controls the lamp  (b) A thermocouple controls the lamp

Fig 2.15  Examples of controlling the lamp

Even a microphone of sufficient voltage and current output could be used to turn the transistor on (Fig 2.16), provided its output is rectified from AC to DC so that the emitter-base PN junction within the transistor will always be forward-biased:

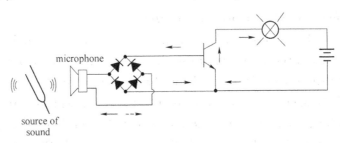

Fig 2.16  Sound controlling the lamp

The point is quite apparent by now: any sufficient source of DC current may be used to turn the transistor on, and that source of current needs only be a fraction of the amount of current needed to energize the lamp. Here we see the transistor functioning not only as a switch, but as a true amplifier: using a relatively low-power signal to control a relatively large amount of power.

Please note that the actual power for lighting up the lamp comes from the battery to the right of the schematic. It is not as though the small signal current from the solar cell, thermocouple, or microphone which is being magically transformed into a greater amount is of high enough frequency, photons absorbed by the semiconductor give bound electrons enough energy to jump into the conduction band. The resulting free electron (and its hole partner) conduct electricity, thereby lowering resistance.

### 2.2.2　The Transistor as a Switch

Because a transistor's collector current is proportionally limited by its base current, it can be used as a sort of current-controlled switch. A relatively small flow of electrons sent through the base of the transistor has the ability to exert control over a much larger flow of electrons through the collector.

For the sake of illustration, let's insert a transistor in place of the switch to show how it can control the flow of electrons through the lamp (Fig 2.14). Remember that the controlled current through a transistor must go between collector and emitter. Since it's the current through the lamp that we want to control, we must position the collector and emitter of our transistor where the two contacts of the switch are now. We must also make sure that the lamp's current will move in the direction of the emitter arrow symbol to ensure that the transistor's junction bias will be correct.

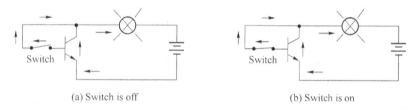

(a) Switch is off　　　　　　　　　(b) Switch is on

Fig 2.14　The transistor as a switch

In this example, an NPN transistor is chosen.

We are faced with the need to add something more so that we can have base current. Without a connection to the base wire of the transistor, base current will be zero, and the transistor cannot turn on, resulting in a lamp that is always off.

If the switch is open, the base wire of the transistor will be left "floating" (not connected to anything) and there will be no current through it (Fig 2.14(a)). In this state, the transistor is said to be cutoff. If the switch is closed (Fig 2.14(b)), however, electrons will be able to flow from the emitter to the base of the transistor, through the switch and up to the left side of the lamp, back to the positive side of the battery. This base current will enable a much larger flow of electrons from the emitter to the collector, thus lighting up the lamp. In this state of maximum circuit current, the transistor is said to be saturated.

Of course, it may seem pointless to use a transistor in this capacity to control the lamp. After all, we're still using a switch in the circuit. If we're still using a switch to control the lamp—if only indirectly—then what's the point of having a transistor to control the current? Why not just use the switch directly to control the lamp current?

There are a couple of points to be made here, actually. First is the fact that when used in this manner, the switch contacts need only handle what little base current is necessary to turn the transistor on, while the transistor itself handles the majority of the lamp's current. This may be an important advantage if the switch has a low current rating: a small switch may be used to control a relatively high-current load. Perhaps what is more important, though, is the fact that the current-controlling behavior of the transistor enables us to use something completely different to turn the lamp on or off.

Consider this example (Fig 2.15 (a)), where a solar cell is used to control the transistor, which in turn controls the lamp.

Or, we could use a thermocouple (Fig 2.15 (b)) to provide the necessary base current to turn the transistor on.

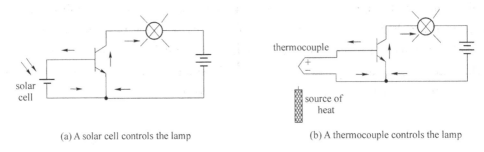

(a) A solar cell controls the lamp       (b) A thermocouple controls the lamp

Fig 2.15   Examples of controlling the lamp

Even a microphone of sufficient voltage and current output could be used to turn the transistor on (Fig 2.16), provided its output is rectified from AC to DC so that the emitter-base PN junction within the transistor will always be forward-biased:

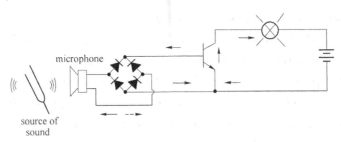

Fig 2.16   Sound controlling the lamp

The point is quite apparent by now: any sufficient source of DC current may be used to turn the transistor on, and that source of current needs only be a fraction of the amount of current needed to energize the lamp. Here we see the transistor functioning not only as a switch, but as a true amplifier: using a relatively low-power signal to control a relatively large amount of power.

Please note that the actual power for lighting up the lamp comes from the battery to the right of the schematic. It is not as though the small signal current from the solar cell, thermocouple, or microphone which is being magically transformed into a greater amount of power. Rather, those small power sources are simply controlling the battery's power to light up the lamp.

Review:

Transistors may be used as switching elements to control DC power to a load. The switched (controlled) current goes between emitter and collector, while the controlling current goes between emitter and base.

When a transistor has zero current through it, it is said to be in a state of cutoff (fully nonconducting).

When a transistor has maximum current through it, it is said to be in a state of saturation (fully conducting).

## 2.3　Application

根据阅读材料连接下面电路,了解器件特性并能正确使用。

应用1:

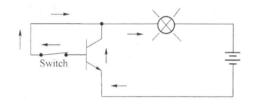

应用2:

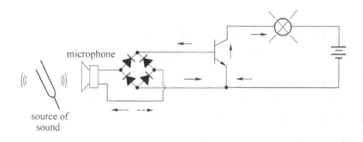

## 2.4　Knowledge(专业词汇)

专业英语中的专业词汇有许多构成方式:在一些较传统学科中往往是从普通英语中借用一些词汇来充当专业词汇。一些较新的学科中通过意义固定的前缀、后缀等复合法来构词,以及缩合法等。

**1. 加前缀**

1) multi-(多的)

multimedia(多媒体),multimeter(万用表),multiply(乘以)等。

2) inter-(在……之间,相互)

Internet(因特网、互联网),interface(接口、界面),interaction(相互作用、影响),

interchange(交换),intercom(内部通话系统),interconnect(相互连接)等。

  3) tele-(远端的、远程的、远距离的)

telecommunications(电信),telegram(电报),television(电视),telephone(电话),telescope(望远镜),teleoperator(远程操作装置)等。

  4) micro-(微)

microsecond(微秒),microwave(微波),microcomputer(微型计算机),microchip(微芯片),microelectronics(微电子学),microprocessor(微处理器)等。

**2．加后缀**

  1) -or,-er(做……的人或物、器)

oscillator(振荡器),amplifier(放大器),trigger(触发器)等。

  2) -scope(可用于观测的仪器设备)

oscilloscope(示波器),microscope(显微镜),telescope(望远镜)等。

  3) -meter(仪器仪表、表)

voltmeter(电压表),multimeter(万用表),amperemeter(电流表)等。

  4) -ic(学科、……学)

electronics(电子学),physics(物理学),mathematics(数学)等。

  5) -(o)logy(技术、技术学)

technology(技术),psychology(心理学)等。

**3．缩合法**

  缩合法即由两个或两个以上的词采用截头去尾的方式构成一个新词的方法。一般来讲,构成方法为:保留第一个词的开头和第二个词的末尾部分,其他的词保留一些有特点的字母。例如:

  modem(modulation+demodulation)(调制解调器)

  transceiver(transmitter+receiver)(收发机)等。

**4．首字母组合法**

  所谓首字母组合法,就是把表达一个专业术语的意群词组中的每一个单词的第一个(或前一两个)字母拿出来顺序拼写成一个新的词,而且所选出的首字母都大写。例如:

  DSP(Digital Signal Processor,数字信号处理器)

  ROM(Read-Only-Memory,只读存储器)

  RAM(Random Access Memory,随机存取存储器)

  PCM(Pulse-Code Modulation,脉冲编码调制)

  CAD(Computer-Aided Design,计算机辅助设计)

  CAM(Computer-Aided Manufacturing,计算机辅助制造)

  MOS(Metal-Oxide Semi-conductor,金属氧化物半导体)

  DOS(Disk Operation System,磁盘操作系统)

**5．缩写法**

  英语中有一些词常采用简略写法,即去掉原单词中的一些拼写字母而使原单词书写起来更简略。例如:

corp=corp.＝corporation
tel=tel.＝telephone
TV＝television
Cn＝centimeter
Hz＝Hertz

## 2.5 Exercises

I. **Translate the following phrases and expressions**
1. 欧姆定律
2. 电子器件
3. 二极管特性
4. 电流增益
5. electrical component
6. transistor biasing circuits
7. Color Code
8. electromagnetic energy
9. semiconductor diode
10. bipolar transistors

II. **Translate the following sentences into Chinese**

1. Resistors are used to limit current flowing to a device, thereby preventing it from burning out, as voltage dividers to reduce voltage for other circuits, as transistor biasing circuits, and to serve as circuit loads.

2. The resistor is generally a linear device and its characteristics form a straight line when plotted on a graph.

3. A capacitor will block DC current, but appears to pass AC current by charging and discharging.

4. Capacitors are available in various shapes and sizes.

5. An inductor is an electrical device, which can temporarily store electromagnetic energy in the field about it as long as current is flowing through it.

6. In this condition, the internal resistance of the diode is low and a large current will flow through the diode (depending on the external circuit resistance).

7. Most transistors used today are NPN because this is the easiest type to make from silicon.

8. The acronym MOS stands for metal-oxide semiconductor, which historically denoted the gate, insulator, and channel region materials respectively.

9. The capacitor values depend on which circuit you use and what signal frequency you are amplifying.

10. When a transistor has zero current through it, it is said to be in a state of cutoff (fully nonconducting).

# Unit 3  Instruments

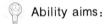 Knowledge aims:

1. Professional glossary.
2. Instruments manual.
3. Passive voice.

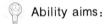 Ability aims:

Can read instrument manual.

 Pre-reading

Read the following passage, paying attention to the questions.
1. What can be measured with a multimeter?
2. What is the function of an oscilloscope?

## 3.1  Text

### 3.1.1  Multimeters

A multimeter is a general-purpose meter capable of measuring DC and AC voltage, current, resistance, and in some cases, decibels. There are two types of meters: analog, using a standard meter movement with a needle (Fig 3.1(a)), and digital, with an electronic numerical display (Fig 3.1(b)). Both types of meters have a positive (+) jack and a common jack (−) for the test leads, a function switch to select DC voltage, AC voltage, DC current, AC current, or ohms and a range switch for accurate readings. The meters may also have other jacks to measure extended ranges of voltage (1 to 5 kV) and current (up to 10 A) there are some variations to the functions used for specific meters.

Besides the function and range switches (sometimes they are in a single switch), the analog meter may have a polarity switch to facilitate reversing the test leads. The needle usually has a screw for mechanical adjust to set it to zero and also a zero adjust control to compensate for weakening batteries when measuring resistance. An analog meter can read positive and negative voltage by simply reversing the test leads or moving the polarity switch. A digital meter usually has an automatic indicator for polarity on its display.

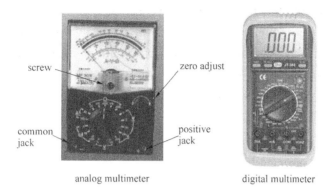

Fig 3.1  Portable multimeters

Meters must be properly connected to a circuit to ensure a correct reading. A voltmeter is always placed across (in parallel) the circuit or component to be measured. When measuring current, the circuit must be opened and the meter inserted in series with the circuit or component to be measured. When measuring the resistance of a component in a circuit, the voltage to the circuit must be removed and the meter placed in parallel with the component.

### 3.1.2 The Digital Oscilloscope

UT2000/3000 oscilloscopes (Fig 3.2) offer user-friendly front panel that allows access to all functions easy operation. The scaling of all channels and the positions of buttons are optimally arranged for direct view operation. As design is based on the mode of traditional instruments, users can use the new units without spending considerable time in learning and familiarizing with operation. For faster adjustment to ease test, there is an AUTO key. The new units also feature more appropriate waveform and range scale positions.

Fig 3.2  UT2000/3000 oscilloscopes

In addition to easy operation, the UT2000/3000 Series have all the high performance indicators and powerful functions that ensure speedy testing and measurement. With 500 MS/s real-time sampling rate and 25 GS/s equivalent sampling rate, these oscilloscopes can display signals much quicker, while powerful trigger and analytical features enable easy capture and analysis of waves, while a clear LCD display and mathematics functions enable the user to observe and analyze signal problems promptly and clearly.

The performance features listed below will explain why the new series can fully satisfy your testing and measurement requirements.

- Dual analog channels
- HD color/mono LCD display system at 320×240 resolution
- Supports plug-and-play USB storage devices and capable of communicating with a computer through the USB storage device
- Automatic waveform and status configuration
- Storage of waveforms, setups and bit map and waveforms, setups recurrence
- Sophisticated window expansion function to analyze waveform details and overview precisely
- Automatic measurement of 28 waveform parameters
- Automatic cursor tracing measurement
- Unique wave recording and replay function
- Built-in FFT
- Multiple waveform mathematics functions (including add, subtract, multiply and divide)
- Edge, video, pulse width and alternate trigger functions
- Multilingual menu displays
- Chinese and English help system

UT2000/3000 Series digital storage oscilloscopes are small and compact bench top oscilloscopes. The user-friendly front panel enables easy operation for basic testing and measuring tasks. The UT2000/3000 Series provides a front panel with at-a-glance functions for easy operation (Fig 3.3). There are buttons and function keys on the front panel. The functions of buttons are similar to other oscilloscopes. The row of 5 keys on the right of the display panel are the menu operation keys (designated as F1 to F5 from top to down). With these keys you can set up different options of the current menu. The other keys are function keys. You can use them to enter different function menus or access particular functions directly.

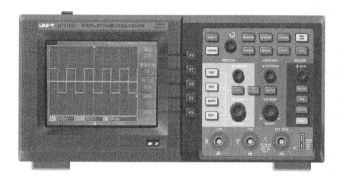

Fig 3.3  Front panel of UT2000/3000 Series oscilloscopes

Schematic diagram operating the UT2000/3000 front panel (Fig 3.4)

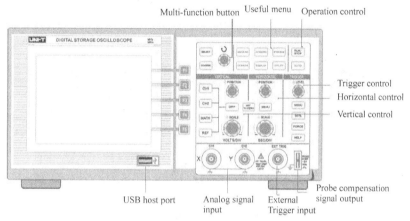

Fig 3.4  Schematic diagram operating the UT2000/3000 front panel

Schematic diagram for the display interface (Fig 3.5)

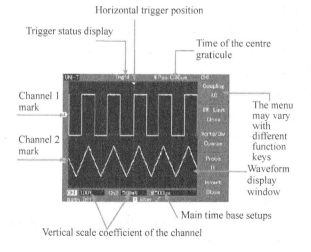

Fig 3.5  Schematic diagram for the display interface

**Functional Check**

Carry out a quick functional check in the following steps to make sure your oscilloscope is operating normally.

**1. Power on the Unit**

Power on the unit. Power supply voltage is 100~240 V AC, 45~440 Hz. After connecting to power, let the unit carry out self-calibration to optimize the oscilloscope signal path for measurement accuracy. Press the [UTILITY] button and then [F1] to start the calibration. Then press [F1] on the next page to display DEFAULT SETUP (Fig 3.6) for details.

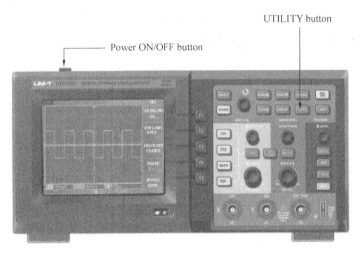

Fig 3.6 Default setup

When the above procedure is complete, press [CH1] to enter the CH1 menu.

WARNING: Ensure oscilloscope is securely grounded to avoid danger.

**2. Accessing Signals**

The UT2000/3000 Series oscilloscopes have dual input channels and one external trigger input channel. Please access signals in the following steps.

(1) Connect the probe to the CH1 input, and set the attenuation switch of the probe to 10×. Fig 3.7 shows setting the attenuation switch.

(2) You have to set the probe attenuation factor of the oscilloscope. This factor changes the vertical range multiple to ensure the measurement result correctly reflects the amplitude of the measured signal. Set the attenuation factor of the probe as follows: Press [F4] to display 10× on the menu.

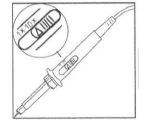

Fig 3.7 Setting the attenuation switch

**Example: Measuring Simple Signals**

To observe and measure an unknown signal, and to quickly display and measure the signal's frequency and peak-to-peak value.

**1. To Quickly Display This Signal, Follow the Steps below.**

(1) In the probe menu, set the attenuation factor to 10× and set the switch on the probe to 10×;

(2) Connect the CH1 probe to the circuitry to be measured;

(3) Press [AUTO].

The oscilloscope will carry out auto setup to optimize waveform display. In this status, you can further adjust the vertical and horizontal range until you get the desired waveform display.

**2. Automatic Measurement of Signal Voltage and Time Parameters**

Your oscilloscope can automatically measure most display signals. To measure signal frequency and peak-to-peak value, follow the steps below.

(1) Press [MEASURE] to display the auto measurement menu;

(2) Press [F1] to enter the measurement type option menu;

(3) Press [F3] to select voltage;

(4) Press [F5] to go to page 2/4, and then press [F3] to select measurement type: peak-to-peak value;

(5) Press [F2] to enter the measurement type option menu, and then press [F4] to select time;

(6) Press [F2] to select measurement type:

frequency values are now displayed in positions [F1] and [F2] respectively.

Fig 3.8 shows auto measurement.

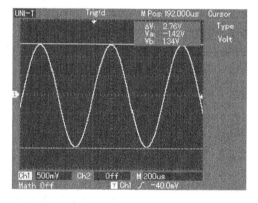

Fig 3.8 Auto measurement

# Technical Words and Phrases

measure         ['meʒə(r)]        n.        量度器，测量

| | | vt. | 测量 |
|---|---|---|---|
| meter | ['mi:tə(r)] | n. | 米,公尺;仪表 |
| needle | ['ni:d(ə)l] | n. | 针 |
| | | vt. | 刺穿 |
| trigger | ['trigə] | vt. | 引发,引起;触发 |
| dual | ['dju:əl] | adj. | 二元的,双的 |
| status | ['steitəs] | n. | 状态 |
| sophisticated | [sə'fistikeitid] | adj. | 精细的,高级的,精致的 |
| precisely | [pri'saisli] | adv. | 精确地;准确地 |
| multilingual | [mʌlti'liŋgwəl] | adj. | 使用多种语言的 |
| compact | [kəm'pækt] | adj. | 紧凑的,紧密的;简洁的 |
| optimize | ['ɔptimaiz] | vt. | 使最优化,优化 |
| calibration | [kæli'breiʃən] | n. | 校准,定标,校正 |
| amplitude | ['æmplitju:d] | n. | 振幅,幅值,幅度 |
| accurate | ['ækjurət] | adj. | 精确的,准确的 |
| facilitate | [fə'siliteit] | vt. | 促进;帮助;使容易 |
| oscilloscope | [ə'siləskəup] | n. | 示波器 |
| period | ['piərid] | n. | 时期,学时,周期 |
| superimposed | [sju:pərim'pəuzd] | adj. | 成阶层的,重叠的 |
| switch | [switʃ] | n. | 开关,转换 |
| | | vt. | 转换,转变 |
| vertically | ['və:tik(ə)li] | adv. | 垂直地 |

| | |
|---|---|
| be connected to | 连接到…… |
| capable of V-ing | 可以做……的,可以……的 |
| cathode-ray tube (CRT) | 阴极射线显像管 |
| dual-trace oscilloscope | 双踪示波器 |
| in parallel with | 与……并联 |
| in series with | 与……串联 |
| peak-to-peak voltage | 电压峰-峰值 |
| polarity switch | 极性开关 |
| rms voltage | 电压有效值(rms 为 root-mean-square 的缩写) |

## 3.2 Reading Materials

### 3.2.1 Analog Oscilloscope

The oscilloscope (Fig 3.9) is basically a graph-displaying device—it draws a graph of an electrical signal. When the signal inputs into the oscilloscope, an electron beam is created, focused, accelerated, and properly deflected to display the voltage waveforms on the face of a cathode-ray tube (CRT).

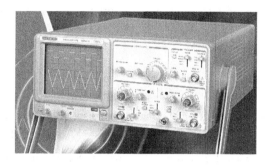

Fig 3.9 Dual-trace oscilloscope

In most applications the graph shows how signals change over time: the vertical (Y) axis represents voltage and the horizontal (X) axis represents time. The amplitude of a voltage waveform on an oscilloscope screen can be determined by counting the number of centimeters (cm), vertically, from one peak to the other peak of the waveform (Fig 3.10) and then multiplying it by the setting of the volt/cm control. As an example, if the amplitude was 5 cm and the control was set on 1 V/cm, the peak-to-peak voltage would be 5 V.

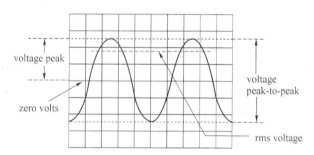

Fig 3.10 Voltage peak and peak-to-peak voltage

Time can be measured using the horizontal scale of the oscilloscope. Time measurements include measuring the period, pulse width, and frequency. Frequency is the reciprocal of the period, so once you know the period, the frequency is one divided by the period.

The frequency of a waveform can be determined by counting the number of centimeters, horizontally, in one cycle of the waveform and multiplying it by the setting time/cm control. For example, if the waveform is 4 cm long and the control is set at 1 ms/cm, the period would be 4 ms. The frequency can now be found from the formula:

$$f=\frac{1}{p}=\frac{1}{4 \text{ ms}}=250 \text{ Hz}$$

If the control was gone on 100 μs/cm, the period would be 400 μs and the frequency would be 2.5 kHz.

A dual-trace oscilloscope is advantageous to show the input signal and output signal of one circuit in the same time, to determine any defects, and indicate phase relationships. The two traces may be placed over each other (superimposed) to indicate better the phase shift between two signals.

### 3.2.2  Signal Generator

A signal generator converts DC to AC or varying DC in the form of sine waves, square waves, triangle waves, or other types of voltage waveforms(Fig 3.11). The signal generator is used to inject a signal into a circuit or piece of equipment for troubleshooting or for calibration. Some generators may be used for audio, RF, or higher frequencies, whereas others have overlapping frequency ranges. All generators will have a function switch, a frequency range switch, and a fine adjustment control for selecting a specific frequency, an amplitude control for varying the peak-to-peak output voltage, and output terminals.

Fig 3.11  Function signal generator

To select a sine wave of, say, 5 kHz, the user would set the function switch to the sine wave, set the range switch to 1 K, and then adjust the frequency fine adjust control to 5. The amplitude control would then be adjusted to establish the desired peak-to-peak voltage output.

## 3.3  Application

根据英文资料了解万用表、示波器和信号发生器的应用。

应用1:测量交直流电压。

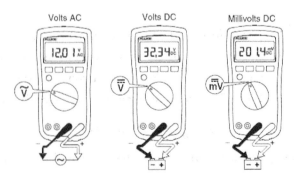

应用 2:判断二极管好坏。

应用 3:用信号发生器产生频率为 150 kHz,峰-峰值为 5 V 的正信号,用示波器测量此信号并迅速显示被测量信号的频率和峰-峰值。

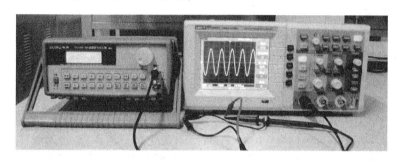

## 3.4　Knowledge(词义)

英语中的单词大多数都是多义词,应注意准确选定英语单词在句中的含义。根据文章涉及的专业内容来确定其含义是一种有效的方法。

**1. 由词性确定词义**

这主要适用于一个词有多种词性的场合,如 characteristic 一词既有名词性(特性、特征),又有形容词性(独特的、特征的),在句子中应根据其不同词性得到不同的翻译。

Capacitors are devices, the principal characteristic of which is capacitance.　电容器属于器件,其主要特性是电容量。

The narrow directive beam is characteristic of radar antennas.　雷达天线所具有的特点是波束窄而定向。

**2. 由上下文背景确定词义**

在专业英语中有的单词有多种含义。如 power(幂、功率、电力、电源等含义),例如:

The third power of 2 is equal to 8.　2 的 3 次幂等于 8。

The power subsystem can provide a maximum current of 10 A.　该电源子系统能提供的最大电流为 10 A。

Voltage multiplying current gives power.　电压乘电流得到电功率。

在阅读电子技术专业文献时,应注意扩大自己的专业词汇。许多平时很熟悉的单词,在电子专业文献中可能有其特定的含义。

**3. 词义引申**

在阅读理解过程中,有时直译的表达方式并不符合中文的表达习惯,这时应采用词义引申。在保持原文意思不变的情况下,用适当的引申词可以更准确地表达原文意思且符合中文表达习惯。

The light in the workshop is poor. 车间中光线不足。

Radar was not invented until the last war. 直到上次战争时,雷达还未发明。

The last war 指什么,在英语中是不言而喻的,但在汉语中就觉得意义不清。根据汉语习惯,应译成"雷达是在第二次世界大战中发明的"。

**4. 词量增减**

由于历史背景、地理位置、自然环境、民情风俗等方面的巨大差异,英、汉两种语言的用词、结构和表达方式不可能完全相同,阅读时应该随时注意两种语言的差别,有时要增补一些词,有时要删减一些词,以符合中国人的阅读习惯。

(1) 词量增补

英语专业文章为了避免用词重复,常常省略一些词语,这是阅读时的难点之一。还有一些词,在英语中并无含义,但译成中文时应增补,方能正确理解。

If you are a bit serious about the electronics hobby, I recommend the "Color Code". 如果你对电子技术颇有兴趣,建议学会"条形码"电阻的识别方法。

He offered to help us. 他提出要帮助我们。

Don't use more material than necessary. 要多少材料用多少,不要多用。

Let those who can serve as teachers. 让那些能当老师的人来当老师(能者为师)。

(2) 词量删简

英语中常用一些关系词、冠词、连词、代词以及同义词、同位语等,在译成汉语时可以免去不译。

It takes only three working processes to machine the part. 加工这个零件只要3道工序。(the 表示特指,故译成这个)It 这里不必译出。

The sixties of 18th century saw the start of the Industrial Revolution. 18世纪60年代开始了产业革命。

Multi-digit displays consist of two or more seven-segment displays contained in a single package or module. 多位数码显示器由封装在一起的两个或更多的7段显示器组成。

**5. 词类转换**

有时中、英文在描述一些现象时用的方法是很不相同的,在专业文献中,常会遇到如若直译其意思很不明确的情况,这时可结合专业知识把原文的意思表达出来,转换原来的词的词性,使其更符合中文的习惯。

How fast a machine works is one of its important characteristics. 运转速度是机器的重要性能指标之一。

## 3.5 Exercises

Ⅰ. Translate the following phrases and expressions

1. 数字万用表

2. 正、负电压

3. 峰-峰值

4. 与元件相并联

5. AC voltage

6. mechanical adjust

7. digital oscilloscope

8. user-friendly front panel

9. external trigger

10. automatic measurement

Ⅱ. **Translate the following sentences into Chinese**

1. A multimeter is a general-purpose meter capable of measuring DC and AC voltage, current, resistance, and in some cases, decibels.

2. An analog meter can read positive and negative voltage by simply reversing the test leads or moving the polarity switch.

3. When measuring current, the circuit must be opened and the meter inserted in series with the circuit or component to be measured.

4. The frequency of a waveform can be determined by counting the number of centimeters, horizontally, in one cycle of the waveform and multiplying it by the setting time/cm control.

5. Depending on how you set the vertical scale (volts/div control), an attenuator reduces the signal voltage or an amplifier increases the signal voltage.

6. Lissajous patterns can be used to show the phase relationship of two signals of the same frequency and to determine an unknown frequency from a known frequency.

7. There are two types of meters: analog, using a standard meter movement with a needle and digital, with an electronic numerical display.

8. If both signals are the same frequency, a circle will appear on the face of the oscilloscope.

9. In most applications the graph shows how signals change over time: the vertical (Y) axis represents voltage and the horizontal (X) axis represents time.

10. All signal generators will have a frequency range switch, a fine adjustment control for selecting a specific frequency, an amplitude control for varying the peak-to-peak output voltage and output terminals.

# Unit 4  Integrated Circuit

 Knowledge aims:

1. Technical words and phrases.
2. Integrated circuit.
3. Passive.

 Ability aims:

Can read integrated circuit materials.

 Pre-reading

Read the following passage, paying attention to the questions.
1. What is an integrated circuit?
2. What is ASIC?
3. What is chip holder?
4. What is a typical IC design process composed of?

## 4.1  Text

### 4.1.1  Information on Integrated Circuits

An integrated circuit (IC) is a small electronic device made out of a semiconductor material. The first integrated circuit was developed in the 1950s by Jack Kilby of Texas Instruments and Robert Noyce of Fairchild Semiconductor.

Integrated circuits (Fig 4.1) are used for a variety of devices, including microprocessors, audio and video equipment, and automobiles. Integrated circuits are often classified by the number of transistors and other electronic components they contain.

- SSI (small-scale integration): up to 100 electronic components per chip
- MSI (medium-scale integration): from 100 to 3,000 electronic components per chip
- LSI (large-scale integration): from 3,000 to 100,000 electronic components per chip
- VLSI (very large-scale integration): from 100,000 to 1,000,000 electronic components per chip

- ULSI (ultra large-scale integration): more than 1 million electronic components per chip

Fig 4.1 Integrated circuits

When an IC is designed and fabricated, it generally follows one of two main transistor technologies: bipolar or metal-oxide semiconductor (MOS). Bipolar processes create BJTs, whereas MOS processes create FETs. Bipolar logic was more common before the 1980s, but MOS technologies have accounted for the great majority of digital logic ICs since then. N-channel FETs are fabricated in an NMOS process, and P-channel FETs are fabricated in a PMOS process. In the 1980s, complementary-MOS, or CMOS, became the dominant process technology and remains so to this day. CMOS ICs incorporate both NMOS and PMOS transistors.

An application-specific integrated circuit (ASIC) is an integrated circuit (IC) customized for a particular use, rather than intended for general-purpose use. For example, a chip designed solely to run a cell phone is an ASIC. In contrast, the 7400 Series and 4000 Series integrated circuits are logic building blocks that can be wired together for use in many different applications.

As feature sizes have shrunk and design tools improved over the years, the maximum complexity (and hence functionality) possible in an ASIC has grown from 5,000 gates to over 100 million gates. Modern ASICs often include entire 32-bit processors, memory blocks including ROM, RAM, EEPROM, Flash and other large building blocks. Such an ASIC is often termed as SoC (System-on-Chip). Designers of digital ASICs use a hardware description language (HDL), such as Verilog or VHDL, to describe the functionality of ASICs.

Field-programmable gate arrays (FPGA) (Fig 4.2) are the modern day equivalent of 7400 Series logic and a breadboard, containing programmable logic blocks and programmable interconnects that allow the same FPGA to be used in many different applications. For smaller designs and/or lower production volumes, FPGAs may be more cost effective than an ASIC design. The non-recurring engineering cost (the cost to setup the factory to produce a particular ASIC) can run into hundreds of thousands of dollars.

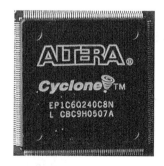

Fig 4.2 Altera FPGA

The general term application specific integrated circuit includes FPGAs, but most designers use ASIC only for non-field programmable devices and make a distinction between ASIC and FPGAs.

### 4.1.2 Bipolar Integrated Circuits & MOS Integrated Circuits

Historically, bipolar integrated circuits used to be much more popular than MOS integrated circuits, particularly for small-scale logic circuits. There were two major reasons for this: first, bipolar-junction transistors (BJT) originally could be manufactured more reliably than MOS transistors; second, they were faster.

As the reliability of MOS transistors improved, and as integrated circuits became more complex, which made the lower power and smaller size of MOS logic more important, the popularity of BJT logic decreased, however, BJT technology is still popular for the highest frequency logic circuits.

### 4.1.3 The Process of IC Design

A typical IC design process is composed of the following four categories.

(1) System (behavioral) design is the process of defining the circuit functionality and the input-output behavior. This level of specification can be expressed in terms of a flowchart or in terms of a high-level hardware description language (HDL).

(2) Logic design is the process of transforming a high-level description of a complex function into a net list of technology independent logic elements such as NAND gates, NOR gates, inverters and latches. This process helps to ensure that minimal logic is used to implement the function that was earlier defined in a high-level language.

(3) Circuit design transforms the basic logic components into networks of transistors and interconnects.

(4) Layout design creates geometrical shapes on various mask layers, which correspond to a silicon implementation of the circuit.

Although these steps are interrelated, each has its primary goals. At the system design level, the goal is to provide a complete and precise functional description. Logic-level design attempts to reduce the power consumption, and the objective of layout design is to realize circuit functions with a high packing density.

## Technical Words and Phrases

| | | | |
|---|---|---|---|
| chip | [tʃip] | n. | 电路芯片;碎片;筹码 |
| delay | [di'lei] | vt. vi | 推迟;延缓;迟延 |
| flowchart | [fləu'tʃɑːt] | n. | 流程图,程序框图 |
| frame | [freim] | n. | 框,框架;环境;背景 |

| | | | |
|---|---|---|---|
| implement | ['implimənt] | n. | 工具；器具 |
| | | vt. | 实现；履行 |
| integrate | ['intigreit] | vt. | 集成，使成整体，使一体化 |
| interrelate | [,intəri'leit] | vt. | （使）互相联系 |
| package | ['pækidʒ] | n. | 包，封装 |
| | | vt. | 打包，封装 |
| pin | [pin] | n. | 引脚，腿 |
| | | vt. | 钉住，牵制 |
| screwdriver | ['skru:draivə(r)] | n. | 螺丝刀，改锥 |
| subcomponents | [sʌbkəm'pəunənt] | n. | 子部件 |
| well-informed | [welin'fɔ:md] | adj. | 消息灵通的，熟悉的，博识的， |
| fabricate | ['fæbrikeit] | vt. | 制造，组装 |

| | |
|---|---|
| metal-oxide semiconductor | 金属氧化半导体 |
| power consumption | 功耗 |
| keep pace with… | 与……保持一致的步伐 |
| physical limit | 物理条件限制（或译成硬件限制） |
| trade-off analysis | 平衡分析，权衡利弊 |
| application-specific | 专用的 |
| be essential for/to… | 对……来说是很重要的，很必要的 |
| in terms of | 以……的观点；就……而说 |
| integrated circuit(IC) | 集成电路 |
| keep pace with… | 与……保持一致的步伐 |
| moderate complexity | 中等规模（指集成电路中线路元件数及电路的复杂度为中等） |

## 4.2 Reading Materials

### Circuit Board

**1. Breadboard (Temporary, no soldering required)**

This is a way of making a temporary circuit, for testing purposes or to try out an idea. No soldering is required and all the components can be reused afterwards. It is easy to change connections and replace components. Almost all projects started life on a breadboard (Fig 4.3(a)) to check whether the circuit worked as intended.

**2. Stripboard (Permanent, soldered)**

Stripboard (Fig 4.3(b)) has parallel strips of copper track on one side. The strips are 0.1 inches(2.54 mm) apart and there are holes every 0.1 inches (2.54 mm). Stripboard requires no special preparation other than cutting to size. It can be cut with a junior hacksaw, or simply snap it along the lines of holes by putting it over the edge of a bench or table and pushing hard.

(a) Breadboard              (b) Stripboard

Fig 4.3 Circuit board

**3. Printed Circuit Board (Permanent, soldered)**

Printed Circuit Boards (PCB) (Fig 4.4) have copper tracks connecting the holes where the components are placed. They are designed specially for each circuit and make construction very easy. However, producing the PCB requires special equipment so this method is not recommended if you are a beginner unless the PCB is provided for you.

Fig 4.4 Printed Circuit Board (PCB)

## 4.3 Application

应用1：根据英文资料了解面包板的使用，并在面包板上连接如下电路。

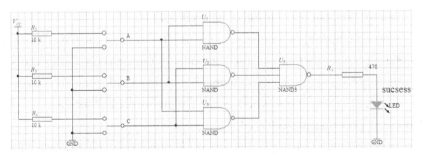

## 4.4 Knowledge(翻译技巧 1——被动语态)

作为专业文献翻译,要做到译文正确、合乎逻辑、文字准确、流畅。翻译首先要求译文正确,这是一个好的译文的最基本要求。它要求译者要具有必备的英语基础知识与专业知识。在正确理解原文的基础上,不仅要正确地将原文含义表达出来,而且还要使译文合乎中文习惯,尽可能使译文语言精确、流畅。一篇译文只有满足了这几点才可称得上好的译文。

根据专业英语的特点,在专业英语翻译中要特别注重被动语态的翻译。

被动语态的处理上,为了突出主语是动作的受体这一特点,一般与原文保持一致而译成被动语态。除了这一基本译法外,被动语态还可根据不同场合译成各种主动形式以使译文更流畅、更符合中文习惯。例如:

Eg. 1 The power switch is placed on the front panel. 前面板上装有电源开关。

Eg. 2 Resistance is measured in Ohm. 电阻测量的单位是欧姆(电阻是以欧姆为单位测量的,欧姆是电阻测量的单位)。

Eg. 3 The discovery is highly appreciated in a circle of science. 该发现在科学界评价很高(科学界对该发现评价很高)。

Eg. 4 Tin can be melted. 锡可以熔化(仍为主语,把动作变为不及物动词)。

**1. 将 by, in, on, at 等介词后面的成分译成主语**

例如,在 Eg. 1,Eg. 2,Eg. 3 中,若要突出 by,in,on,at 等后面的成分时往往要用这种译法,特别是该成分为专有名词时。例如,具体人名、地理名称等。有时也是为了使译文更符合中文习惯而采取这种译法。

**2. 将主语译成宾语**

The bias resistor $R1$ may be bypassed to maintain the voltage drop across it constant. 为了保持它两边的电压降不变,我们往往将偏置电阻 $R1$ 旁路。

在文章翻译过程中,为了保持原文的描述、解释、说明思路,往往采用这种译法。

**3. 译成不及物动词**

The system may be further subdivided. 该系统可进一步划分。

**4. "人为"添加一个"我们、人们"等主语**

The method of connection is called forward bias. 我们将这种连接方法称为正偏。

Two basic types of transistors can be formed, depending upon the sequence of materials. 根据材料的组合顺序,我们可构成两种基本类型的晶体管。

Such currents of free electrons are utilized in television, X-rays, electron microscope and many other modern devices. 人们把自由电子的这种定向流动应用于电视、X 光、电子显微镜和许多其他现代设备中。

**5. 一些特殊的以 It 作主语的被动语态**

专业英语中有相当数量的以 It 作形式主语的被动语态固定结构,它们常常译成主动结构且译文较固定,在专业英语翻译中要加以注意。常见的有:

It is said that…　　　　　　　据说……

It is reported that…　　　　　据报道……

| | |
|---|---|
| It is supposed that… | 假设……假定…… |
| It is well known that… | 众所周知…… |
| It should be pointed out that… | 应当指出的是…… |
| It is estimated that… | 据估计…… |
| It is announced that… | 据称……，据公布…… |
| It can be seen that… | 可见…… |
| It has been proved that… | 业已证明…… |

需要说明的是，在被动语态的中英文互译中，1、4 两条规则我们要牢记。通常在写作时也是这样，主语是专有名词且用被动语态表达句意时，该主语一定要用 by 引导出，而主语是"我们、人们"时就可省去。

## 4.5 Exercises

**Ⅰ. Translate the following phrases and expressions**

1. 半导体材料
2. MOS 技术
3. 逻辑构建模块
4. 高频逻辑电路
5. field-programmable gate arrays
6. very large-scale integration
7. MOS transistors
8. high-level language
9. System-on-Chip
10. digital logic IC

**Ⅱ. Translate the following sentences into Chinese**

1. Moore's law, which predicted that the number of devices integrated on a chip would be doubled every two years, was accurate for a number of years.

2. Advances in silicon technology have allowed IC designer to integrate more than a few million transistors on a chip; even a whole system of moderate complexity can now be implemented on a single chip.

3. However, producing the PCB requires special equipment so this method is not recommended if you are a beginner unless the PCB is provided for you.

4. In any case, what really matters is the ratio of channel width to channel length.

5. Through this platform, customers will be able to use their mobile phones to enjoy services previously only available with IC cards.

6. This is fortunate for us, because gamma rays, X-rays, and ultraviolet rays can harm living things.

7. Potential applications of the technology could include electronic ticketing and online credit which would provide convenience and asked value for both providers and customers.

8. The clear input must be maintained at logic 1 during normal clocked operation.

9. A ripple counter contains a chain of flip-flops with the output of each one feeding the input of the next.

10. Electrons also flow in a television tube, where they are made to hit the screen, causing a flash of light.

# Unit 5  Datasheet

 Knowledge aims:

1. Technical words and phrases.
2. Datasheet.
3. Translation of long sentences.

 Ability aims:

Can read IC's datasheet.

 Pre-reading

Read the following passage, paying attention to the questions.

1. How many pins does the 74LS194 have?
2. What are the features of 74LS194?
3. What are the features of NE555?

## 5.1  Text

### 5.1.1  DM74LS194A Datasheet

**DM74LS194A**
**4 Bit Bidirectional Universal Shift Register**
**General Description**
This bidirectional shift register is designed to incorporate virtually all of the features a system designer may want in a shift register; it features parallel inputs, parallel outputs, right-shift and left-shift serial inputs, operating-mode-control inputs, and a direct overriding clear line. The register has four distinct modes of operation, namely:

Parallel (broadside) load
Shift right (in the direction $Q_A$ toward $Q_D$)
Shift left (in the direction $Q_D$ toward $Q_A$)
Inhibit clock (do nothing)
Synchronous parallel loading is accomplished by applying the four bits of data and

taking both mode control inputs, S0 and S1, HIGH. The parallel data (A toward D) is loaded into the associated flip-flops and appear at the outputs ($Q_A$ toward $Q_D$) after the positive transition of the clock input. During loading, serial data flow ($D_{SR}$, $D_{SL}$) is inhibited.

Shift right is accomplished synchronously with the rising edge of the clock pulse when S0 is HIGH and S1 is LOW. Serial data for this mode is entered at the shift-right data input. When S0 is LOW and S1 is HIGH, data shifts left synchronously and new data is entered at the shift-left serial input. Clocking of the flip-flop is inhibited when both mode control inputs are LOW.

**Features**
- Parallel inputs and outputs
- Four operating modes:
  Synchronous parallel load
  Right shift
  Left shift
  Do nothing
- Positive edge-triggered clocking
- Direct overriding clear

**Port**
- Clock
- Clear
- A—D: parallel inputs
- Shift left serial input
- Shift right serial input
- S0, S1: mode control
- $Q_A$—$Q_D$: output

**Absolute Maximum Ratings**

The "Absolute Maximum Ratings" are those values beyond which the safety of the device cannot be guaranteed. The device should not be operated at these limits. The parametric values defined in the Electrical Characteristics tables are not guaranteed at the absolute maximum ratings. The Recommended Operating Conditions table will define the conditions for actual device operation.

- Supply Voltage             7 V
- Input Voltage              7 V
- Operating Free Air Temperature Range    $0 \sim +70$ ℃
- Storage Temperature Range              $-65 \sim +150$ ℃

**Connection Diagram** (Fig 5.1)

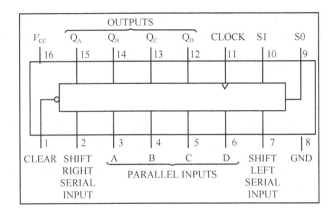

Fig 5.1  Connection diagram

**Function Table**

| Clear | Mode | | Clock | Serial | | Parallel | | | | Outputs | | | |
|---|---|---|---|---|---|---|---|---|---|---|---|---|---|
| | S1 | S0 | | Left | Right | A | B | C | D | $Q_A$ | $Q_B$ | $Q_C$ | $Q_D$ |
| L | X | X | X | X | X | X | X | X | X | L | L | L | L |
| H | X | X | L | X | X | X | X | X | X | $Q_{A0}$ | $Q_{B0}$ | $Q_{C0}$ | $Q_{D0}$ |
| H | H | H | ↑ | X | X | a | b | c | d | a | b | c | d |
| H | L | H | ↑ | X | H | X | X | X | X | H | $Q_{An}$ | $Q_{Bn}$ | $Q_{Cn}$ |
| H | L | H | ↑ | X | L | X | X | X | X | L | $Q_{An}$ | $Q_{Bn}$ | $Q_{Cn}$ |
| H | H | L | ↑ | H | X | X | X | X | X | $Q_{Bn}$ | $Q_{Cn}$ | $Q_{Dn}$ | H |
| H | H | L | ↑ | L | X | X | X | X | X | $Q_{Bn}$ | $Q_{Cn}$ | $Q_{Dn}$ | L |
| H | L | L | X | X | X | X | X | X | X | $Q_{A0}$ | $Q_{B0}$ | $Q_{C0}$ | $Q_{D0}$ |

**Physical Dimensions**(Fig 5.2)

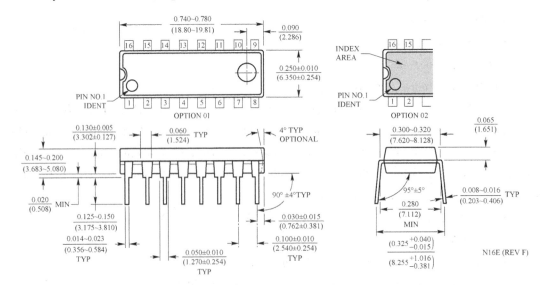

Fig 5.2  Package number N16E

## 5.1.2 NE555 Datasheet

NE555 timer is usually used in electronic circuits. The following is a partial list of its datasheet:
- Timing from microseconds to hours
- Astable or monostable operation
- Adjustable duty cycle
- TTL-Compatible output can sink or source up to 200 mA
- Designed to be interchangeable with signetics NE555, SA555, and SE555

**Description**

NE555 is a precision timing circuit capable of producing accurate time delays or oscillation. In the time-delay or monostable mode of operation, the timed interval is controlled by a single external resistor and capacitor network. In the astable mode of operation, the frequency and duty cycle can be controlled independently with two external resistors and a single external capacitor.

The threshold and trigger levels normally are two-thirds and one-third, respectively, of $V_{CC}$. These levels can be altered by use of the control-voltage terminal (CONT). When the trigger input (TRIG) falls below the trigger level, the flip-flop is set and the output goes high. If the trigger input is above the trigger level and the threshold input (THRES) is above the threshold level, the flip-flop is reset and the output is low. The reset (RESET) input can override all other inputs and can be used to initiate a new timing cycle. When RESET goes low, the flip-flop is reset and the output goes low. When the output is low, a low-impedance path is provided between discharge (DISCH) and ground (GND).

The output circuit is capable of sinking or sourcing current up to 200 mA. Operation is specified for supplies of 5 V to 15 V. With a 5 V supply, output levels are compatible with TTL inputs.

The NE555 is characterized for operation from 0 ℃ to 70 ℃. The SA555 is characterized for operation from −40 ℃ to 85 ℃. The SE555 is characterized for operation over the full military range of −55 ℃ to 125 ℃. The package and definition of pins of NE555 are shown in Fig 5.3.

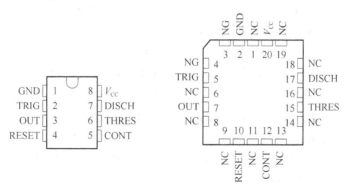

Fig 5.3  The package of NE555

**Physical Dimensions** (Fig 5.4)

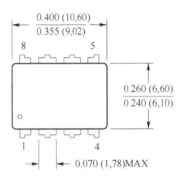
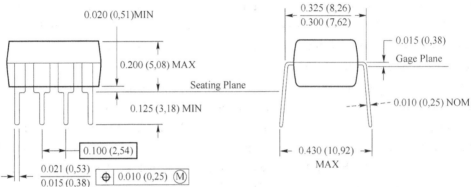

Fig 5.4　The package and definition of pins of NE555

# Technical Words and Phrases

| | | | |
|---|---|---|---|
| bidirectional | [baidiˈrekʃənəl] | adj. | 双向的;双向作用的 |
| incorporate | [inˈkɔːpəreit] | vt. | 包含;体现 |
| distinct | [disˈtiŋkt] | adj. | 明显的;独特的 |
| inhibit | [inˈhibit] | vt. | 抑制;禁止 |
| synchronous | [ˈsiŋkrənəs] | adj. | 同步的,同时的 |
| guaranteed | [ˈgærənˈtiːd] | adj. | 保证的 |
| timer | [ˈtaimə] | n. | 定时器;计时器;时钟 |
| interchangeable | [intəˈtʃeindʒəbl] | adj. | 可互换的;可交换的 |
| oscillation | [ɔsiˈleiʃən] | n. | 振荡,振动;摆动 |
| monostable | [ˈmɔnəuˌsteibl] | adj. | 单稳的,单稳态的 |
| interval | [ˈintəvəl] | n. | 间隔,间距;幕间休息 |
| astable | [eiˈsteibl] | adj. | 非稳态的,非稳态多谐振荡器 |
| threshold | [ˈθreʃhəuld] | n. | 阈值,阈限 |
| altered | [ˈɔːltəd] | vt. | 改变(alter 的过去分词) |

| terminal | [ˈtəːminəl] | n. | 终端机；终端 |
| flip-flop | [ˈflipfləp] | n. | [电子]触发器 |
| military | [ˈmilitəri] | adj. | 军事的 |

| definition of | | | 定义 |
| shift register | | | 移位寄存器 |
| general description | | | 产品说明 |
| rising edge | | | 上升沿 |
| duty cycle | | | 占空比 |
| trigger level | | | 触发电平 |

## 5.2 Reading Materials

### AD574 Datasheet

AD574 is a A/D converter which converts analogy signal into digital signal, and is usually used in electronic circuits. The following is a partial list of its handbook.

1. **Features**
   - Complete 12 bit A/D converter with reference and clock
   - 8 bit and 16 bit microprocessor bus interface
   - Guaranteed linearity over temperature 0 ℃ to +70 ℃ —AD574AJ, K, L; −55 ℃ to +125 ℃ —AD574AS, T, U
   - No missing codes over temperature
   - 35 ms maximum conversion time
   - Ceramic DIP, Plastic DIP or PLCC Package
   - Available in higher speed, pinout-compatible versions (15 ms AD674B)

2. **Product Description**

The AD574A (Fig 5.5) is a complete 12 bit successive-approximation analog-to-digital converter with 3-state output buffer circuitry for direct interface to an 8 bit or 16 bit microprocessor bus.

The AD574A integrates all analog and digital functions on one chip. Offset, linearity and scaling errors are minimized by active laser-trimming of thin-film resistors at the wafer stage. The voltage reference uses an implanted buried Zener for low noise and low drift. On the digital side, 12 bit logic is used for the successive-approximation register, control circuitry and 3-state output buffers.

The AD574A is available in six different grades. The AD574A J, K and L grades are specified for operation over the 0 ℃ to +70 ℃ temperature range. The AD574A S, T and U are specified for the −55 ℃ to +125 ℃ range. All grades are available in a 28-pin hermetically-sealed ceramic DIP. Also, the J, K and L grades are available in a 28-pin plastic DIP and PLCC, and the J and K grades are available in ceramic PLCC.

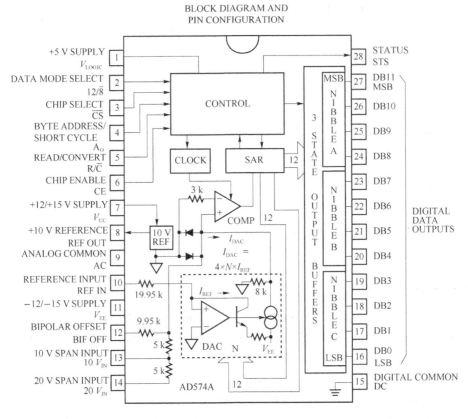

Fig 5.5　AD574A

## 5.3　Application

根据74LS194的数据手册了解其功能、特点及应用,并用74LS194按图制作一个彩灯电路。

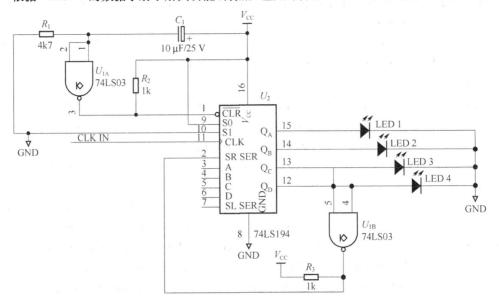

## 5.4 Knowledge(翻译技巧2——长句翻译)

科技文章要求叙述准确,用词严谨,因此一句话里常常包含多个分句,这种复杂且长的句子居科技英语难点之首。较长句子看上去显得很复杂,但一般来讲,往往是因为其含有较多的修饰成分显得冗长。若能正确区分哪一些是句子主干成分,哪一些是附加的修饰成分,就能正确理解原文意思。不过长句翻译往往不在理解英文原意上,而在于怎样把这个较复杂、冗长的原文意思准确、通畅地翻译成中文。

由于汉语与英语两种语言之间存在着很多差异,多数情况下用顺序翻译法得到的译文往往不符合汉语习惯。这种情况下就要采取一些其他的方法与技巧,如变序翻译法、分句翻译法等。

**1. 变序翻译法**

在翻译那些包含较多修饰成分的句子时就要适当改变原文成分的顺序。

The difficulties that would have to be encountered by anyone who attempted to explore the Moon would be in comparably greater than those that have to be faced in the endeavor to reach the summit of Mount Qomolangma. 对任何试图登月探险的人来讲,其所要遇到的困难将比那些力图登上珠穆朗玛峰的人所遇到的困难大得无法比拟。

在这里,把原句中的一个定语从句改变顺序后放在了句首,同时也变成了状语的功能。

**2. 分句译法**

当一个长句所论述的多个含义之间逻辑关系不是非常密切时,往往可将其各含义分别译成许多分句,这样可使译文不仅简洁明了,而且符合中文习惯。

Such students will have acquired a set of engineering tools consisting essentially of mathematics and one or more compute languages and the language of engineering graphics, and the ability to use the English language to express themselves in both forms, and will also have studied a number of basic engineering sciences, including engineering mechanics, materials and processes and thermal fluids. 这些学生将能获得一系列工程技能、英语表达运用能力以及许多工程学基础知识。所谓工程技能主要包括数字、计算机语言及工程制图语言。所谓工程学基础知识则包括工程机械学、材料与工艺学以及流学。

在这里,整个句子主干是学生将获得的知识与技能,而每个分词短语引导的定语是说明每种技能或知识都包括哪些内容。这些定语成分不但冗长,且与主干内容并没有密不可分的关系,所以采取了分句译法。

## 5.5 Exercises

Ⅰ. Translate the following phrases and expressions

1. 双向移位寄存器
2. 工作模式控制
3. 时钟上升沿触发
4. 触发电平

5. Parallel (broadside) load
6. Synchronous parallel loading
7. Absolute Maximum Ratings
8. Recommended Operating Conditions
9. Astable or Monostable Operation
10. Physical Dimensions

**II. Translate the following sentences into Chinese**

1. This bidirectional shift register is designed to incorporate virtually all of the features a system designer may want in a shift register.

2. Synchronous parallel loading is accomplished by applying the four bits of data and taking both mode control inputs, S0 and S1, HIGH. The Parallel data (A toward D) is loaded into the associated flip-flops and appear at the outputs ($Q_A$ toward $Q_D$) after the positive transition of the clock input.

3. The threshold and trigger levels normally are two-thirds and one-third, respectively, of $V_{CC}$.

4. In the astable mode of operation, the frequency and duty cycle can be controlled independently with two external resistors and a single external capacitor.

5. Shift right is accomplished synchronously with the rising edge of the clock pulse when S0 is HIGH and S1 is LOW. Serial data for this mode is entered at the shift-right data input.

6. These devices (NE555) are precision timing circuits capable of producing accurate time delays or oscillation.

7. If the trigger input is above the trigger level and the threshold input (THRES) is above the threshold level, the flip-flop is reset and the output is low.

8. The reset (RESET) input can override all other inputs and can be used to initiate a new timing cycle.

9. AD574 is a A/D converter which converts analogy signal into digital signal, and usually used in electronic technology.

10. The AD574A integrates all analog and digital functions on one chip.

# Unit 6  User Manual

 Knowledge aims:

1. Technical words and phrases.
2. User manual.

 Ability aims:

Can read and write user's manual.

 Pre-reading

Read the following passage, paying attention to the questions.
1. What can you do with iPhone 4?
2. How can we scan reflective originals?

## 6.1  Text

### 6.1.1  Introduction to iPhone 4

In 2007 iPhone reinvented what we thought of as a smart phone. iPhone 3GS offers incredible speed and performance, on average up to twice as fast as iPhone 3G. Now, this is really hot. There are over 100 new features. We introduce several new features here.

**1. New Design**

iPhone 4 has glass on the front and back, and steel around the sides. It's like a beautiful old Leica Camera. It is 24% thinner than the iPhone 3GS. As a matter of fact, it is the thinnest smartphone on the planet. Here are the volume controls, a front facing camera, micro SIM tray, camera and LED flash on the back, bottom, mic, top, headset jack, noise cancellation mic.

**2. Retina Display**

Something we call the retina display. What's that? In any display there are pixels. We dramtically increased the pixel density four times the amount. We get really, really sharp text. Now the retina display is 326 pixels per inch.

**3. 300 Hours of Standby**

Because we've been able to make the battery bigger and the A4 is so good, we've improved the battery life. 7 hours of 3G talk, 6 hours of 3G browsing, 10 hours of Wi-Fi browsing, 10 hours of video, 40 hours of music, and 300 hours of standby.

**4. Quad Band HSDPA, 7.2 Mbit/s**

**5. Dual Mics, 802.11n Wi-Fi, GPS, Compass, Accelerometer**

**6. Adding a Gyroscope**

We're adding a 3 axis gyro, and we tied the gyro and accelerometer, compass, and gyro together for six axis. It's perfect for gaming.

**7. Megapixels**

These cameras are really about capturing photons and low light photography. So we've gone from 3 megapixels to 5 megapixels, but we're using a backside illuminated sensor. In addition to that, when most people increase megapixels they make them smaller, but we've kept ours the same size. It has $5\times$ digital zoom, tap to focus, and we've got an LED flash.

**8. HD Video**

It also records HD video, 720 p at 30 fps.

**9. iPhone OS 4**

iPhone OS 4 is the most advanced mobile operating system in the world.

### 6.1.2 iPhone User Guide

iPhone 4 overview (Fig 6.1)

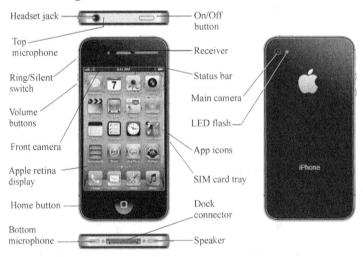

Fig 6.1 iPhone 4 overview

Your Home screen may look different, depending on the model of iPhone you have and whether you've customized your Home screen.

**1. Buttons**

**On/Off button** (Fig 6.2)

When you're not using iPhone, you can lock it to turn off the display and save the battery.

Lock iPhone: press the On/Off button. When iPhone is locked, nothing happens if you touch the screen. iPhone can still receive calls, text messages, and other updates. You can also:

- Listen to music.
- Adjust the volume using the buttons on the side of iPhone (or on the iPhone earphones) while you're on a phone call or listening to music.
- Use the center button on iPhone earphones to answer or end a call, or to control audio playback.

By default, if you don't touch the screen for a minute, iPhone locks automatically.

| Unlock iPhone | Press the Home button ☐ or the On/Off button, then drag the slider. |
| --- | --- |
| Turn iPhone off | Press and hold the On/Off button for a few seconds until the red slider appears, then drag the slider. |
| Turn iPhone on | Press and hold the On/Off button until the Apple logo appears. |

Fig 6.2  On/Off button

**Home button**

The Home button lets you get back to the Home screen at any time. It also provides other convenient shortcuts.

Go to the Home screen: press the Home button. At the Home screen, just a tap opens an app. See "Opening and switching apps" on page 19.

**Volume buttons** (Fig 6.3)

When you're on the phone or listening to songs, movies, or other media, the buttons on the side of iPhone adjust the audio volume. Otherwise, the buttons control the volume for the ringer, alerts, and other sound effects.

WARNING: For important information about avoiding hearing loss, see the Important Product Information Guide at www.apple.com/support/manuals/iphone.

To limit the volume for music and videos, go to Settings > Music.

You can also use the volume up button to take a picture or record a video.

**Ring/Silent switch** (Fig 6.4)

Flip the Ring/Silent switch to put iPhone in ring mode  or silent mode 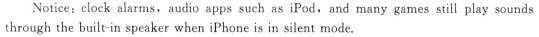.

Notice: clock alarms, audio apps such as iPod, and many games still play sounds through the built-in speaker when iPhone is in silent mode.

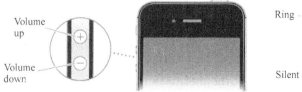

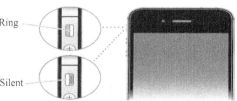

Fig 6.3  Volume buttons                                    Fig 6.4  Ring/Silent switch

## 2. Installing the SIM Card

If you were given a SIM card to install, install it before setting up iPhone.

Install the SIM card: insert the end of a small paper clip or SIM eject tool into the hole on the SIM card tray. Pull out the SIM card tray and place the SIM card in the tray. With the tray aligned and the SIM card on top, carefully replace the tray.

Install the SIM card in iPhone 4(Fig 6.5).

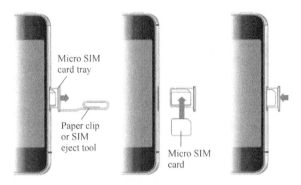

Fig 6.5　Installing the SIM card in iPhone 4

## 3. Basics

**Using apps**

The high-resolution Multi-Touch screen and simple finger gestures make it easy to use iPhone apps.

**Opening and switching apps**

Press the Home button ☐ to go to the Home screen and see your apps.

Open an app: tap it (Fig 6.6).

To return to the Home screen, press the Home button ☐ again.

Switch to main screen: flick left or right to see another Home screen (Fig 6.7).

Fig 6.6　Open an app　　　　Fig 6.7　Flick left or right to see another Home screen

Double-click the Home button ☐ to reveal the multitasking bar, which shows your most recently used apps (Fig 6.8). Tap an app to reopen it, or flick to see more apps.

**Zooming in or out** (Fig 6.9)

Recently used apps

Fig 6.8  Recently used apps

Fig 6.9  Zooming in or out

When viewing photos, web pages, email, or maps, you can zoom in or out. Pinch your fingers together or apart. For photos and web pages, you can double-tap (tap twice quickly) to zoom in, and then double-tap again to zoom out. For maps, double-tap to zoom in and tap once with two fingers to zoom out.

**Viewing in portrait or landscape orientation** (Fig 6.10)

Many iPhone apps let you view the screen in either portrait or landscape orientation. Rotate iPhone and the display rotates too, adjusting automatically to fit the new screen orientation.

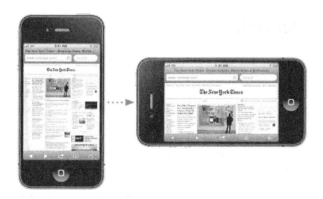

Fig 6.10  Viewing in portrait or landscape orientation

# Technical Words and Phrases

| | | | |
|---|---|---|---|
| reinvent | [ri:in'vent] | vt. | 重新使用,重复发明 |
| tray | [trei] | n. | 托盘;文件盒 |
| cancellation | ['kænsə'leiʃən] | n. | 取消;删除 |
| retina | ['retinə] | n. | 视网膜,网膜;屏幕 |
| pixel | ['piksəl] | n. | 像素,象素,像素点 |

| | | | |
|---|---|---|---|
| density | [ˈdensəti] | n. | 密度 |
| standby | [ˈstændbai] | n. | 待机 |
| browsing | [ˈbrauziŋ] | n. | 浏览 |
| compass | [ˈkʌmpəs] | n. | 指南针 |
| accelerometer | [əkˌseləˈrɔmitə] | n. | 加速计 |
| gyroscope | [ˈdʒaiərəskəup] | n. | 陀螺仪 |
| axis | [ˈæksis] | n. | 轴；轴线 |
| capturing | [ˈkæptʃəriŋ] | vt. | 捕捉（capture 的 ing 形式） |
| capture | [ˈkæptʃə] | n. | 捕获 |
| flick | [ˈflik] | vt. | 轻弹 |
| double-click | [ˈdʌblˌklik] | n. | 双击 |
| pinch | [pintʃ] | vt. | 挤压，收缩 |
| portrait | [ˈpɔːtrit] | n. | 肖像 |
| rotate | [rəuˈteit] | vi. | 旋转 |

| | |
|---|---|
| touch screen | 接触式屏幕；触感屏幕 |
| landscape orientation | 横向，横向打印 |
| digital zoom | 数码变焦；数字变焦 |
| zoom in | 放大 |
| App Store | 应用软件 |

## 6.2　Reading Materials

### Introduction to MiraScan

MiraScan is the driver for your scanner. It is TWAIN compliant and designed to be user-friendly. With its iconized user interface and fully logical task flow design, you can complete a satisfactory scanning job with only a few mouse clicks.

You can perform all of the following tasks using MiraScan.

(1) Preview, scan and import the reflective originals or transparencies into your image editing software.

(2) Adjust the quality of your scanned image before you actually start editing the image in your image editing software.

(3) Apply batch scan functionality, allowing you to specify and switch among multiple scanning sessions in an image.

(4) Create special effects to the scanned image by applying invert and mirror functions.

(5) Use the Color Wizard to adjust the image easily and quickly.

**Scanning Reflective Originals**

Step 1. Place the original face down on the scanner glass plate. Note the direction of the original so that you will not scan the image in the wrong direction (Fig 6.11). Close the scanner lid.

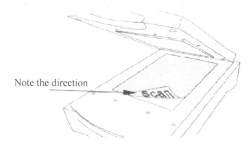

Fig 6.11  Scanning reflective originals

Step 2. Open your application software.

Step 3. If this is your first time to scan, you may have to select the TWAIN source by choosing "Select source" in the "File" menu and then selecting "MiraScan" in your application software (You only need to do this once, unless you re-install your application software).

Please note that the way to select the TWAIN source may differ according to the software you use. For details, please refer to the documents that come with your application software.

Step 4. Choose "Acquire" from your application software to bring up MiraScan (this may also differ according to the application you use).

Step 5. From the MiraScan main screens (Fig 6.12), select "Reflective" in the "Original" combo box, and then click "Preview". A preview image will appear in the Preview Area.

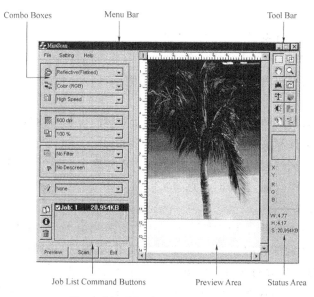

Fig 6.12  MiraScan main screens

Step 6. Adjust the scan area in the Preview Area.

Step 7. Use the options in the Combo Boxes to specify the Resolution, Scale … etc. That will apply to the scanned image.

Step 8. Use the options in the Tool Bar to adjust the image.

Step 9. If you need to add another scan area (scan job) to the original, push the Duplicate button in the Job List to add a new job (Fig 6.13). Then repeat Step 6 and 7 to do the settings for that scan job.

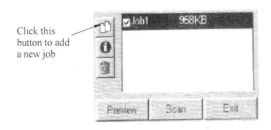

Fig 6.13　Add a new job

Step 10. After you have finished the settings for each scan job, press the Scan button to scan.

Step 11. A few seconds later, the scanned image(s) will be imported into your application software. You can start to edit the image(s).

## 6.3　Knowledge(用户使用说明书)

使用说明书是随各种产品设备附带的书面材料,其形式有书本、小册子或散页之分,现在还有光盘,主要根据所说明的设备大小与复杂程度而定。其内容包括设备的安装、试验、维护等。

**1. 特点**

英语说明书在编写体裁等方面的特点如下。

(1) 文句简短、扼要。

(2) 内容严格按照使用和维修时的先后顺序编排、划分类别章节,并给出醒目的标题及不同的序号。

(3) 作参考用的附图和附表比较多,用以辅助文字的说明,直观性强。

(4) 重要的零部件和操作程序均用大写字体标出。

(5) 在操作与测试过程的说明中,祈使句的出现频率大,被动语态也很常见。

(6) 常用到很多组合词,翻译时注意与实际结合。

**2. 说明书的编写**

(1) 序——说明书的最前面往往有个序,用来简洁强调本产品的优点或特点,有时也说明本产品使用前应特别注意的事项,如关于安全使用,电视机、录像机等的电源要求,对所接收信号的要求等,这一部分有时直接标明本产品特点、注意事项等。

**WARNING**：This VTR can be used with a power (mains) voltage of 100 to 110 V,115 to

127 V，200 to 220 V or 230 to 250 V. 这句话说明了这个录像机的电源适用范围。

其主要用途是让用户在选购产品时可以一目了然地了解该产品的最主要特征及是否适用。还有常用的 Features(特点)、Precautions(保护措施)等。

(2)目录(Contents)——列出说明书说明内容的目录,便于查寻。

(3)正文——对设备的各个部分进行描述和说明,如本单元课文及阅读材料所摘选的内容,一般采用图文结合的方式,写作和翻译时都要注意对照。

如果有多项功能时,要注意按顺序逐项介绍,重复步骤可写参见……,文字要简洁。如课文中用 step1,step2…,可以让使用者操作方便。

正文可以采用章节结构,也可以采用项目结构或列表结构,视具体需要说明的内容而定。在使用英语大写字母缩写时,第一次必须用全称表示,考虑到说明书(手册)的阅读对象并非都是专业人员,使用专业术语最好也要用通俗的语言甚至图片加以说明。

## 6.4 Exercises

Ⅰ. **Translate the following phrases and expressions**

1. 视网膜显示
2. 移动终端操作系统
3. 高清晰视频
4. 使用应用程序
5. Home screen
6. Volume buttons
7. 326 pixels per inch
8. 300 hours of standby
9. Install the SIM card
10. Zooming in or out

Ⅱ. **Translate the following sentences into Chinese**

1. These cameras are really about capturing photons and low light photography.

2. When you're on the phone or listening to songs, movies, or other media, the buttons on the side of iPhone adjust the audio volume.

3. When iPhone is locked, nothing happens if you touch the screen. iPhone can still receive calls, text messages, and other updates.

4. For photos and web pages, you can double-tap (tap twice quickly) to zoom in, and then double-tap again to zoom out.

5. Adjust the quality of your scanned image before you actually start editing the image in your image editing software.

6. With its iconized user interface and fully logical taskflow design, you can complete a satisfactory scanning job with only a few mouse clicks.

7. Please note that the way to select the TWAIN source may differ according to the software you use.

8. MiraScan can record the settings you make for each scan session in a configuration file. With this feature, you can specify different settings for each scan job in each configuration file.

9. The default unit is inch. To change the unit, press in the list box with your mouse, and choose the desired unit from the list by clicking it.

10. A high precision voltage reference and clock are included on-chip, and the circuit guarantees full-rated performance without external circuitry or clock signals.

# Unit 7　Appliances

 Knowledge aims:

1. Technical words and phrases.
2. Electronic appliances.
3. Letters of applying for a job.

 Ability aims:

Can read electrical appliances material.

 Pre-reading

Read the following passage, paying attention to the questions.
1. What is CRT?
2. What difference between the color TV and black-white TV?
3. What is the basic principle of a refrigerator?
4. What is the function of refrigerant inside a refrigerator?

## 7.1　Text

### 7.1.1　Television

**1. About Television**

Television is certainly one of the most influential forces of our time.

To understand TV, let's start at the beginning with a quick note about your brain. There are two amazing things about your brain that make television possible.

The first principle is this: If you divide a still image into a collection of small colored dots, your brain will reassemble the dots into a meaningful image. On a TV or computer screen, the dots are called pixels.

The human brain's second amazing feature relating to television is this: if you divide a moving scene into a sequence of still pictures and show the still images in rapid succession, the brain will reassemble the still images into a single, moving scene.

**2. The Cathode Ray Tube**

Some TVs in use today rely on a device known as the cathode ray tube, or CRT, to display their images. Let's start with the CRT, because CRTs are used to be the most common way of displaying images.

In a cathode ray tube (Fig 7.1), the "cathode" is a heated filament (unlike the filament in a normal light bulb). The heated filament is in a vacuum created inside a glass "tube". The "ray" is a stream of electrons that naturally pour off a heated cathode into the vacuum.

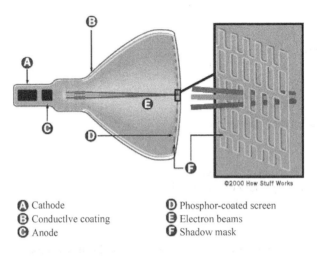

Ⓐ Cathode
Ⓑ Conductlve coating
Ⓒ Anode
Ⓓ Phosphor-coated screen
Ⓔ Electron beams
Ⓕ Shadow mask

Fig 7.1   CRT

Electrons are negative. The anode is positive, so it attracts the electrons pouring off the cathode. In a TV's cathode ray tube, the stream of electrons is focused by a focusing anode into a tight beam and then accelerated by an accelerating anode. This tight, high-speed beam of electrons flies through the vacuum in the tube and hits the flat screen at the other end of the tube. This screen is coated with phosphor, which glows when struck by the beam.

There are coils, which are able to create magnetic fields inside the tube. One set of coils creates a magnetic field that moves the electron beam vertically, while another set moves the beam horizontally. By controlling the voltages in the coils, you can position the electron beam at any point on the screen.

In a CRT, phosphor coats the inside of the screen. When the electron beam strikes the phosphor, it makes the screen glow. In a black-and-white screen, there is one phosphor that glows white when struck. In a color screen, there are three phosphors arranged as dots or stripes that emit red, green and blue light. There are also three electron beams to illuminate the three different colors together.

### 3. Black-and-White TV Signal

In a black-and-white TV, the electron beam "paints" an image onto the screen by moving the electron beam across the phosphor a line at a time. As the beam paints each line from left to right, the intensity of the beam is changed to create different shades of black, gray and white across the screen. Because the lines are spaced very closely together, your brain integrates them into a single image. A TV screen normally has about 480 lines visible from top to bottom.

When a television station wants to broadcast a signal to your TV, or when your VCR (Video Cassette Recorder) wants to display the movie on a video tape on your TV, the signal needs to mesh with the electronics controlling the beam so that the TV can accurately paint the picture that the TV station or VCR sends. The TV station or VCR therefore sends a well-known signal to the TV that contains three different parts.

- Intensity information for the beam as it paints each line
- Horizontal-retrace signals to tell the TV when to move the beam back at the end of each line
- Vertical-retrace signals 60 times per second to move the beam from bottom-right to top-left

**4. Color TV**

A color TV screen differs from a black-and-white screen in three ways.

- There are three electron beams that move simultaneously across the screen. They are named the red, green and blue beams.
- The screen is not coated with a single sheet of phosphor as in a black-and-white TV. Instead, the screen is coated with red, green and blue phosphors arranged in dots or stripes. If you turn on your TV or computer monitor and look closely at the screen with a magnifying glass, you will be able to see the dots or stripes.
- On the inside of the tube, very close to the phosphor coating, there is a thin metal screen called a shadow mask. This mask is perforated with very small holes that are aligned with the phosphor dots (or stripes) on the screen (Fig7.2).

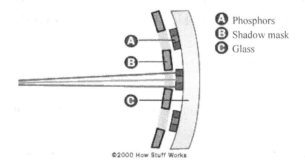

Fig 7.2 The shadow mask works

When a color TV needs to create a red dot, it fires the red beam at the red phosphor. It is similar for green and blue dots. To create a white dot, red, green and blue beams are fired simultaneously—the three colors mix together to create white. To create a black dot, all three beams are turned off as they scan past the dot. All other colors on a TV screen are combinations of red, green and blue.

A color TV signal starts off looking just like a black-and-white signal. An extra chrominance signal is added by superimposing a 3.579 545 MHz sine wave onto the standard black-and-white signal. A phase shift in the chrominance signal indicates the color to display. The amplitude of the signal determines the saturation. Tab 7.1 shows you the relationship between color and phase.

Tab 7.1  A phase shift in the chrominance

| Color | Phase | Color | Phase |
| --- | --- | --- | --- |
| Burst | 0 degrees | Blue | 195 degrees |
| Yellow | 15 degrees | Cyan | 255 degrees |
| Red | 75 degrees | Green | 315 degrees |
| Magenta | 135 degrees | | |

A black-and-white TV filters out and ignores the chrominance signal. A color TV picks it out of the signal and decodes it, along with the normal intensity signal, to determine how to modulate the three color beams.

### 7.1.2  Refrigerator

The basic idea behind a refrigerator is very simple. It uses the evaporation of a liquid to absorb heat. You probably know that when you put water on your skin, it makes you feel cool. As the water evaporates, it absorbs heat, creating that cool feeling. Rubbing alcohol feels even cooler because it evaporates at a lower temperature.

The liquid, or refrigerant, used in a refrigerator evaporates at an extremely low temperature, so it can create freezing temperatures inside the refrigerator. If you place your refrigerator's refrigerant on your skin (definitely NOT a good idea), it will freeze your skin as it evaporates.

There are five basic parts to any refrigerator (Fig 7.3):
- Compressor
- Heat-exchanging pipes—serpentine or coiled set of pipes outside the unit
- Expansion valve
- Heat-exchanging pipes—serpentine or coiled set of pipes inside the unit
- Refrigerant—liquid that evaporates inside the refrigerator to create the cold temperatures. Many industrial installations use pure ammonia as the refrigerant. Pure ammonia evaporates at −32 degrees Celsius.

The basic mechanism of a refrigerator works like this.

The compressor compresses the refrigerant gas. This raises the refrigerant's pressure and temperature, so the heat-exchanging coils outside the refrigerator allow the refrigerant to dissipate the heat of pressurization.

As it cools, the refrigerant condenses into liquid form and flows through the expansion valve.

When it flows through the expansion valve, the liquid refrigerant is allowed to move from a high-pressure zone to a low-pressure zone, so it expands and evaporates (light blue). In evaporating, it absorbs heat, making it cold.

The coils inside the refrigerator allow the refrigerant to absorb heat, making the inside of the refrigerator cold. The cycle then repeats.

Pure ammonia gas is highly toxic to people and would pose a threat if the refrigerator was to leak, so all home refrigerators don't use pure ammonia. You may have heard of refrigerants known as Freon, a non-toxic replacement for ammonia. It has about the same boiling point as ammonia. However, Freon is not toxic to humans, so it is safe to use in your kitchen, but many large industrial refrigerators still use ammonia.

In the 1970s, it was discovered that the Freon then in use are harmful to the ozone layer, so as of the 1990s, all new refrigerators and air conditioners use refrigerants that are less harmful to the ozone layer.

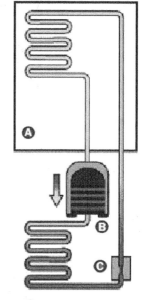

Ⓐ Inside the refrigerator
Ⓑ Compressor
Ⓒ Expansion valve

Fig 7.3　Structure of refrigerator

## Technical Words and Phrases

| | | | |
|---|---|---|---|
| antenna | [æn'tenə] | n. | 天线 |
| cable | ['keib(ə)l] | n. | 电缆,此处指有线电视 |
| channel | ['tʃænəl] | n. | 海峡;信道,频道 |
| chrominance | ['krəuminəns] | n. | 色度 |
| dot | [dɔt] | n. | 点,圆点 |
| | | vt. | 在……上打点 |
| intensity | [in'tensiti] | n. | 强烈,剧烈;强度,亮度 |
| phosphor | ['fɔsfə(r)] | n. | 磷;启明星 |
| plasma | ['plæzmə] | n. | 等离子体;等离子显示器 |
| influential | [influ'enʃəl] | adj. | 有影响的;有势力的 |
| reassemble | [ri:ə'sembl] | vi. | 重新集合 |
| sequence | ['si:kwəns] | n. | [数][计] 序列;顺序 |
| filament | ['filəmənt] | n. | 灯丝;细丝 |
| absorb | [əb'sɔ:b] | vt. | 吸收;吸引 |
| alcohol | ['ælkəhlɔ] | n. | 酒精,乙醇;含酒精的饮料 |
| ammonia | [ə'məuniə] | n. | [化]氨,氨水 |

| chamber | [ˈtʃeimbə(r)] | n. | 室,房间;(枪)膛 |
| condense | [kənˈdens] | vi. | (使)浓缩,精简 |
| dissipate | [ˈdisipeit] | vt. | 驱散,消散;浪费 |
| evaporation | [ivæpəˈreʃ(ə)n] | n. | 蒸发,蒸发作用 |
| Freon | [ˈfriːɔn] | n. | 氟利昂 |
| joule | [dʒuːl] | n. | [物]焦耳(功和能量的单位) |
| liquid | [ˈlikwid] | n. | 液体,流体 |
| | | adj. | 液体的 |
| magnetron | [ˈmægnitrɔn] | n. | 磁电管,磁控管 |
| molecule | [ˈmɔlikjuːl] | n. | 分子 |
| refrigerant | [riˈfridʒərənt] | n. | 致冷剂 |
| | | adj. | 致冷的,冷却的 |
| refrigerator | [riˈfridʒəreitə(r)] | n. | 冰箱 |
| shield | [ˈʃiːld] | n. | 护罩 |
| | | vt. | 保护,防护 |
| toxic | [ˈtɔksik] | adj. | 毒的;中毒的,有毒的 |
| twist | [twist] | n. | 扭曲 |
| | | vt. | 拧,扭曲 |
| valve | [vælv] | n. | 阀,活门;气门 |
| zone | [zəun] | n. | 存储区;带,层;区域,范围 |

| covert … into | | | 把……转换…… |
| integrate … into | | | 把……整体组合成…… |
| VCR(Video Cassette Recorder) | | | 盒式录像机,磁带式录像机 |
| a stream of | | | 一连串 |
| pour off | | | 流出 |
| cathode ray tube | | | 阴极射线管 |

## 7.2 Reading Materials

### 7.2.1 Digital TV

The horizontal resolution is something like 500 dots for a color analog TV set. This level of resolution was amazing 50 years ago, but today it is rather passed. The lowest resolution computer monitor that anyone uses today has 640×480 pixels, and most people use a resolution like 800×600 pixels or 1024×768 pixels. We have grown comfortable with the great clarity and solidity of a computer display, and analog TV technology pales by comparison.

Many of the new satellite systems, as well as DVDs, use a digital encoding scheme that provides a much clearer picture. In these systems, the digital information is converted to the analog format to display it on your analog TV. The image looks great compared to a VHS tape, but it would be twice as good if the conversion to analog didn't happen.

There is now a big push underway to convert all TV sets from analog to digital, so that digital signals drive your TV set directly.

When you read and hear people talking about digital television (DTV), what they are talking about is the transmission of pure digital television signals, along with the reception and display of those signals on a digital TV set. The digital signals might be broadcasted over the air or transmitted by a cable or satellite system to your home. In your home, a decoder receives the signal and uses it, in digital form, to directly drive your digital TV set.

There is a class of digital television that is getting a lot of press right now. It is called high-definition television, or HDTV. HDTV is high-resolution digital television combined with Dolby Digital surround sound (AC-3). This combination creates a stunning image with stunning sound. HDTV requires new production and transmission equipment at the HDTV stations, as well as new equipment for reception by the consumer. The higher resolution picture is the main selling point for HDTV. Imagine 720 or 1080 lines of resolution compared to the 525 lines people are used to in the United States (or the 625 lines in Europe)—it's a huge difference!

### 7.2.2 The Microwave Oven

A microwave oven (Fig 7.4) consists of:
- a magnetron
- a magnetron control circuit (usually with a microcontroller)
- a waveguide
- a cooking chamber (or cooking cavity)

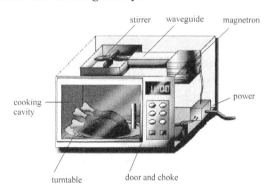

Fig 7.4 Structure of microwave oven

A microwave oven works by passing microwave radiation, usually at a frequency of 2,450 MHz (a wavelength of 12.24 cm), through the food. Water, fat, and sugar molecules in the food absorb energy from the microwave beam in a process called dielectric heating. Most molecules are electric dipoles, meaning that they have a positive charge at one end and a negative charge at the other, and is therefore twisted to and from as it tries to align itself with the alternating electric field induced by the microwave beam. This molecular movement creates heat. Microwave heating is most efficient on liquid water, and much less so on fats, sugars, and frozen water. Microwave heating is sometimes incorrectly explained as resonance of water molecules, but this occurs only at much higher frequencies, in the tens of gigahertz.

The cooking chamber itself is a Faraday cage enclosure to prevent the microwaves escaping into the surroundings. The oven door is usually a glass panel, but has a layer of conductive mesh to maintain the shielding. Since the mesh width is much less than the wavelength of 12 cm, the microwave radiation can not pass through the door, while visible light (with a much shorter wavelength) can.

Microwaves are radio waves. In the case of microwave ovens, the commonly used radio wave frequency is 2,450 MHz. Radio waves in this frequency range have an interesting property: they are absorbed by water, fats and sugars. When they are absorbed, they are converted directly into atomic motion—heat. Microwaves in this frequency range have another interesting property: they are not absorbed by most plastics, glass or ceramics. Metal reflects microwaves, which is why metal pans do not work well in a microwave oven.

With wireless computer networks gaining in popularity, microwave interference has become a concern among those with wireless networks. Microwave ovens are capable of disrupting wireless network transmissions due to the fact that the microwave creates radio waves at about 2,450 MHz.

## 7.3 Application

你能说出吸尘器的原理吗？

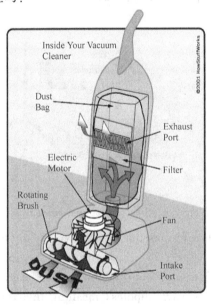

Fig 7.5 Structure of vacuum cleaner

## 7.4　Knowledge(求职信)

一份好的英文简历、求职信是展示你个人信息的绝佳机会。一流的简历将使你在激烈的竞争中脱颖而出。只要掌握以下诀窍,就可以写出出类拔萃的简历,从而赢得工作机会。

### 1. 简历(Resume)

(1) Organise your experience

第一步:组织好你的经历

In functional CVs, you put your skills into categories then briefly list past job titles at the bottom. These are suitable for those who have been unemployed for long periods, held different types of jobs in the past, changed jobs too frequently, are returning to work after a long period or who wish to change career.

功能型简历——强调技能、资质以及成就。适合于以下情况:有很长时间没有工作过、过去频繁更换工作不想给招聘者留下不好的印象、工作经历有中断、跨专业求职,但你具有申请职位所需的相关技能。

Recent graduates and others on a consistent career path usually opt for the chronological format. These CVs list your jobs and duties for each in reverse chronological order.

时序性简历——按照逆时序记录你曾就职的职位。适合于应届毕业生,或者工作不曾间断过的情况。

(2) Categorize your achievements

第二步:给你的成就分类

When making a chronological CV, you should outline sections of your experience, education and skills to show what you've accomplished. HR personnel and employers take less than a minute to scan your CV, so it's imperative to highlight and organize items into several concise and relevant segments.

写时序性简历时,应该着重概括你的经历、教育和技能。HR人员和你的雇主会对你的简历一扫而过,所以简历上必须突出重点和分成几个简洁、相关的部分。

If you're a recent graduate and therefore have not yet been employed, put your Education section first. In addition to the basics—university name, degree and graduation date—you can include relevant coursework, honors or awards.

如果你刚刚毕业还没有工作经验,那么把你的教育经历放在首位。包括一些基本的方面,比如大学名称、学位和毕业日期。当然也包括你修过的相关课程、所获荣誉或奖项等。

Other categories might include Relevant Work Experience, Volunteer Experience, Computer Skills, Publications, Activities, Language Skills and so on.

其他分类还包括相关工作经验、志愿者经历、电脑技能、发表过的文章、参加过的活动、语言能力等。

(3) Appearance can make or break your CV

第三步:格式可以成就你的简历,也可能毁了它

—Fonts: Whether you email, fax or post your CV, keep your font plain and easy to read. And select a reasonable size—anywhere between 9 and 12 points should be acceptable. Use a sans serif font like Arial or Verdana, not Times New Roman.

—字体:无论你是发电子邮件、传真或是邮寄你的简历,都应该让你的字体看上去舒服、易于阅读。记得要选择一个合适的字号,最好是9号到12号之间。字体方面,最好用Arial或Verdana,而不是Times New Roman。

—Formatting: Too many different fonts, colors and graphic styles will hold the readers up. Simple bullets are best for separating your duties and skills; use bold and italics sparingly. Formatting should highlight your accomplishments, not draw attention away from them.

—格式:过多的字体、颜色和样式会分散读者的注意力。简单的项目符号能最好地表明你的职责和技能,同时,有节制地使用粗体和斜体。使用格式是为了突出你的成就,而非分散别人的注意力。

(4) Content is king

第四步:内容才是王道

—Action verbs: Use strong action verbs to highlight your job experience and duties. Instead of starting your sentence with a noun, kick off with an active verb. For example, assisted customers, trained and supervised 15 new employees, organized special promotional events.

—行为动词:使用简洁有力的动词来突出你的工作经验和职责,而不是用名词开头。比如,帮助客户,培训和监管15名新员工,组织专门的销售活动。

—Numbers: It's a good idea to include numbers, percentages and amounts in your job descriptions to back up your achievements. For example, increased monthly sales by ￡100,000 over a 6-month period, increased turnover by 20% in the first year, supervised a team of 10 people.

—数字:在简历中使用数字或百分比使成就更具有说服力是个不错的主意。例如,销售额在6个月间以每个月￡100 000的速度增长,第一年增加了20%的营业额,监管一个10人的团队。

—Length: No one wants to scan through two or more pages of long-winded accomplishments and experience. If it doesn't all fit, cut it down to the most relevant and impressive items.

—长度:没人愿意看长篇大论的简历。遇到不必要的部分就删减掉,留下最相关、给人印象最深刻的部分。

例1

Personnnal Data

Name: Your Name

Gender: Male

Height: 185 cm

Weight: 80 kg
Health: Excellent
Birthdate: March 3, 1990
Birthplace: Hainan
Marital Status: Single
Address: 23 South Seaside Avenue, South China Computer Company, Haikou 571000
Mobile: xxx
E-mail: xxx@xxx.com
Position Sought:
Computer Programmer with a foreign enterprise in Beihai City
Qualifications:
Four years' work experience operating computers extensively, coupled with educational preparation
Professional Experience:
—Computer Programmer, South China Computer Company, Haikou, from 2002 to date.
—Coded well-defined systems logic flow charts into computer machine instructions using Java or C.
—Coded subroutines following specifications, file size parameters, block diagrams.
—Performed maintenance tasks and patching to established straightforward programs.
—Documented all programs as completed.
—Tested, debugged and assembled programs.
—Adept at operating IBM-PC and Legend computers.
Educational Background:
Beijing University of Technology
B. S. degree in Computer Science, July 2002
Courses included:
—Computer Science Systems Design and Analysis
—PASCAL Programming Operating Systems
—COBOL Programming Java Programming
—FORTRAN Programming D-BASE Programming
—Systems Management
Beihai No. 14 Middle School, 1992~1998
English Proficiency:
A good command of English in science and technology
Hobbies:
Home page building and on-line chitchatting
References:
Will be supplied upon request

**2. 求职信(Letters of Applying for a Job)**

求职信的内容一般包括以下部分。

(1) 写信的缘由;

(2) 个人情况简介。例如,年龄、性别、文化程度、工作经历、工作技能、个人专长等;

(3) 推荐人或证明人姓名以供录用方查询;

(4) 约定面试时间。通常随求职信附上个人简历和两三封推荐信。

Directions:You are a senior of computer science. You'd like to be an intern for an IT company. Write a letter to present your willings. You should clear:

1) your education background

2) your purpose of being an intern

You should write about 100 words and don't need to write the address.

例 2

Dear sirs,

I am a senior student of computer science in Beijing University of Technology. I would like to work as an intern in your company. As I have a wide interest in computer, I will do whatever job assigned to me, in software development or in technical support. One of my advantages is that I am able to work conscientiously under pressure. The more challenging my task is, the better it will be done.

My main purpose is just to put into practice what I have learned from the classroom in the past few years and to learn about my own ability in practical work. Remuneration is not yet taken into consideration.

I am enclosing a resume and looking forward to hearing from you.

Yours respectfully!

×××

## 7.5 Exercises

**Ⅰ. Translate the following phrases and expressions**

1. 静止图像

2. 与电视有关的

3. 阴极射线管,显像管

4. 建立电磁场

5. move the beam horizontally

6. electron beam

7. emit red, green and blue light

8. electrical signals

9. cable TV programs

10. select the channel

## II. Translate the following sentences into Chinese

1. As the water evaporates, it absorbs heat, creating that cool feeling.

2. If you place your refrigerator's refrigerant on your skin (definitely NOT a good idea), it will freeze your skin as it evaporates.

3. Pure ammonia gas is highly toxic to people and would pose a threat if the refrigerator were to leak.

4. The Freon liquid runs through an expansion valve, and in the process it evaporates to become cold, low-pressure Freon gas.

5. Microwave heating is most efficient on liquid water, and much less so on fats, sugars, and frozen water.

6. With wireless computer networks gaining in popularity, microwave interference has become a concern among those with wireless networks.

7. The first food to be deliberately cooked with microwaves was popcorn, and the second was an egg (which exploded in the face of one of the experimenters).

8. By the late 1970s the technology had improved to the point where prices were falling rapidly.

9. It may look like a complicated machine, but the conventional vacuum cleaner is actually made up of only six essential components.

10. You can put the vacuum-cleaner bag anywhere along the path between the intake tube and the exhaust port, as long as the air current flows through it.

# Unit 8 EDA Software

 Knowledge aims:

1. Technical words and phrases.
2. EDA software.
3. Letters of applying for study chance.

 Ability aims:

Can read EDA software application materials.

 Pre-reading

Read the following passage, paying attention to the questions.
1. What is Quartus II Design Flow?
2. What modules is the complier?
3. How many parts does the protel software have?

## 8.1 Text

### 8.1.1 Quartus II

The Altera Quartus II design software provides a complete, multi-platform design environment that easily adapts to your specific design needs. It is a comprehensive environment for system-on-a-programmable-chip (SOPC) design. The Quartus II software includes solutions for all phases of FPGA and CPLD design.

Quartus II Design Flow is shown in Fig 8.1.

In addition, the Quartus II software allows you to use the Quartus II graphical user interface and command-line interface for each phase of the design flow. You can use one of these interfaces for the entire flow.

**1. Graphical User Interface**

You can use the Quartus II software graphical user interface (GUI) to perform all stages of the design flow. Fig 8.2 shows QuartusII GUI as it appears when you first start the software.

Unit 8　EDA Software

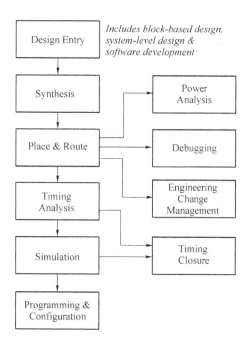

Fig 8.1　Quartus II Design Flow

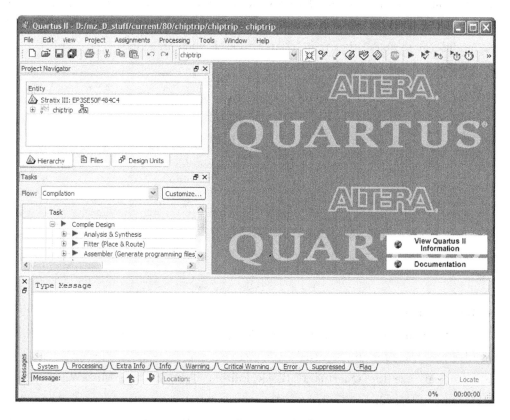

Fig 8.2　Quartus II graphical user interface

## 2. Compiler

The Quartus II software includes a modular Compiler. The Compiler includes the following modules (modules marked with an asterisk are optional during a compilation, depending on your settings):
- Analysis & Synthesis
- Partition Merge*
- Fitter
- Assembler*
- TimeQuest Timing Analyzer*
- Design Assistant*
- EDA Netlist Writer*
- HardCopy Netlist Writer*

To run all Compiler modules as part of a full compilation, on the "Processing" menu, click "Start Compilation". You can also run each module individually by pointing to "Start" on the "Processing" menu, and then clicking the command for the module you want to start.

In addition, you can use the Tasks window (Fig 8.3) to start Compiler modules individually. The Tasks window also allows you to change settings or view the report file for the module, or to start other tools related to each stage in a flow.

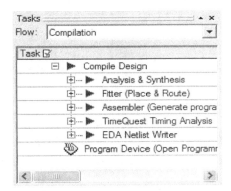

Fig 8.3 Tasks window

## 3. Design Entry

A Quartus II project includes all of the design files, software source files, and other related files necessary for the eventual implementation of a design in a programmable logic device. You can use the Quartus II Block Editor, Text Editor, MegaWizard Plug-In Manager, and EDA design entry tools to create design files that include Altera megafunctions, library of parameterized modules (LPM) functions, and intellectual property (IP) functions. Fig 8.4 shows the Design Entry Flow.

Unit 8　EDA Software

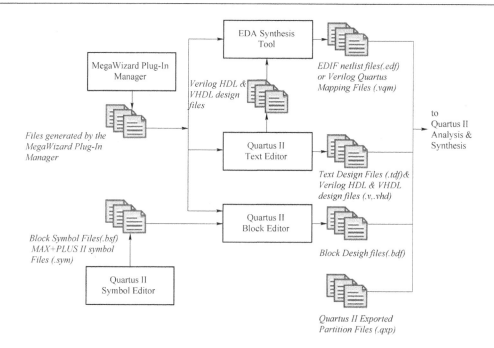

Fig 8.4　Design Entry Flow

**4. Menu**

Quartus Ⅱ commonly used menu commands are mainly: File, Edit, Project, Assignments, Processing. These menu commands are used Quartus Ⅱ applicatians, is commonly used in processing commands. The corresponding menu are shown in Fig 8.5～Fig 8.9.

Fig 8.5　File menu

Fig 8.6　Edit menu

· 79 ·

Fig 8.7　Project menu

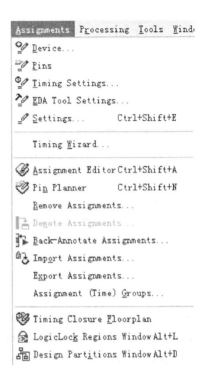

Fig 8.8　Assignments menu

Fig 8.9　Processing menu

### 8.1.2　Protel

Protel is a kind of EDA software the Portel Company launched in the late 1980s. As a CAD software in electronics industry, it is deservedly ranked in front of the number of

EDA software and it is the preferred software for electronic designers. It is used earlier in the domestic and has the highest penetration rate in the country. Some colleges and universities, professional e-opened special courses to learn it, almost all electronics companies should use it, many large companies in the recruitment of electronics design talent in the bar of its conditions often written request will use Protel.

### 1. Protel's Composition

Protel software includes schematic design systems, printed circuit board design, signal simulation systems, programmable logic design system, Protel 99 built-in editor.

Schematic design system is used to design schematic of Advanced Schematic system. This section includes schematics design for the schematic editor Sch and used to modify the generated parts of the parts database editor SchLib.

Printed circuit board design system is used for circuit board design, Advanced PCB. This section includes circuit board editor for the design of circuit board PCB and used to modify the parts package that generates parts package editor PCBLib.

Signal simulation system is used on the schematic diagram of the signal simulation SPICE 3f5 system.

Programmable logic design system is an integrated schematic design system PLD design system.

Protel 99 built-in editor is used to display a text editor, edit text, display and edit the spreadsheet editor of Spread.

### 2. Circuit Diagram Design Flow (Fig 8.10)

(1) Design document size: first of all to the idea of a good parts diagram, design document size. The document size is designed based on the scale and complexity of the circuit diagram.

(2) Set the Protel 99 Schematic design environment: including setting the grid size and type, the cursor type, etc.

(3) Place components: according to the needs of the schematic, some parts are removed from the part library and placed on the drawings, the part number, part package definitions and settings are also placed.

(4) Schematic wiring: using a variety of tools of Protel 99/Schematic, Components in the drawings to connect the wire with electrical significance, symbols, constitute a complete schematic.

(5) Output statements: generate various reports with a variety of reporting tools provided by Protel 99/Schematic. One of the most important statements is network table through which we can prepare for the follow-up circuit board design.

Fig 8.10 Circuit diagram design flow

(6) Save, Print: the final step is to save the file and print output.

## 3. Menu

The main interface of Protel is shown in Fig 8.11.

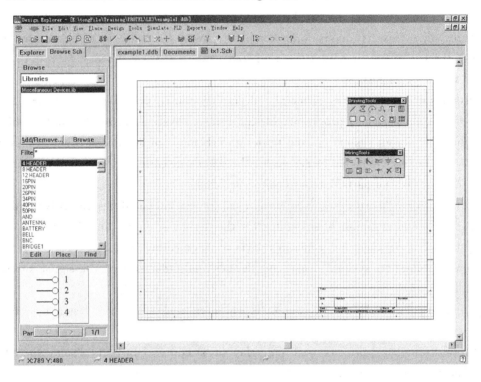

Fig 8.11　The main interface of Protel

There is a main menu upon the main interface of Protel. Protel commonly processing menu commands are mainly: File, Edit, View, Place, Tools, Design, Simulate. The corresponding menu are shown in Fig 8.12～Fig 8.18.

Fig 8.12　File menu

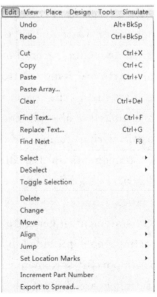

Fig 8.13　Edit menu

Unit 8　EDA Software

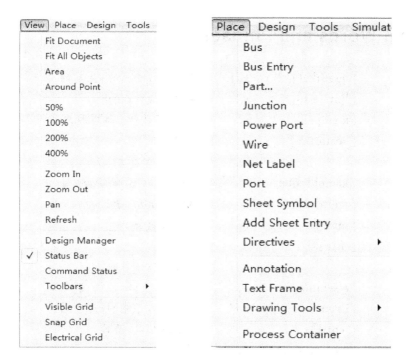

Fig 8.14　View menu　　　　Fig 8.15　Place menu

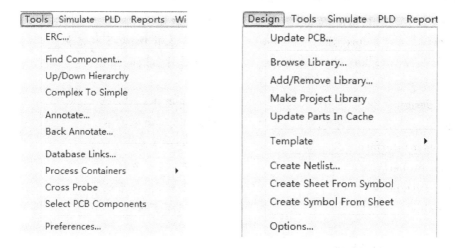

Fig 8.16　Tools menu　　　　Fig 8.17　Design menu

Fig 8.18　Simulate menu

## Technical Words and Phrases

| | | | |
|---|---|---|---|
| graphical | ['græfikəl] | adj. | 图解的;绘画的;生动的 |
| interface | ['intəfeis] | n. | 界面;接口;接触面 |
| compiler | [kəm'pailə] | n. | 编译器;[计]编译程序 |
| asterisk | ['æstərisk] | n. | 星号 |
| | | vt. | 注上星号 |
| compilation | [kɔmpi'leiʃən] | n. | 编辑,编译,编绘,编制 |
| partition | [pɑː'tiʃən] | n. | 划分,分开;分区 |
| merge | [məːdʒ] | vi. | 合并;融合 |
| fitter | ['fitə] | n. | 装配工 |
| | | adj. | 胜任的;适当的 |
| assembler | [ə'semblə] | n. | 汇编程序;汇编机;装配工 |
| eventual | [i'ventʃuəl] | adj. | 最后的,可能的;终于的 |
| entry | ['entri] | n. | 进入;入口;条目 |
| parameterized | [pə'ræmitəraizd] | adj. | 参数化的 |
| deservedly | [di'zəːvidli] | adv. | 理所当然地;应得报酬地 |
| domestic | [dəu'mestik] | adj. | 国内的;家庭的 |
| recruitment | [ri'kruːtmənt] | n. | 补充;招募 |
| spreadsheet | ['spredʃiːt] | n. | 电子制表软件;电子数据表 |
| cursor | ['kəːsə] | n. | 光标;[计]游标,指针 |

| | |
|---|---|
| schematic design | 原理图设计 |
| grid size | 网格大小;栅格大小 |
| graphical user interface | 图形用户界面 |
| intellectual property | 知识产权;著作权 |
| simulation system | 仿真系统,模拟系统 |
| programmable logic | 可编程序逻辑 |

## 8.2 Reading Materials

MATLAB

MATLAB is a numerical computing environment and programming language. Maintained by the Math Works, the MATLAB integrates computation, visualization, and programming in an easy-to-use environment where problems and solutions are expressed in familiar mathematical notation.

MATLAB is an interactive system whose basic data element is an array. It allows you to solve many technical computing problems, especially those with matrix and vector formulations, and an additional package, Simulink, adds graphical multi-domain simulation and Model-Based Design for dynamic and embedded systems.

MATLAB is easy to use, here are two examples.

### 1. Start & Quit MATLAB

When you start MATLAB, the desktop appears, containing tools (graphical user interfaces) for managing files, variables, and applications associated with MATLAB.

Fig 8.19 shows the default desktop. You can customize the arrangement of tools and documents to suit your needs.

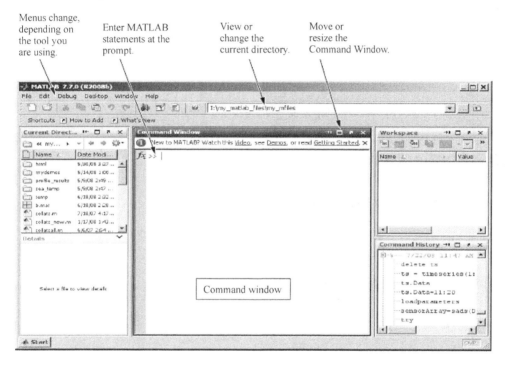

Fig 8.19  Desktop of MATLAB

To end your MATLAB session, select File > Exit MATLAB in the desktop, or type "quit" in the Command Window.

### 2. Plotting Process

The MATLAB environment provides a wide variety of techniques to display data graphically. Interactive tools enable you to manipulate graphs to achieve results that reveal the most information about your data.

For example, the following statement creates a variable $x$ that contains values ranging from $-1$ to 1 in increments of 0.1. The second statement raises each value in $x$ to the third power and stores these values in $y$:

```
x = -1:.1:1;           % define x array
y = x.^3;              % find the third power of each value in x and store as y
```

```
plot (x, y);          % draw a curve of y-x
```

A simple line graph (Fig 8.20) is a suitable way to display $x$ as the independent variable and $y$ as the dependent variable.

You can also annotate and print graphs for presentations, or export graphs to standard graphics formats for presentation in Web browsers or other media.

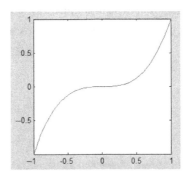

Fig 8.20  A simple line graph

## 8.3  Application

试用 EDA 软件 Protel 绘制如下原理图：

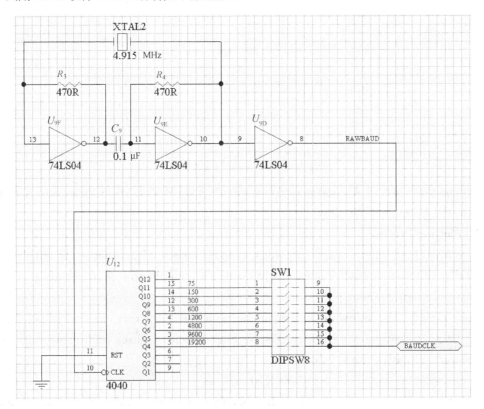

## 8.4 Knowledge(求学信)

求学信(Letters of Applying for Study Chance)

改革开放以来,出国留学的热潮一直有增无减。对于一个渴望出国深造的人来说,写一封好的求学信至关重要。

总的来说,第一封求学信不要过长,只需写明自己的姓名、职业、学历、专业、入学时间以及通讯地址即可。待所申请的学校复函后,再按要求寄去所需材料,例如,简历、成绩单、学位证明、推荐信、经济担保书、健康证明、外语考试成绩等。

Directions: If you are a student of Tianjin University and you want to apply for the Graduate School for pursuit of the International Business Program of the New York University. Write the application letter like following:

1) Declare all your situations in Tianjin University.

2) What do you want to apply for?

You should write about 100 words and don't need to write address.

例

Dear Mr. Smiths,

Thank you for your last letter.

As you require, I have written a personal statement to give a detailed description of my academic and work experience in Tianjin University. I also wrote my reasons for my applying for your Graduate School for pursuit of the International Business Program.

I have two letters of recommendation. One of them is from an English Professor, which proves that my English has reached an advanced level. The other is from an economics professor, which certificates that I am good in the field of economics and business management. Both of the letters will be mailed directly to you.

My GMAT score is 2160. I haven't received my TOFEL score yet. But I will send it to you as soon as I know.

Best Wishes

Yours sincerely,

×××

申请出国的求学信应包括个人陈述、推荐信和相关英语考试的成绩,诸如 TOFEL、GRE 以及 GMAT 等,一般来说,GRE 和 GMAT 有一个即可申请,而 TOFEL 成绩则是去英语国家留学的必要条件。

## 8.5 Exercises

### Ⅰ. Translate the following phrases and expressions

1. 信号仿真系统
2. 可编程片上系统

3. 设计流程

4. 模块化编译器

5. multiplatform design environment

6. graphical user interface

7. Analysis & Synthesis

8. full compilation

9. schematic design system

10. printed circuit board design

Ⅱ. Translate the following sentences into Chinese

1. The Altera Quartus II design software provides a complete, multiplatform design environment that easily adapts to your specific design needs.

2. The Quartus II software includes solutions for all phases of FPGA and CPLD design.

3. The Quartus II software allows you to use the Quartus II graphical user interface and command-line interface for each phase of the design flow.

4. A Quartus II project includes all of the design files, software source files, and other related files necessary for the eventual implementation of a design in a programmable logic device.

5. It is deservedly ranked in front of the number of EDA software and it is the preferred software for electronic designers.

6. Printed circuit board design system is used for circuit board design, Advanced PCB.

7. One of the most important statements is the network table, through the network table to prepare for the follow-up circuit board design.

8. MATLAB is a numerical computing environment and programming language.

9. It allows you to solve many technical computing problems, especially those with matrix and vector formulations, and an additional package, Simulink, adds graphical multi-domain simulation and Model-Based Design for dynamic and embedded systems.

10. Unfortunately, that approach would make theft of cable services very easy, so the signals are encoded in funny ways.

# Unit 9  3G

Knowledge aims:

1. Technical words and phrases.
2. Third-Generation mobile communications system.
3. Abstract.

Ability aims:

Can read Mobile information.

Pre-reading

Read the following passage, paying attention to the questions.
1. Which merits does the third generation mobile communication system have?
2. What is the IMT-2000 migration communications network's merit?
3. What is the function of the W-CDMA?
4. What technology does the TD-SCDMA have?

## 9.1  Text

Third-Generation Mobile Communications System

**1. IMT-2000 Mobile Communications Network**

Various systems were developed and used around the world for first-generation analog mobile communications, and three systems now coexist for second-generation digital communications (PDC in Japan, GSM in Europe and TIA standards in the US). The global standard for third-generation wireless communications has been determined by the International Telecommunication Union (ITU) under the integrated name of IMT-2000.

IMT-2000 realizes mobile communications systems that offer high quality equivalent to that of fixed networks under global standard radio interfaces and can provide a wide range of services. In addition to making it possible to easily communicate with anybody, anywhere and anytime on a global scale, it also permits high-speed, large-volume data communications and image transmissions.

NTT DoCoMo has been active in research and development activities relating to IMT-

2000, and the W-CDMA (wideband code-division multiple access) radio interface that NTT DoCoMo has promoted is included in IMT-2000.

In 2001, NTT DoCoMo has launched FOMA, which is the first service in the world based on IMT-2000, FOMA realizes clearer and more comfortable communications environments than ever before and provides a new mobile environment where voice, still images and video are freely handled through the introduction of new technologies. These include large-volume communications using broad frequency bands and intelligent networks that can select the optimal communications rates and paths according to the type and volume of information being transmitted.

Mobile communications in the 21st century will enter an era of mobile multimedia service and universal mobility. Various technological developments are being carried forward towards this goal, including the development of an advanced intelligent network that will integrate different communications systems to establish a sophisticated mobile communications network that will realize these servies. As part of these efforts, NTT DoCoMo is working towards expanding its new "IMN" intelligent mobile communications network.

In addition, we are aiming at structuring our third-generation mobile communications system (IMT-2000) as a global standard that is capable of handing communications requirements ranging from low-speed (e. g., E-mail) up to high-speed (e. g., video-on-demand) communications. The technologies to achieve this include the W-CDMA system for radio transmissions, and the ATM system for wired transmissions. Because ATM carries out communications by transmitting data in fixed-length cells, a single transmission path can handle multiple communications speeds simultaneously.

## 2. W-CDMA

W-CDMA technology supports the third-generation mobile communications system. CDMA can efficiently utilize the limited frequency resources available and accommodate as many users as possible. This is achieved by sharing frequencies on the basis of spectrum-spread codes assigned to each user, rather than through dividing broadband channels by frequency or time.

Among the various systems, DoCoMo is promoting the introduction of W-CDMA that can transmit high-quality moving images in addition to voice and fax, and also allows for connections to the Internet. As it offers many benefits such as high transmission quality and needs little power for transmissions, W-CDMA is the most suitable technology to meet the objectives of third-generation mobile communications—namely, multimedia, personal and intelligent systems.

## 3. TD-SCDMA

Time Division-Synchronous Code Division Multiple Access, or TD-SCDMA, is a 3G mobile telecommunications standard, being pursued in the People's Republic of China by the Chinese Academy of Telecommunications Technology (CATT), Datang and Siemens AG. TD-SCDMA is based on spread spectrum technology.

A TD-SCDMA system has three parts: RNC, Node B and UE. A pseudo uplink direction of arrival (DoA) measurement is included in 3GPP Release 5 for Node B to facilitate beam switching in the downlink. The Node B measures the average uplink signal-to-interference ratio (SIR) on the dedicated physical control channel (DPCCH) received from each UE in all the cell portions. The four highest SIR values and the corresponding cell portion IDs are sent to the RNC. These measurements are used to implement the beam switching functionality that is required when fixed beam forming is used in the downlink. Based on the cell portion specific SIR measurements, the RNC will typically inform the Node B to transmit the data to a UE under the beam (cell portion) corresponding to the highest uplink measured SIR, as well as informing the UE which S-CPICH should be used for phase reference via a radio resource control (RRC) message. Notice that beam switching only includes measurements from the Node B, i.e. no measurements from the UE are used to trigger beam switching.

## Technical Words and Phrases

| | | | |
|---|---|---|---|
| scale | [skeil] | n. | 标度 |
| goal | [gəul] | n. | 目标 |
| coexist | ['kəuig'zist] | vi. | 同时存在，与……共存 |
| environment | [in'vaiərənmənt] | n. | 环境，周围 |
| optimal | ['ɔptəməl] | adj. | 最佳的，最理想的，最适宜的 |
| transmit | [træns'mit] | vt. | 传送，传播 |
| | | vi. | 播送信号 |
| establish | [i'stæbliʃ] | vt. | 建造，确立；认可，证实 |
| combine | [kəm'bain] | vt. | 使结合，混合 |
| | | vi. | 结合 |
| flexibly | ['fleksəbli] | adv. | 易弯曲地，柔韧地 |
| simultaneously | [saiməl'teinjəsli] | adv. | 同时进行地，同步地 |
| measurement | ['meʒəmənt] | n. | 测量，测量法 |
| equivalent to | | | 等于，相当于；与……等值 |
| fixed-length | | | 定长；固定长度 |

## 9.2  Reading Materials

### 9.2.1  The Cell Approach

One of the most interesting things about a cell phone is that it is actually a radio.

The genius of the cellular system is the division of a city into small cells. (Cells are normally thought of as hexagons on a big hexagonal grid.) In a typical analog cell-phone system in the United States, the cell-phone carrier receives about 800 frequencies to use across the city. The carrier chops up the city into cells. Each cell is typically sized at about 10 square miles (26 square kilometers). This allows extensive frequency reuse across a city, so that millions of people can use cell phones simultaneously.

Each cell has a base station that consists of a tower and a small building containing the radio equipment (more on base stations later).

Cell phones have low-power transmitters in them. Many cell phones have two signal strengths: 0.6 W and 3 W. The base station is also transmitting at low power. Low-power transmitters have two advantages.

1) The transmissions of a base station and the phones within its cell do not make it very far outside that cell. Therefore, the unconnected cells can reuse the same frequencies. The same frequencies can be reused extensively across the city.

2) The power consumption of the cell phone, which is normally battery-operated, is relatively low. Low power means small batteries, and this is what has made handheld cellular phones possible.

The cellular approach requires a large number of base stations in a city of any size. A typical large city can have hundreds of towers. But because so many people are using cell phones, costs remain low per user.

### 9.2.2 The Phone's Internal Structure

On a "complexity per cubic inch" scale, cell phones are some of the most intricate devices people play with on a daily basis. Modern digital cell phones can process millions of calculations per second in order to compress and decompress the voice stream.

If you take a cell phone apart, you find that it contains just a few individual parts:

- An amazing circuit board containing the brains of the phone
- An antenna
- A liquid crystal display (LCD)
- A keyboard (not unlike the one you find in a TV remote control)
- A microphone
- A speaker
- A battery

In Fig 9.1, you see several computer chips. Let's talk about what some of the individual chips do. The analog-to-digital and digital-to-analog conversion chips translate the outgoing audio signal from analog to digital and the incoming signal from digital back to analog. The digital signal processor (DSP) is a highly customized processor designed to perform signal-manipulation calculations at high speed.

Fig 9.1  The parts of a cell phone

The microprocessor handles all of the housekeeping chores for the keyboard and display, deals with command and control signaling with the base station and also coordinates the rest of the functions on the board.

The ROM and Flash memory chips provide storage for the phone's operating system and customizable features, such as the phone directory. The radio frequency (RF) and power section handles power management and recharging, and also deals with the hundreds of FM channels. Finally, the RF amplifiers handle signals traveling to and from the antenna.

Some phones store certain information in internal Flash memory, while others use external cards that are similar to Smart Media cards.

Cell phones have such tiny speakers and microphones that it is incredible how well most of them reproduce sound. As you can see in the picture above, the speaker is about the size of a dime and the microphone is no larger than the watch battery beside it. Speaking of the watch battery, this is used by the cell phone's internal clock chip.

What is amazing is that all of that functionality—which only 30 years ago would have filled an entire floor of an office building—now fits into a package that sits comfortably in the palm of your hand!

## 9.3  Knowledge(摘要)

### 摘要(Abstract)

摘要分成两种,一种是文章摘要,另一种是论文摘要。文章摘要就是给一篇文章写一个摘要,文章摘要是对文章主要内容的简练概括,内容上要涵盖全文,语言上要尽量简练。写摘要前一定要仔细阅读全文,弄懂文章大意;摘要涵盖原文的主要观点并与原文的观点保持一致;摘要应该简明扼要,字数在规定的字数范围内;摘要最好不要照搬原文,应该用自己的话概括原文的主要观点；并且注意千万不要照抄，也千万不要评论，只需要写出中心思想或者段落大意即可。第二种摘要是论文摘要。比方说大家写一篇学术论文，硕士论文、博士论文需要写一个英文摘要。相对来讲，我们认为考论文摘要的可能性稍微大一些。写这种摘要时要注意时态和语态。叙述研究过程，多采用一般过去时；说明某课题现已取得的成果，宜采用现在完成时。摘要中多数情况下可采用被动语态。但在某些情况下，特别是表达作者或有关专家的观点时，又常用主动语态。英文摘要有一些常用句型，比如表示研究目的，可以用 In order to…, This paper describes…, The purpose of this study is…, 表示结论、观点或建议可以用 The authors (suggest/conclude/consider) that…。

将下面这篇约 500 词的原文按要求写成约 150 词的摘要。

原文

How New York Became America's Largest City

In the 18th century, New York was smaller than Philadelphia and Boston. Today it is the largest city in America. How can the change in its size and importance be explained?

To answer this question, we must consider certain facts about geography, history, and economics. Together these three will explain the huge growth of America's most famous city.

The map of the Northeast shows that four of the most heavily populated areas in this region are around seaports. At these points materials from across the sea enter the United States, and the product of the land are sent there for export across the sea.

Economists know that places where transportation lines meet are good places for making raw materials into finished goods. That is why seaports often have cities nearby. But cities like New York needed more than their geographical location in order to become great industrial centers. Their development did not happen simply by chance.

About 1815, when many Americans from the east coast had already moved toward the west, trade routes from the ports to the central regions of the country began to be a serious problem. The slow wagons of that time, drawn by horses or oxen, were too expensive for moving heavy freight very far. Americans had long admired Europe's canals. In New York State a canal seemed the best solution to the transportation problem. From the eastern end of Lake Erie all the way across the state to the Hudson River, there is a long strip of low land. Here the Erie Canal was constructed. After several years of work, it was completed in 1825.

The canal produced an immediate effect. Freight costs were cut to about one-tenth of what had been. New York City, which had been smaller than Philadelphia and Boston, quickly became the leading city of the coast. In the years that followed transportation routes on the Great Lakes were joined to routes on the Mississippi River. Then New York City became the end point of a great inland shipping system that extended from the Atlantic Ocean far up the western branches of the Mississippi.

The coming of the railroads made canal shipping less important, but it tied New York even more closely to the central regions of the country. It was easier for people in the central states to ship their goods to New York for export overseas.

Exports from New York were greater than imports. Consequently, shipping companies were eager to fill their ships with passengers on the return trip from Europe. Passengers could come from Europe very cheaply as a result.

Thus New York became the greatest port for receiving people from European countries. Many of these people remained in the city. Others stayed in New York for a few weeks, months, or years, and then moved to other parts of the United States. For these great number of new Americans, New York had to provide homes, goods, and services. Their labor helped the city become great.

摘要

How New York Became America's Largest City

New York was once smaller than Philadelphia and Boston, but now it is America's largest city because of geography, history and economics.

New York was located at the seaport where materials were imported to the US and the products of the US were sent abroad across the sea. The city was further developed when the Erie Canal was completed in 1825. This linked Lake Erie to New York via the Hudson River and the cost of transporting goods to those who had settled inland was cut down. In addition, the Great Lakes were soon linked to the Mississippi. Later, railroads tied New York closer to the central states, whose goods were exported via New York. Fewer goods were imported, so cheap passages were available from Europe. New York became the main port for receiving Europeans, many of whom stayed in the city and helped it become great.

## 9.4 Exercises

### I. Translate the following phrases and expressions

1. 多种不同的系统
2. 智能网络
3. 图像传输
4. online services
5. data communications
6. global standard

### II. Translate the following sentences into Chinese

1. In 2001, NTT DoCoMo has launched FOMA, which is the first service in the world based on IMT-2000.

2. Various systems were developed and used around the world for first-generation analog mobile communications, and three systems now coexist for second-generation digital communications (PDC in Japan, GSM in Europe and TIA standards in the US).

3. IMT-2000 realizes mobile communications systems that offer high quality equivalent to that of fixed networks under global standard radio interfaces and can provide

a wide range of services.

4. CDMA can efficiently utilize the limited frequency resources available and accommodate as many users as possible.

5. Time Division-Synchronous Code Division Multiple Access, or TD-SCDMA, is a 3G mobile telecommunications standard, being pursued in the People's Republic of China by the Chinese Academy of Telecommunications Technology (CATT), Datang and Siemens AG.

# Unit 10  Microcomputers

  Knowledge aims:

1. Technical words and phrases.
2. Micocomputers.

  Ability aims:

Can read microcomputers data.

 Pre-reading

Read the following passage, paying attention to the questions.
1. What make up a computer system?
2. What is the system bus?
3. What is the function of the main memory?

## 10.1  Text

### 10.1.1  Basic Computer

The computer that everyone thinks of first is typically the personal computer, or PC. The basic components that make up a computer system include CPU, memory, I/O, and the bus that connects them. Although you can write software that is ignorant of these concepts, high performance software requires a complete understanding of this material.

The basic operational design of a computer system is called computer architecture. John Von Neumann, a pioneer in computer design, gave the architecture of most computers in use today. A typical Von Neumann system has three major components: the central processing unit (or CPU), memory, and input/output (or I/O). In a system, the way to these components design impacts system performance. In VNA machines, like the 80x86 family, the CPU is where all the action takes place. All computations occur inside the CPU. Data and CPU instructions reside in memory until required by the CPU. To the CPU, most I/O devices look like memory because the CPU can store data to an output device and read data from an input device. The major difference between memory and I/O locations is the fact that I/O locations are generally associated with external devices in the outside world.

### 10.1.2 The Motherboard

The motherboard is the main circuit board inside the PC which holds the processor, memory and expansion slots and connects directly or indirectly to every part of the PC (Fig 10.1).

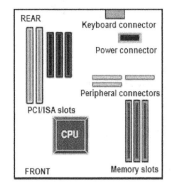

Fig 10.1 The motherboard various components

It's made up of a chipset (known as the "glue logic"), some code in ROM and the various interconnections or buses. PC designs today use many different buses to link their components. Wide, high-speed buses are difficult and expensive to produce. The signals travel at such a rate that even distance of just a few centimeters cause timing problems; while the metal tracks on the circuit board act as miniature radio antennae, transmitting electromagnetic noise that introduces interference with signals elsewhere in the system. For these reasons, PC design engineers try to keep the fastest buses confined to the smallest area of the motherboard and use slower, more robust buses, for other parts.

### 10.1.3 The System Bus

The system bus connects the various components of a VNA machine. The 80x86 family has three major buses: the address bus, the data bus, and the control bus. A bus is a collection of wires on which electrical signals pass between components in the system. These buses vary from processor to processor. However, each bus carries comparable information on all processors. For example, the data bus may have a different implementation on the 80386 than on the 8086, but both carry data between the processor, I/O, and memory.

**1. Data Bus**

The 80x86 processors use the data bus to transfer data between the various components in a computer system. The size of this bus varies widely in the 80x86 family. Indeed, this bus defines the "size" of the processor.

**2. Address Bus**

The data bus on an 80x86 family processor transfers information between a particular memory location or I/O device and the CPU. The only question is, "Which memory location or I/O device?" The address bus answers this question.

To differentiate memory locations and I/O devices, the system designer assigns a unique memory address to each memory element and I/O device. When the software wants to access some particular memory location or I/O device, it places the corresponding address on the address bus. Circuitry associated with the memory or I/O recognizes this address and instructs the memory or I/O device to read the data from or place data on the data bus.

**3. Control Bus**

The control bus is a collection of signals that control how the processor communicates with the rest of the system. Consider for a moment the data bus. The CPU sends data to memory and receives data from memory on the data bus. This prompts the question. "Is it sending or receiving?" There are two lines on the control bus, read and write, which specify the direction of data flow. Other signals include system clocks, interrupt lines, status lines, and so on. The exact make up of the control bus varies among processors in the 80x86 families. However, some control lines are common to all processors and are worth a brief mention.

The read and write lines control the direction of data on the data bus. When both contain logic one, the CPU and memory, I/O does not have communication with one another. If the read line is low (logic zero), the CPU is reading data from memory (that is, the system is transferring data from memory to the CPU). If the write line is low, the system transfers data from the CPU to memory.

### 10.1.4  Main Memory

The main memory is the central storage unit in a computer system. It is a relatively large and fast memory used to store programs and data during the computer operation. The principal technology used for the main memory is based on semiconductor integrated circuits. Integrated circuits RAM (Read Random Memory) chips are available in two possible operation modes, static and dynamic. The static RAM consists essentially of internal flip-flops that store the binary information. The stored information remains valid as long as power is applied to the unit. The dynamic RAM stores the binary information in the form of electric charges that are applied to the capacitors. The capacitors are provided inside the chip by MOS transistors. The stored charges on the capacitors tend to discharge with time and refreshing the dynamic memory must periodically recharge the capacitors. The dynamic RAM offers reduced power consumption and large storage capacity in a single memory chip. The static RAM is easier to use and has shorter read and write cycles.

### 10.1.5  BIOS (Basic Input/Output System)

**1. Introduction to BIOS**

One of the most common uses of Flash memory is for the basic input/output system of your computer, commonly known as the BIOS (Fig 10.2). The BIOS makes sure all the other chips, hard drives, ports and CPU function together.

The BIOS is special software that interfaces the major hardware components of your computer with the operating system. It is usually stored on a Flash memory chip on the motherboard, but sometimes the chip is another type of ROM (Read Only Memory).

Fig 10.2 BIOS uses Flash memory

## 2. What BIOS Does

The BIOS software has a number of different roles, but its most important role is to load the operating system. When you turn on your computer and the microprocessor tries to execute its first instruction, it has to get that instruction from somewhere. It cannot get it from the operating system because the operating system is located on a hard disk, and the microprocessor cannot get to it without some instructions that tell it how. The BIOS provides those instructions. The BIOS also offers some other instructions (program), such as

A power-on self-test (POST) for all of the different hardware components in the system to make sure everything is working properly.

Activating other BIOS chips on different cards installed in the computer. For example, SCSI and graphics cards often have their own BIOS chips.

Providing a set of low-level routines that the operating system uses to interface to different hardware devices—It is these routines that give the BIOS its name. They manage things like the keyboard, the screen, and the serial and parallel ports, especially when the computer is booting.

The first thing the BIOS does is to check the information stored in a tiny (64 bytes) amount of RAM located on a CMOS chip. The CMOS setup provides detailed information particular to your system and can be altered as your system changes. The BIOS uses this information to modify or supplement its default programming as needed.

Interrupt handlers are small pieces of software that act as translators between the hardware components and the operating system. For example, when you press a key on your keyboard, the signal is sent to the keyboard interrupt handler, which tells the CPU what it is and passes it on to the operating system. The device drivers are other pieces of software that identify the base hardware components such as keyboard, mouse, hard drive and floppy drive.

In order to run faster (computer startup) general BIOS copied to RAM because the BIOS is the received signal and the output signal from the hardware to the hardware.

## Technical Words and Phrases

| | | | |
|---|---|---|---|
| address | [ə'dres] | vt. | 访问 |
| | | n. | 地址 |
| architecture | ['ɑːkitektʃə(r)] | n. | 计算机的物理结构 |
| assign | [ə'sain] | vt. | (与 to 连用)分配;指定 |
| bus | [bʌs] | n. | (计算机)总线 |
| cycle | ['saik(ə)l] | n. | 循环,周期;循环期 |
| differentiate | [difə'renʃieit] | vt. | 区分,区别,辨别 |
| dynamic | [dai'næmik] | adj. | 动力的;动态的 |
| family | ['fæmili] | n. | 系列;家族 |
| ignorant | ['ignərənt] | adj. | (常与 of, in 连用)无知识的 |
| location | [ləu'keiʃ(ə)n] | n. | 地点,位置 |
| motherboard | ['mʌðəbɔːd] | n. | (计算机)主板 |
| periodically | [piəri'ɔdikəli] | adj. | 周期的,期刊的 |
| prompt | [prɔmpt] | vt. | (常与 to 连用)提出,提示 |
| | | n. | 提示,提词,提示符 |
| | | adj. | 迅速的;及时的 |
| refresh | [ri'freʃ] | vt. | 刷新,消除疲劳;恢复精神 |
| size | ['saiz] | n. | 计算机数据的二进制位数 |

communicate with…            与……联络;通信;交换(看法等)
give sb. credit for sth.     为……赞扬某人,认为某人具有
                             (某种品德、才能等)

## 10.2 Reading Materials

### Microcontroller

The AT89C51 is a low-power, high-performance CMOS 8 bit microcomputer with 4 k bytes of Flash programmable and erasable read only memory (PEROM). The device is manufactured using Atmel's high-density nonvolatile memory technology and is compatible with the industry-standard MCS-51 instruction set and pinout. The on-chip Flash allows the program memory to be reprogrammed in-system or by a conventional nonvolatile memory programmer. By combining a versatile 8 bit CPU with Flash on a monolithic chip, the Atmel AT89C51 is a powerful microcomputer which provides a highly-flexible and cost-effective solution to many embedded control applications.

## 1. Features

- Compatible with MCS-51™ Products Partition
- 4 k bytes of In-System Reprogrammable Flash Memory
- Endurance: 1,000 Write/Erase Cycles
- Fully Static Operation: 0 Hz to 24 MHz
- Three-level Program Memory Lock
- 128×8 bit Internal RAM
- 32 Programmable I/O Lines
- Two 16 bit Timer/Counters
- Six Interrupt Sources
- Programmable Serial Channel
- Low-power Idle and Power-down Modes

The AT89C51 provides the following standard features: 4 k bytes of Flash, 128 bytes of RAM, 32 I/O lines, two 16 bit timer/counters, a five vector two-level interrupt architecture, a full duplex serial port, on-chip oscillator and clock circuitry. In addition, the AT89C51 is designed with static logic for operation down to zero frequency and supports two software selectable power saving modes. The Idle Mode stops the CPU while allowing the RAM, timer/counters, serial port and interrupt system to continue functioning. The Power-down Mode saves the RAM contents but freezes the oscillator disabling all other chip functions until the next hardware reset.

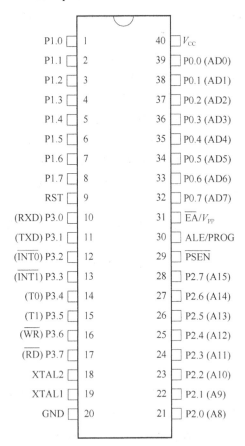

Fig 10.3 Pin configurations

## 2. Pin Description

**V$_{CC}$**

Supply voltage.

**GND**

Ground.

**Port 0**

Port 0 is an 8 bit open-drain bi-directional I/O port. As an output port, each pin can sink eight TTL inputs. When 1s are written to port 0 pins, the pins can be used as high impedance inputs. Port 0 may also be configured to be the multiplexed low order address/

data bus during accesses to external program and data memory. In this mode P0 has internal pullups. Port 0 also receives the code bytes during Flash programming, and outputs the code bytes during program verification. External pullups are required during program verification.

**Port 1**

Port 1 is an 8 bit bi-directional I/O port with internal pullups. The Port 1 output buffers can sink/source four TTL inputs. When 1s are written to Port 1 pins they are pulled high by the internal pullups and can be used as inputs. As inputs, Port 1 pins that are externally being pulled low will source current ($I_{IL}$) because of the internal pullups. Port 1 also receives the low-order address bytes during Flash programming and verification.

**Port 2**

Port 2 is an 8 bit bi-directional I/O port with internal pullups. The Port 2 output buffers can sink/source four TTL inputs. When 1s are written to Port 2 pins they are pulled high by the internal pullups and can be used as inputs. As inputs, Port 2 pins that are externally being pulled low will source current ($I_{IL}$) because of the internal pullups. Port 2 emits the high-order address byte during fetches from external program memory and during accesses to external data memory that use 16 bit addresses (MOVX @ DPTR). In this application, it uses strong internal pullups when emitting 1s. During accesses to external data memory that use 8 bit addresses (MOVX @ RI), Port 2 emits the contents of the P2 Special Function Register. Port 2 also receives the high-order address bits and some control signals during Flash programming and verification.

**Port 3**

Port 3 is an 8 bit bi-directional I/O port with internal pullups. The Port 3 output buffers can sink/source four TTL inputs. When 1s are written to Port 3 pins they are pulled high by the internal pullups and can be used as inputs. As inputs, Port 3 pins that are externally being pulled low will source current ($I_{IL}$) because of the pullups. Port 3 also serves the functions of various special features of the AT89C51 as listed in Tab 10.1. Port 3 also receives some control signals for Flash programming and verification.

Tab 10.1 AT89C51 Port 3 second function table

| Port Pin | Alternate Functions |
| --- | --- |
| P3.0 | RXD (serial input port) |
| P3.1 | TXD (serial output port) |
| P3.2 | $\overline{INT0}$ (external interrupt 0) |
| P3.3 | $\overline{INT1}$ (external interrupt 1) |
| P3.4 | T0 (timer 0 external input) |
| P3.5 | T1 (timer 1 external input) |
| P3.6 | $\overline{WR}$ (external data memory write strobe) |
| P3.7 | $\overline{RD}$ (external data memory read strobe) |

**RST**

Reset input. A high on this pin for two machine cycles while the oscillator is running resets the device.

**ALE/PROG**

Address Latch Enable output pulse for latching the low byte of the address during accesses to external memory. This pin is also the program pulse input (PROG) during Flash programming. In normal operation ALE is emitted at a constant rate of 1/6 the oscillator frequency, and may be used for external timing or clocking purposes. Note, however, that one ALE pulse is skipped during each access to external Data Memory. If desired, ALE operation can be disabled by setting bit 0 of SFR location 8EH. With the bit set, ALE is active only during a MOVX or MOVC instruction. Otherwise, the pin is weakly pulled high. Setting the ALE-disable bit has no effect if the microcontroller is in external execution mode.

**PSEN**

Program Store Enable is the read strobe to external program memory. When the AT89C51 is executing code from external program memory, PSEN is activated twice each machine cycle, except that two PSEN activations are skipped during each access to external data memory.

**EA/$V_{PP}$**

External Access Enable. EA must be strapped to GND in order to enable the device to fetch code from external program memory locations starting at 0000H up to FFFFH. Note, however, that if lock bit 1 is programmed, EA will be internally latched on reset. EA should be strapped to $V_{CC}$ for internal program executions. This pin also receives the 12 V programming enable voltage ($V_{PP}$) during Flash programming, for parts that require 12 V $V_{PP}$.

**XTAL1**

Input to the inverting oscillator amplifier and input to the internal clock operating circuit.

**XTAL2**

Output from the inverting oscillator amplifier.

## 10.3 Application

根据英文资料了解计算机,并动手组装一台计算机。

## 10.4　Knowledge(科技论文写作知识)

A research paper is a form of written academic communication that can be used to give useful information and to share academic ideas with others. Most of the research papers are written for publication in journals or conference proceedings in one's field. Publication is one of the fastest ways for propagating ideas and for professional recognition and advancement. If you have clear idea about the features and styles, get your paper published in the target journal or accepted by an international conference.

一篇研究论文是指用写作方式进行学术交流的一种形式,它用来提供有用信息和与其他人共享学术思想。大部分学术论文都是为某一学术领域的出版物(杂志)或某一领域的学术会议而写的。出版物是传播学术思想、受到学术界公认和倡导学术进步的最快途径之一。如果你在写论文时对论文的格式和特征很了解,你的论文就能在学术杂志上发表或被一个国际学术会议认可(允许你在会上宣读你的论文)。

**Features of Academic Papers(学术论文的特征)**

The first feature of an academic paper is the content. It is no more and no less than an objective and accurate account of a piece of research you did, either in the humanities, social sciences, natural sciences or applied sciences. It should not be designed to teach or to provide general background.

The second feature is the style of writing for this purpose. Your paper should contain three ingredients: precise logical structure, clear and concise language, and the specific style demanded "Appendixes A to E" you may get a brief idea of different styles required by different journals.

The third, which is indeed a part of the second, is the system of documenting the sources used in writing the article. At every step in the process of writing, you must take into account the ideas, facts, and opinions you have gained from sources you have consulted.

One of the most convenient features of academic papers is that they are divided into clearly delineated sections. This is helpful because you only have to concentrate on one section at a time. You can thus visualize more or less completely the whole paper while you are working on any part of it. Though papers of the humanities and social sciences do not always have the clearly divided sections, they share some of the common requirements with the scientific papers.

学术论文的第一个特征是内容,每篇论文叙述一个观点,准确描述你所进行的研究中的一个部分,无论是人文科学、社会科学、自然科学或应用科学。不要把论文写成像教材或给出一般的背景(泛泛而谈)。

学术论文的第二个特征是为写作目的所采用的写作格式。论文应包含三个部分,合理的逻辑结构、清晰精练的语言和按准备投稿的杂志所要求的特定的格式。不同的杂志有不同的"投稿须知",你可以通过它来了解各种杂志对格式的要求。

学术论文的第三个特征实际上是第二个特征的一部分,是在写文章中所用的资料系统,在写作过程的每一步中,你都要考虑你已从查阅、参考的资料中所获取的思想(实验、试验)、事实和观点。

学术论文最明显的特征之一是学术论文清晰地分成几个部分。这一点很有用,因为每次你只需集中考虑一个部分。当你撰写任一部分时,你就可以看到整篇论文在逐步形成。虽然人文科学和社会科学的学术论文的几个部分之间并不总是分得很清楚,但它们都和科学论文一样共同遵守某些普遍要求。

Divisions of Academic Papers

For the average scientific paper the following suggested outline of the divisions of a paper is normally acceptable to, and demanded by, the editors of journals or compilers of conference proceedings.

一般学术会议或杂志的编辑要求学术论文按如下的大纲分成几个部分。

(1) Title of the Paper (subtitle if necessary):标题,副标题

(2) By lines:标题下写作者的名字和地址

Name(s) of author(s)

Affiliation(s) of author(s): present and/or permanent address

(3) Abstract:摘要

The purpose and scope of the paper 论文涉及的范围及写作目的

The method of study or experiment 实验研究的方法

A very brief summary of the results, conclusion, and /or recommendations 结果、结论或建议的一个简短的总结介绍

(4) Introduction:引言

A statement of the exact nature of the problem 问题本质的介绍

The background of previous work on this problem done either by the author or others of different approaches 关于这个问题其他人或作者做的前期工作的情况,或采用其他方法做的情况

The purpose of this paper 这篇论文的目的

The method by which the problem will be attacked 处理问题的方法

The primary findings, conclusions and significance of this work 主要的发现、结论和这项工作的意义

A statement of the organization of the material in the paper 论文中材料的组织方法介绍

(5) Body of Paper：论文主体

The organization of this main part of the paper is left to the discretion of the author. The information should be presented in some logical sequence, the major points emphasized with suitable illustrations, and the less important ideas subordinated in some appropriate way. This portion of the paper should be styled for the specialist and should not be designed to teach or to provide background for the general reader.

论文的主要部分的组织方法是作者自己确定的,文中所提供的信息应按逻辑顺序,主要观点要强调,并加以适当的说明,不重要的观点则用适当的附属的方法表示(注意突出重点)。这部分的内容是给专家(同行)看的,不要把论文写成像教材或给出一般的背景(泛泛而谈)。

(6) Conclusion：结论

Summary and evaluation of the results 小结并评价(实验)结果

Significance and advantages over previous work 这些工作的意义和优点

Gaps and limitations in the work 工作中的局限性和存在的问题

Directions for future work and applications 对未来工作和应用的描述

(7) Acknowledgments：致谢,对论文(研究)有帮助的人表示感谢

(8) References：参考文献

## 10.5  Exercises

Ⅰ. **Translate the following phrases and expressions**

1. 动态随机存储器
2. 高性能的软件
3. 输入输出器件
4. 控制信号线
5. interrupt lines
6. impact system performance
7. be generally associated with external devices
8. 80x86 family microprocessor
9. read data from an input device
10. storage capacity in a single memory chip

Ⅱ. **Translate the following sentences into Chinese**

1. To the CPU, most I/O devices look like memory because the CPU can store data to an output device and read data from an input device.

2. A bus is a collection of wires on which electrical signals pass between components in the system.

3. The signals travel at such a rate that even distances of just a few centimeters cause timing problems.

4. When the software wants to access some particular memory location or I/O device, it places the corresponding address on the address bus.

5. The main memory is a relatively large and fast memory used to store programs and data during the computer operation.

6. The stored information remains valid as long as power is applied to the unit.

7. In VNA machines, like the 80×86 family, the CPU is where all the action takes place.

8. The static RAM is easier to use and has shorter read and write cycles.

9. One of the most common uses of Flash memory is for the basic input/output system of your computer, commonly known as the BIOS.

10. The BIOS software has a number of different roles, but its most important role is to load the operating system.

# Appendix 1 译文

## UNIT 1 电子技术简介

### 1.1 文章

#### 1.1.1 电子技术的历史

在 20 世纪五六十年代,最具代表性的先进电子技术就是无线电技术,包括无线电广播、收音、无线通信(电报)、业余无线电台、无线电定位、导航等遥测、遥控、遥信技术。早期就是这些电子技术带领着许多青少年步入了奇妙的电子世界,无线电技术展示了当时科技生活美妙的前景。电子科学开始形成了一门新兴学科。无线电电子学、无线通信开始了电子世界的历程。

早期的无线电技术推动了电子技术的发展,其中最主要的是真空管电子技术向半导体电子技术的发展。半导体电子技术使有源器件实现了微型化和低成本,使无线电技术有了更大普及和创新,并大大地开阔了许多非无线电的控制领域。

1947 年,John Bardeen、Walter Brattain 和 William Shockley 发明了晶体管。将多个晶体管组装在一个电路上的唯一方法就是购买多个分离的晶体管,并将它们连在一起。1959 年,Jack Kilby 和 Robert Noyce 各自发明了一种将多个晶体管做在同一片半导体材料上的方法。这个发明就是集成电路或 IC,是我们现代电脑化世界的基础。集成电路之所以被这样命名,是因为它将多个晶体管和二极管集成到同一块小的半导体芯片上。IC 包含按照形成电路所要求的拓扑结构连在一起的许多小元件,而无须再将分立元件的导线焊接起来。大量数字逻辑电路,如门电路、计数器、定时器、移位寄存器以及模拟开关、比较器等,为电子数字控制提供了极佳的条件,使传统的机械控制转向电子控制。

进入 20 世纪 70 年代,大规模集成电路出现,促进了常规的电子电路单元向专用电子系统发展。许多专用电子系统单元变成了集成化器件,如收音机、电子钟、计算器等,在这些领域的电子工程师从电路、系统的精心设计、调试转变为器件选择、外围器件适配工作。电子技术和电子产品使电子工程师降低了工作难度。

#### 1.1.2 电子专业介绍

电子技术专业培养目标:培养适应 21 世纪电子技术发展需求,德、智、体、美全面发展,初步掌握电子科学技术、信号分析与处理、自动控制等专业理论基础,具有以电路分析与综合设计能力和以微处理器(单片机、可编程控制器 PLC、嵌入式系统等)为基本平台,较熟练地运用计算机 EDA 技术和现代电子设计与制作技术,拥有从事各种实用性电子设备或产品的应用、开发、设计能力,具备较强创新和实践能力的高等技术应用型专门人才。

主要课程:工程设计制图及 CAD、Protel 技术、计算机系统及应用、C 语言程序设计、电工与电子技术、电路综合设计、高频电路、单片机原理及应用、嵌入式系统、EDA 技术、微处理器应用开发与制作、自动控制原理、PLC 技术及应用、信号分析与处理、电力电子技术、家用电子电器设备与维修、现代通信技术、专业英语等。

本专业毕业生能获得以下几方面的知识和能力。

(1) 掌握应用电子技术的基本理论、专业知识和基本技能。

(2) 具备分析、开发、维修电子产品与电子设备的基本能力,较强的计算机应用能力。在工业生产监控仪器仪表,家用电器开发、设计、维护和 EDA 技术方面见长。

(3) 掌握文献检索、查询的基本方法,具有一定的英文文献阅读能力,具有一定专业可持续发展能力。

### 1.1.3 课程介绍

作为一个电子技术专业的学生,要学习下列课程。

**1. 直流电路与交流电路**

这门课程包括无源器件(电阻、电容和电感)的基本理论和用直流电源供电的电路网络,接着介绍无源电路中的交流电流和交流电压的作用,这个课程模块还包括直流电机、三相电机和变压器。

**2. 模拟电子技术**

这个课程模块介绍半导体器件在线性应用范围中的特征和由这些器件组成的电路(图1.1)。内容包括半导体二极管:PN 结二极管、特殊二极管;三极管:场效应三极管、晶体三极管;信号放大电路:实际放大电路、偏置电路、运算放大器电路;其他电路:整流、稳压、直流电压源电路。

**3. 数字电子技术**

这个单元学习以下内容:逻辑电路的基本概念、数字表示方法、组合逻辑电路、时序逻辑电路、CMOS 数字电路、逻辑运算定律和布尔代数、数字运算(二进制、十六进制、整数)、组合逻辑电路的分析与综合、时序逻辑电路的分析与综合、寄存器、计数器、总线系统以及逻辑电路设计中的计算机辅助设计工具(软件)。

**4. 微处理器系统**

当前,计算机及微处理器在电子工业的各个领域中应用十分广泛,随着计算机变得更加复杂和功能不断强大,微处理器的应用将继续快速增长。对日益增长的电子工业来说,一个具有微处理器编程能力的学生将会是无价的人才。这个模块中安排学生对一个简单的微处理器编程来完成工业上典型的控制任务。用汇编语言和 C 语言对微处理器进行编程时,学生将用到一些内部的器件,如 RS232 接口、定时器、中断器件、计数器、输入/输出口、模/数转换器等,利用这些器件通过编程完成控制(系统)等操作。

**5. 计算机编程及其在工程中的应用**

该课程继续学习更高级的编程技术,教学中采用 C 语言,重点放在如何运用编程技术解决工程应用的实际问题。电子技术专业将为毕业生打下一个牢固的基础,学生毕业后可以从事的行业有:电气工程、电力能源和控制工程、电子技术、计算机工程、通信工程等。

## 1.2 阅读材料

**你了解这些电子系统吗？**

有些电子系统在日常生活中很常见，例如，收音机、电视机、电话、家用计算机。有些电子系统也是日常生活中常用的，但很少引起人们注意，如汽车中用电子系统来控制燃料混合和点火时间，使发动机的性能可以达到最佳，尾气排放最少；又如人造气象卫星中的电子系统（图 1.2）为我们提供地球（周围气象）的连续、详细的图像。

另有一些电子系统可能更少见，例如称为全球定位系统（GPS）的卫星系统，用于为位于地球上任何位置的船舶、飞机和汽车提供三维定位信息。当它们接收到来自于几颗卫星所发射的信号后，通过比较信号到达的时间和信号中所含的卫星轨道信息，可以确定它们的位置。

其他电子系统还有航空飞行控制系统，各种雷达、光盘录音设备和播放器，制造业生产控制系统和导航系统。

# UNIT 2 元件

## 2.1 文章

### 2.1.1 电阻器

电阻器是一种电子器件，它能阻碍电流的流动。在电阻器中流过的电流与加在电阻两端的电压成正比，与电阻的阻值成反比。这就是欧姆定律，可以用公式表示成 $I=\dfrac{U_R}{R}$。电阻器一般是线性器件，画出来的（伏安）特性曲线形成一条直线。

电阻器常用作限流器，限制流过器件的电流以防止器件因流过的电流过大而烧坏。电阻器也可用作分压器，以减小其他电路的电压，如晶体管偏置电路。电阻器还可用作电路的负载。

一般来说，电阻有碳（膜）电阻、线绕电阻和金属膜电阻（图 2.1），电阻器的尺寸与电阻的（额定）功率有关，尺寸比较大的电阻器通常是高功率电阻器。可变电阻器是电阻值可调节的电阻器，如变阻器、电位器和微调电位器。精密电阻器是指其误差率在 1% 或更小的电阻器。

如果你对电子技术颇有兴趣，建议学会"彩色条形码"电阻的识别方法，这样会带来很多方便。而且这种彩色条形码标注方法在其他器件也适用，如线圈（电感）、电容等。每条彩条表示一个数字，如黑色＝0，棕色＝1，红色＝2等。

图 2.2 给出彩色条形码电阻的例子，这是一个有四色条码的电阻，其中第一条是十位数，第二条是个位数，第三条是以 10 为基的指数值，第四条表示电阻的精度。如果没有第四条，则电阻的精度为 ±20%；如果第四条为银色，表示电阻的精度为 ±10%；而金色表示精度

为±5%。

对5色条码的电阻来说,第一条是百位数,第二条是十位数,第三条是个位数,第四条是以10为基的指数值。褐色(精度1%),红色(2%),绿色(0.5%),蓝色(0.25%)和紫色(0.1%)只在5色条的电阻上用来表示精度。所有5色条的电阻都有表示精度的彩色条。

可以自己制作一个电阻(器)吗?当然可以,而且不难。这里教你如何做一个电阻(器),用一支软铅笔(HB铅笔或2HB铅笔更好),在纸上画一段大约2英寸(5 cm)长的粗线。用万用表测量这段线的欧姆值,(方法是)把万用表的两个表笔分别与铅笔线的两端相接触,一定要让表笔与线段的碳接触。根据线的(粗细)电阻值大约在800 kΩ~1.5 MΩ。如果你擦掉一些线,使线明显变短,电阻值就会变小。你也可以用含硅胶的碳来制作电阻器,当硅胶干了以后测量其电阻值。

### 2.1.2 电容器

电容器是可以暂时储存电能的电子器件。电容器一般由两块导体(金属极板)组成(图2.3(a)),中间用一层不导电的绝缘材料隔开,这层绝缘材料可以增加电容储存电荷的本领(即增大电容量)。绝缘材料可以是纸、塑料片、云母、陶瓷材料、空气或真空。极板可能是铝薄板,铝箔或在一片绝缘板的两面各贴上一层金属薄膜。可以直接把一个这种导体—绝缘体—导体(三明治式)制成平板电容器,也可以把它卷起来成为圆柱形电容器,电容的符号如图2.3(b)所示。

电容器隔直流,但能以充电和放电的方式通过交流。它构成的交流电阻抗,称为容抗。容抗与电容量和交流电的频率有关,容抗的公式为 $X_C=1/(2\pi f_C C)$,其单位为欧姆。

电容器有各种形状,大小不一(图2.4)。通常电容值和加在电容两端的直流工作电压值是标在电容器上面的,但有些电容值和电阻值一样,是用彩色条形码来表示的。用云母和陶瓷作为电介质的小电容器以皮法拉($10^{-12}$ F)作为电容单位,但在电容器上只印上有效值,如105(图2.4(7))表示其电容为 $10\times 10^5$ pF$=1$ μF(1微法拉)。旋转电容器(如收音机中所用的)是用空气作为电介质的,由一组静止的平行电极板和一组可转动的电极板组成,当可转的电极板转进或转出时,电容量增大或减小。微调电容器用螺丝来进行精确调节,其绝缘材料有空气介质、云母介质和陶瓷介质。

### 2.1.3 电感器

当电流流过电感器时,电感器周围就有电磁场,电感器是以电磁场的形式暂时储存电磁能量的电子器件。电感器是一组线圈,有的电感器是空心的(空气芯),有的线圈中有可增加其电感量的铁心,(可调电感)有一个强磁的圆柱状铁心,通过调节铁心可以增加电感量或减少电感量。

电感器总是反抗电流变化,对直流电而言,电感器是没有阻碍作用的,但对交流电来说,电感器有一个交流阻抗,称为感抗。这个感抗与电感量和交流电的频率有关,可以用公式表示为 $X_L=2\pi f_L L$,其单位为欧姆。电感器可以用来滤波,增加射频(无线电频率)放大器的输出。

电感器有各式各样的形状(图2.5),空气芯的、铁心的(铁心的有时看起来像个变压器,但只有两个输出端)、环状的(圆环形的)、管状的,在一个圆柱体上有一些分开的线圈构成的射频扼流线圈和带有调节螺丝的可调射频线圈等。

## 2.1.4 半导体二极管

一个半导体二极管(简称二极管)可能是最简单的半导体器件。二极管是由半导体材料制成的 PN 结构成的。P 型材料(端)称为正极,而 N 型材料(端)称为负极(图 2.6)。

当二极管的正极电位高于负极电位(其差值大于开启电压,对锗管近似为 0.3 V,对硅管近似为 0.7 V)时称二极管是正向偏置,这时二极管的内部电阻是很小的,有一个较大的电流流过二极管,流过电流的大小取决于外部电路的电阻值。

当二极管的正极电位低于负极电位时称二极管反向偏置,这时二极管的内部电阻非常高,所以一个理想二极管可以阻挡反向电流而让正向电流通过。

二极管有很多用途,例如一个用电池的电器通常串联一个二极管来保护电器,以防止电池反接。如果电池放反了,二极管就阻挡(电池)的反向电流,起到保护电器的作用。

一个二极管的实际特性曲线并不是十分理想的,如图 2.7 所示。当理想二极管反向偏置时,电流不能通过,而实际二极管反向偏置时却有约 $10~\mu A$ 的电流流过(虽然很小,但仍不够理想)。如果加上足够大的反向电压,PN 结会被击穿,让电流(反向)通过。选择二极管时一般要使其反向击穿电压远大于电路中可能出现的电压,二极管就不会击穿。

当二极管正向偏置时,只要很小的电压就可以使它导通。对硅管来说,正偏电压约为 0.7 V。虽然二极管正向偏置时,流过的电流可以比较大,但无论正向偏置还是反向偏置,电流过大时都会损坏二极管。

图 2.8 给出一些二极管的图片。

## 2.1.5 NPN 双极型晶体管

有两类标准的双极型晶体管(通常中文称为三极管):NPN 型和 PNP 型,用不同的电路符号表示(图 2.9)。字母 N、P 表示制作三极管各层的材料,现在用的三极管大多数是 NPN 型,因为这种类型的硅管比较容易制作。

NPN 三极管由一块 N 型发射极(E)、一块 P 型基极(B)和一块 N 型集电极(C)组成。

一个晶体管可用于构成一个放大器。图 2.10 所示的电路用两个标准的 5 mm 的红色发光二极管和一个通用低功率 NPN 三极管构成(可以看到三极管中流过两个电流)。

当开关合上时,一个小电流流入三极管的基极,这个电流恰好使 B 极的发光二极管 B 微微发光,三极管放大这个小电流,使一个较大的电流通过 C 极流到 E 极。这个集电极电流很大,使发光二极管 C 很亮。

集电极电流 $I_C$ 与基极电流 $I_B$ 成正比,小于发射极电流 $I_E$,因为要使三极管导通必须有一个小的基极电流流入(发射极),三个电流之间的关系是 $I_E = I_C + I_B$。

$I_C$ 与 $I_B$ 的比值称为三极管的电流放大系数,用来表示三极管放大电流的能力,这个电流放大系数称为 $\beta$,当 C、E 两端的电压($U_{CE}$)保持不变时,有 $\beta = \Delta I_C / \Delta I_B$。

要使一个 NPN 型的双极型晶体管导通,基极必须略高于发射极的正向电压(对硅管来说约为 +0.6 V)。当晶体管逐渐趋于饱和时,这个电压大约是 +0.7 V,这时 C 极与 E 极之间的电阻很小,甚至几乎可以看成是短路。

当图 2.10 中的开关断开时,没有基极电流流过,所以三极管切断集电极电流,两个发光二极管都不亮(三极管截止),此时 C 极与 E 极之间的电阻很大,可以看成是开路(不通)。

实际上三极管的性能没这么理想,这时仍有一个极小的漏电流($I_{CBO}$)从集电极流到基极,这个漏电流可能引起一个晶体管电路的稳定性(不好)的问题。

图 2.11 给出各种晶体三极管的图片。

## 2.2 阅读材料

### 2.2.1 非线性电阻器

标准类型的电阻器阻值通常不受外部条件如电压、温度和光的影响,这种电阻器称作线性电阻器。而非线性电阻器的阻值则随温度(热敏电阻器)、电压(压敏变阻器)或光(光敏电阻器)的变化而变化。

热敏电阻器(图 2.12)是用金属如锰、镍、铜或铁的氧化物制成的。通常,热敏电阻器有一个负的温度系数,当温度升高时它的阻值下降。典型的阻值变化约是 $-5\%/°C$,电阻的阻值范围为 $1\sim50$ M$\Omega$。

热敏电阻可以放在晶体管的偏置电路中来控制稳定晶体管电路(的静态工作点)。把一个热敏电阻安放在晶体管边上(并连接在电路中),当温度升高时,热敏电阻器的阻值下降,这就导致从发射极到基极的正向偏置电压的减小,从而流过晶体管的电流减小,电路就变得比较稳定。当温度降低时,热敏电阻器恢复其初值,正向偏置电压也就恢复为正常值。

压敏变阻器在外形上与热敏电阻器相似,但它们的两端的电压增大时阻值减小,流过压敏变阻器的电流随其两端的电压按指数关系变化。对一个给定的压敏变阻器来说,电流可以增大到原来的 64 倍。大部分压敏变阻器都用作其他电路的保护器件,如并联在一个开关的两端以防止电火花或连接在一个感应电路中防止突然产生的电压波动。

光敏电阻(图 2.13)是用高阻的半导体材料制作的,如果足够高频率的光照在光敏电阻上,则半导体吸收光子(能量)使束缚电子能够跃迁到导通带成为自由电子,自由电子(和相应产生的空穴)可以导电,则光敏电阻的阻值变小了。

### 2.2.2 三极管用作开关

因为一个三极管的集电极电流是正比于其基极电流的,所以可以把三极管作为一种电流控制开关。通过输入一个相当小的基极电流,可以起到控制一个较大的集电极电流的作用。

为了便于说明,我们通过用一个三极管取代开关来说明三极管如何控制流过电灯的电流(图 2.14)。记住通过三极管的受控电流是从集电极流到发射极。因为这个流过灯泡的电流是我们想要控制的,所以我们必须把三极管的集电极和发射极放在开关的两个接触端,我们还必须保证灯泡的电流流向与发射极箭头的方向一致,以保证三极管的 PN 结偏置是正确的。

这个例子选用 NPN 型三极管构成。

要有基极电流,我们还要加一条电路,因为三极管的基极不接,基极电流为零,这个三极管就不能导通,灯也不亮。

如果基极开关断开,三极管的基极悬空(即不与任何地方相连接),没有电流流过。这种状态称三极管截止(图 2.14(a))。如果基极开关合上(图 2.14(b)),则电子将从三极管的发射极流到基极,通过开关,流过左边的灯泡,回到电池的正极(注:电子的流向与电流方向相反)。这个基极电流将使更大量的电子从发射极流到集电极,点亮灯泡,这时电路电流达到最大值,这种状态称三极管饱和。

当然这样利用三极管去控制一个灯看起来毫无意义,毕竟只要用一个开关就可以控制一个灯了。如果这个电路仍用一个开关间接地去控制灯,三极管控制电流的意义是什么呢?为什么不干脆就用开关直接控制灯的电流?

实际上这里有两点:首先是采用这种方法控制时,开关中仅流过很小的基极电流使三极管导通,而三极管(集电极)流过的是灯中的大电流。这是一个优点,如果开关只允许流过小电流,就可以用一个小(额定电流)开关去控制一个相当大电流的负载。另一点可能更重要,就是三极管的电流控制特性可以使我们用其他各种方法来控制灯。

图 2.15(a)中用一个太阳能电池来控制三极管从而控制灯。

或者图 2.15(b)用一个热电耦来提供基极电流使三极管导通(用温度控制灯)。

如果通过整流,把话筒输出的交流信号变成直流信号,使三极管的发射极-基极的 PN 结正偏,甚至一个话筒的输出电压和电流可用来使三极管导通(图 2.16)(用声音控制灯)。

现在意义应该很清楚了,一个小小的直流电流源可以用来使三极管导通,直流电源的电流与灯泡中所流过电流相比是很小的。这里我们看到三极管的作用不但是一个开关,而且是一个放大器:用一个相当小功率的信号去控制一个相当大功率(的电器)。

请注意实际点亮灯的能量来自于示意图右侧的电池,并不是来自太阳能电池、热电耦或话筒的信号被神奇地放大了(转换成一个大能量的信号),这些小信号源只是简单地起一个控制电池能源点亮灯泡的作用。

小结:

三极管可用作控制直流电源连接到负载的开关,当控制电流流过发射极和基极时,被控制电流流过发射极和集电极。

当三极管中没有电流流过时,称三极管处于截止状态(非导通)。

当三极管中流过的电流达到最大值时,称三极管处于饱和状态(完全导通)。

# UNIT 3　仪器仪表

## 3.1　文章

### 3.1.1　万用表

万用表是一种通用仪表,能用来测量直流和交流电压、电流、电阻,有的还能测量分贝(放大倍数)。有两种万用表:一种是用指针在标准刻度上的移动来指示测量值的模拟万用表[图 3.1(a)],另一种是用电子数字显示器显示测量值的数字万用表[图 3.1(b)]。这两种万用表都有一个正极(+)插孔和一个公共端(-)插孔用来插入测试笔,一个功能选择开关用来选择(测量对象)——直流电压、交流电压、直流电流、交流电流或欧姆(电阻),一个范围选择开关用来(选择范围以做)精确测量。万用表也可能还有其他插孔用来测量高电压(1~5 kV)和大电流(高达 10 A),对一些特殊的万用表来说还有一些其他功能的变化。

除了功能选择开关和范围选择开关(有时它们合成一个开关),模拟万用表可能还有一个极性开关,可以很方便地交换测试笔的极性。通常有一个螺丝可调节指针,(在无电流时)

使指针指在零处,当测量电阻时另有一个零点调节控制(钮)用来在电池电压不足时进行补偿调节(即保证电阻为 0 时指针指向零值)。模拟万用表可以测量正电压和负电压,只要简单地对调一下两个测试笔或拨一下极性开关,数字万用表通常会自动在显示器上指示出极性。

为了保证读数正确,万用表必须与电路正确连接。一个电压表(万用表测量电压时)应与被测电路或元件并联。当测量电流时,电路必须断开,插入万用表表笔使万用表与被测电路或元件相串联。当测量电路中局部电路(或元件)的(等效)电阻时,必须除去电路中的电源,万用表与这局部电路(或元件)并联。

### 3.1.2 数字示波器

UT2000/3000 系列数字存储示波器(图 3.2)向用户提供简单而功能明晰的前面板,以进行所有的基本操作。各通道的标度和位置旋钮提供了直观的操作,符合传统仪器的使用习惯,用户不必花大量的时间去学习和熟悉数字存储示波器的操作,即可熟练使用。为加速调整,便于测量,用户可直接按 AUTO 键,仪器则显现适合的波形和档位设置。

除易于使用之外,UT2000/3000 系列数字存储示波器还具有更快完成测量任务所需的高性能指标和强大功能。通过 500 MS/s 的实时采样和 25 GS/s 的等效采样,可在 UT2000/3000 数字存储示波器上观察更快的信号。强大的触发和分析能力使其易于捕获和分析波形。清晰的液晶显示和数学运算功能,便于用户更快更清晰地观察和分析信号问题。

从下面给出的性能特点,可以了解此系列数字存储示波器如何满足用户的测量要求。
- 双模拟通道
- 高清晰彩色/单色液晶显示系统,320×240 分辨率
- 支持即插即用 USB 存储设备,并可通过 USB 存储设备与计算机通信
- 自动波形、状态设置
- 波形、设置和位图存储以及波形和设置再现
- 精细的视窗扩展功能,精确分析波形细节与概貌
- 自动测量 28 种波形参数
- 自动光标跟踪测量功能
- 独特的波形录制和回放功能
- 内嵌 FFT
- 多种波形数学运算功能(包括加、减、乘、除)
- 边沿、视频、脉宽、交替触发功能
- 多国语言菜单显示
- 中英文帮助信息显示

UT2000/3000 系列数字存储示波器是小型、轻便的台式数字存储示波器。向用户提供方便且易操作的前面板(图 3.3),可以进行基本的测试。UT2000/3000 向用户提供简单而功能明晰的前面板,以进行基本的操作。面板上包括旋钮和功能按键,旋钮的功能与其他数字存储示波器类似。显示屏右侧的一列 5 个按键为菜单操作键(自上而下定义为 F1 键至 F5 键)。通过它们,用户可以设置当前菜单的不同选项;其他按键为功能键,通过它们,用户可以进入不同的功能菜单或直接获得特定的功能应用。

UT2000/3000 面板操作说明如图 3.4 所示。

显示界面说明如图 3.5 所示。

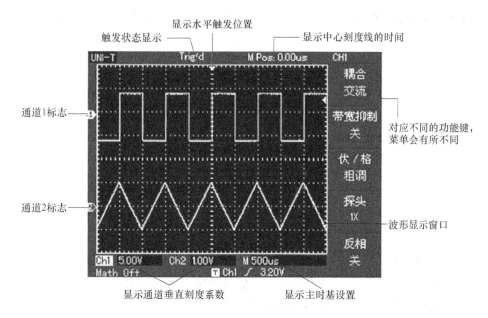

图 3.5 显示界面说明图

**功能检查**

做一次快速功能检查,以核实本仪器运行是否正常。请按如下步骤进行。

**1. 接通仪器电源**

用户可将本机接通电源,电源的供电电压为交流 100~240 V,频率为 45~440 Hz。接通电源后,让仪器以最大测量精度优化数字存储示波器信号路径执行自校正程序,按 U-TILITY 按钮,按 F1 执行。然后进入下一页按 F1,调出出厂设置,如图 3.6 所示。上述过程结束后,按 CH1,进入 CH1 菜单。

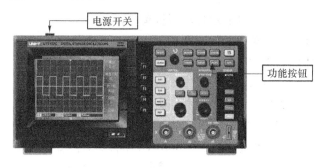

图 3.6 默认设置

警告:为避免危险,请确认数字存储示波器已经安全接地。

**2. 数字存储示波器接入信号**

UT2000/3000 系列数字存储示波器为双通道输入,另有一个外触发输入通道。请按如下步骤接入信号。

(1) 将数字存储示波器探头连接到 CH1 输入端,并将探头上的衰减倍率开关设定为 10×(图 3.7)。

(2) 在数字示波器上需要设置探头衰减系数,此衰减系数改变仪器的垂直档位倍率,从而使得测量结果正确反映被测信号的幅值。设置探头衰减系数的方法如下,按[F4],使菜单显示 10×。

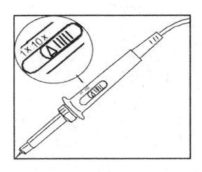

图 3.7 探头衰减倍率开关设定

例一:测量简单信号

观测电路中一未知信号,迅速显示和测量信号的频率和峰-峰值。

**1. 欲迅速显示该信号,请按如下步骤操作**

(1) 将探头菜单衰减系数设定为 10×,并将探头上的开关设定为 10×;

(2) 将 CH1 的探头连接到电路被测点;

(3) 按下 AUTO 按钮。

数字存储示波器将自动设置使波形显示达到最佳。在此基础上,用户可以进一步调节垂直、水平档位,直至波形的显示符合用户的要求。

**2. 进行自动测量信号的电压和时间参数**

数字存储示波器可对大多数显示信号进行自动测量。欲测量信号频率和峰-峰值,请按如下步骤操作:

(1) 按 MEASURE 按键,以显示自动测量菜单;

(2) 按下 F1,进入测量菜单种类选择;

(3) 按下 F3,选择电压类;

(4) 按下 F5 翻至 2/4 页,再按 F3 选择测量类型,峰-峰值;

(5) 按下 F2,进入测量菜单种类选择,再按 F4 选择时间类;

(6) 按 F2 即可选择测量类型,频率。

此时,峰-峰值和频率的测量值分别显示在 F1 和 F2 的位置。自动测量如图 3.8 所示。

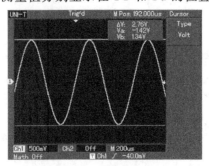

图 3.8 自动测量

## 3.2 阅读材料

### 3.2.1 模拟示波器

示波器(图 3.9)是一个图像显示设备,它显示一个电子信号的图像。当信号输入到示波器中时,一个电子束被产生、聚焦、加速并适当偏离,在阴极射线管(CRT)的显示屏上显示电压的波形。

通常,示波器图像显示电压信号如何随时间变化的:其垂直轴 $Y$ 表示电压,水平轴 $X$ 表示时间。在示波器屏幕上的电压波形的幅度可以通过输出电压波峰与波谷之间纵向距离的厘米值来确定(图 3.10),将这厘米值乘上 V/cm 控制钮的设定值就得到电压的幅度值。例如,如果电压的峰-峰间幅度为 5 cm,控制钮设在 1 V/cm 处,则峰-峰电压值为 5 V。

用示波器的水平标尺可以测量时间值,时间测量包括测量信号的周期、脉冲宽度和频率。频率是周期的倒数,所以一旦知道了周期,频率就是用 1 除以周期。

一个波形的频率可以通过在水平方向数出波形一个周期的厘米值来确定,将这厘米值乘上时间/厘米控制钮的设定值就得到它的一个周期所需的时间。例如,如果一个波形长 4 cm,控制钮设在 1 ms/cm,则周期是 4 ms,则频率可以用下面的公式求出:

$$f = \frac{1}{p} = \frac{1}{4 \text{ ms}} = 250 \text{ Hz}$$

如果控制钮设在 100 $\mu$s/cm,则周期是 400 $\mu$s,频率为 2.5 kHz。

一个双踪示波器具有同时显示输入信号和输出信号的优点,可以显示输出信号是否有失真和表示输入/输出信号的相位关系。两路信号的波形可以重叠在一起,较好地显示出输入信号与输出信号相位的差别。

### 3.2.2 信号发生器

信号发生器是把直流电转换成交流电或变化的直流电的仪器(图 3.11),即把直流电转换成正弦波、方波、三角波或其他波形的电压信号。信号发生器是用来给电路或设备输入一个信号,以便对电路或设备进行维修或校正。有些信号发生器可以用来专门产生音频、射频或高频信号,而另一些则可以产生多种频率范围的信号。所有的信号发生器有函数(波形选择)旋钮,有频率范围选择旋钮、频率细调旋钮,用来选择一个特定的频率,有一个幅度控制旋钮用来改变输出电压的峰-峰值(或幅值),还有一些输出端口。

如果要选一个 5 kHz 的正弦波,可把波形选择旋钮调在正弦波上,把频率范围选择旋钮放在 1 K 上,然后调节频率细调旋钮到 5,再通过调节输出幅度控制旋钮便可得到想要的峰-峰值电压的输出信号。

# UNIT 4　集成电路

## 4.1　文章

### 4.1.1　关于集成电路

集成电路是用半导体材料制成的小电子器件,第一块集成电路是在20世纪50年代由德克萨斯仪器公司的 Jack Kilby 和 Fairchild 半导体公司的 Robert Noyce 开发的。

集成电路应用于各种设备中,如微处理器、音频和视频设备以及汽车(图4.1)。集成电路通常根据其包含的晶体管和其他电路元件的数量来归类。

SSI(小规模集成电路):每个芯片中有100个以下电子元件。

MSI(中规模集成电路):每个芯片中有100~3 000个电子元件。

LSI(大规模集成电路):每个芯片中有3 000~100 000个电子元件。

VLSI(很大规模集成电路):每个芯片中有100 000~1 000 000个电子元件。

ULSI(超大规模集成电路):每个芯片中有100万个以上的电子元件。

在集成电路的设计和制造过程中,常用两种主要晶体管技术:双极和金属氧化物半导体(MOS)。双极工艺生产出来的是 BJT(双极型晶体管),而 MOS 工艺生产出来的是 FET(场效应晶体管)。在20世纪80年代以前更常用的集成电路是双极逻辑,但是此后 MOS 技术在数字逻辑集成电路中占据了大多数。N 沟道 FET 是采用 NMOS 工艺生产的,而 P 沟道 FET 是采用 PMOS 工艺生产的。到了20世纪80年代,互补 MOS 即 CMOS 成为占主导地位的加工技术,并且延续至今。CMOS 集成电路包含了 NMOS 和 PMOS 两种晶体管。

专用集成电路(ASIC)是为了特殊应用而定制的集成电路,而不是通用的。比如,一片仅被设计用于运行蜂窝式电话的芯片是专用集成电路(ASIC)。相比之下,7400系列与4000系列集成电路是可以用导线连接的逻辑构建模块,适用于各种不同的应用。

随着逐年来特征尺寸的缩小和设计工具的改进,ASIC 中的最大复杂度从5 000个门电路增长到了1亿个门电路,因而功能也有极大的提高。现代 ASIC 常包含32位处理器,包括 ROM、RAM、EEPROM、Flash 等存储器,以及其他大规模组件。这样的 ASIC 经常被称为 SoC(片上系统)。数字 ASIC 的设计者们使用硬件描述语言(HDL),比如 Verilog 或 VHDL 语言来描述 ASIC 的功能。

现场可编程门阵列(FPGA 如图4.2所示)是7400系列和面包板的现代版,它包括可编程逻辑块和可编程模块之间的相互连接,使得相同的 FPGA 能够用于许多不同的场合。对于较小规模的设计或(与)小批量生产,FPGA 可能比 ASIC 设计有更高的成本效率。不能循坏的工程费用(建立工厂生产特定 ASIC 的成本)可能会达到数十万美元。

专用集成电路这一通用名词也包括 FPGA,但是大多数设计者仅将 ASIC 用于非现场可编程的器件,将 ASIC 和 FPGA 两者区别开来。

### 4.1.2 双极型(晶体管)集成电路和 MOS 集成电路

历史上,双极型集成电路曾经比 MOS 集成电路更普及,尤其是对小规模集成逻辑电路而言。主要的原因有两个,一是最初双极晶体管(即三极管)要比 MOS 管更可靠,其次是三极管的速度比 MOS 管快。

但随着 MOS 管可靠性的改进以及集成电路变得越来越复杂,使得 MOS 逻辑电路的体积小及(损耗)功率小这两个优点显得更重要了,双极型逻辑电路的使用也减少了,然而,双极型晶体管(集成电路)技术在高频逻辑电路中仍然很有用。

### 4.1.3 集成电路的设计过程

一个典型的集成电路设计过程由 4 个部分组成。

(1) 系统(性能)设计是定义电路功能和输入输出特性的过程。这一级的设计说明可以用流程图或用一种高级硬件描述语言(HDL)来表示。

(2) 逻辑设计是把一个复杂功能的高级描述(定义)转换成由独立逻辑部件如与非门、非门、转换器、锁存器构成的功能列表,这个过程有助于保证用最小化的逻辑来实现前面用高级语言定义的功能。

(3) 电路设计是把基本逻辑部件转换成晶体管和内部连接构成的电路的过程。

(4) 线路板设计是根据硅材料电路的需要,在各层面上创建几何形状(即制作具体的晶体管元件等)。

虽然这些步骤相互之间是有联系的,但每一步都有它自己的基本目标。在系统设计阶段,目标是提供一个完整和精确的功能描述。逻辑阶段的设计目标是减小能量消耗,线路板设计目标则是以高集成度实现一个电路的功能。

## 4.2 阅读材料

### 电路板

**1. 面包板(临时的,不要焊接)**

面包板是在需要测试电路和验证一个(设计)想法时用来搭建一个临时电路的。用面包板搭电路不要焊接,所有的元器件都可以反复使用,可以很方便地改变电路连接及更换元件。几乎所有的设计都是先用面包板(图 4.3(a))来检查电路是否符合设计要求的。

**2. 条形焊接板(永久的,需焊接)**

条形焊接板(图 4.4(b))有一面有平行的铜条,铜条的间距是 0.1 英寸(2.54 mm),铜条上面每隔 0.1 英寸(2.54 mm)有小孔。条形焊接板只要取适当大小就可以用了,可以用一般的钢锯锯开,也可以简单地把它放在长凳、桌子边上,沿着一排有孔的直线用力折断。

**3. 印刷电路板(PCB)(永久的,需焊接)**

印刷电路板(PCB)(图 4.5)用铜条(线)连接到各个器件的焊接孔上,每块电路板都是专门设计的,焊接比较容易。但制作 PCB 板需要专用的设备,所以不推荐新手(初学者)用 PCB 板,除非已有现成的 PCB 板。

# UNIT 5　数据手册

## 5.1　文章

### 5.1.1　DM74LS194A 数据手册

DM74LS194A
4 位双向通用移位寄存器
一般描述：
这种双向移位寄存器的设计包含了系统设计师想在一个移位寄存器上实现的几乎所有的移位功能，它可实现并行输入，并行输出，右移串行数据输入和左移串行数据输入，工作方式控制，异步复位功能。这个移位寄存器有四种工作方式：
并行装载
右移（数据移动方向由 $Q_A$—$Q_D$）
左移（数据移动方向由 $Q_D$—$Q_A$）
保持
同步并行加载：当工作方式控制端 S0、S1 均为高电平时，在时钟（CLOCK）上升沿作用下，并行数据（A—D）被送入相应的输出端 $Q_A$—$Q_D$。此时串行数据（$D_{SR}$、$D_{SL}$）被禁止。
当 S0 为高电平、S1 为低电平时，在 CLOCK 上升沿作用下进行右移操作，数据由 $D_{SR}$ 送入。当 S0 为低电平、S1 为高电平时，在 CLOCK 上升沿作用下进行左移操作，数据由 $D_{SL}$ 送入。当 S0 和 S1 均为低电平时，CLOCK 被禁止。
特点：
- 并行输入和输出
- 四种工作方式：
  同步并行输入
  右移
  左移
  保持
- 时钟上升沿触发
- 异步清零

端口：
- CLOCK 时钟端
- CLEAR 清零端
- A—D：并行数据输入端
- 左移串行数据输入端
- 右移串行数据输入端
- S0，S1：工作方式控制端
- $Q_A$—$Q_D$：输出端

绝对最大额定值

"绝对最大额定值"是那些超出不能保证器件正常工作的安全值。器件不能工作在这些极限值条件下。在绝对最大额定值条件下不能保证在电气特性表中定义的参数值。推荐工作条件表将确定实际器件的操作条件。

电源电压　　　　　7 V
输入电压　　　　　7 V
工作环境温度　　　0～+70 ℃
储存温度　　　　　-65～+150 ℃

器件连接图如图 5.1 所示。

功能表

| 清零 | 工作方式 | | Clock | 输入 | | | | | | 输出 | | | |
|---|---|---|---|---|---|---|---|---|---|---|---|---|---|
| | | | | 串行 | | 并行 | | | | $Q_A$ | $Q_B$ | $Q_C$ | $Q_D$ |
| | S1 | S0 | | 左移 | 右移 | A | B | C | D | | | | |
| L | X | X | X | X | X | X | X | X | X | L | L | L | L |
| H | X | X | L | X | X | X | X | X | X | $Q_{A0}$ | $Q_{B0}$ | $Q_{C0}$ | $Q_{D0}$ |
| H | H | H | ↑ | X | X | a | b | c | d | a | b | c | d |
| H | L | H | ↑ | X | H | X | X | X | X | H | $Q_{An}$ | $Q_{Bn}$ | $Q_{Cn}$ |
| H | L | H | ↑ | X | L | X | X | X | X | L | $Q_{An}$ | $Q_{Bn}$ | $Q_{Cn}$ |
| H | H | L | ↑ | H | X | X | X | X | X | $Q_{Bn}$ | $Q_{Cn}$ | $Q_{Dn}$ | H |
| H | H | L | ↑ | L | X | X | X | X | X | $Q_{Bn}$ | $Q_{Cn}$ | $Q_{Dn}$ | L |
| H | L | L | X | X | X | X | X | X | X | $Q_{A0}$ | $Q_{B0}$ | $Q_{C0}$ | $Q_{D0}$ |

物理尺寸如图 5.2 所示。

## 5.1.2 NE555 数据手册

NE555 是电子技术中常用的定时器集成芯片,这里从其使用手册中摘录了一部分:
- 定时器,定时范围从微秒到数小时
- 非稳态(中文中也称双稳态)或单稳态输出
- 占空比可调
- 与 TTL 兼容的输出,吸收(灌电流)和输出(拉电流)可达 200 mA
- 可与 Signetics(公司)的 NE555,SA555,SE555 互换(使用)

(性能)描述

NE555 是精密定时器电路,可产生精确的时间延时和振荡。在用于延时或单稳态模式工作时,定时间隔是由一外接的电阻电容电路控制的;在非稳态(振荡)模式下,其输出频率和占空系数可分别用两个外接电阻和一个外接电容来控制。

门槛电平和触发电平一般分别是 $V_{CC}$ 的 2/3 和 1/3。利用控制电压端(CONT)也可以改变门槛电平和触发电平。当触发端(TRIG)输入电平低于触发电平,触发器被置 1,输出高电平。如果触发输入高于触发电平且门槛端(THRES)输入也高于门槛电平,则触发器清零,输出低电平。清零(RESET)输入端可以不管任何其他端的输入情况(将输出清零),常用于定时器一个新的工作循环的初始化。当清零端低电平时,触发器被清零,输出为低电平。当输出是低电平时,在放电端(DISCH)和地(GND)之间有一条低阻抗通路。

输出电路可以接收高达 200 mA 的灌电流或输出拉电流。电源电压可以是 5~15 V。当用 5 V 电源时,输出与 TTL 芯片的输入兼容(即可以直接相接)。

NE555 的工作温度范围是 0~70 ℃,SA555 是 -40~85 ℃,SE555 是军用芯片,其工作温度范围是 -55~125 ℃。图 5.3 给出 NE555 的封装及引脚定义。

物理尺寸如图 5.4 所示。

## 5.2 阅读材料

### AD574 数据手册

AD574 是一种模数转换芯片,即把模拟信号转换成数字信号的芯片,是电子技术中常用的芯片,这里从它的说明书中摘录了一部分。

**1. 特点(图 5.5)**

自带参考电压和时钟的 12 位 A/D 转换器

8 位或 16 位微处理器总线接口

在下列温度范围确保线性度:

0~+70 ℃——对 AD574AJ,K,L 类型

-55~+125 ℃——对 AD574AS,T,U 类型

在工作温度范围内没有误码

最长转换时间 35 ms

陶瓷双列直插、塑料双列直插或 PLCC(塑料有引线芯片载体,一种封装形式)封装

另有与它的引脚输出兼容的高速类型(15 ms AD674B)

**2. 产品性能描述**

AD574A(图 5.5)是 12 位连续模-数转换器,带有三态输出缓冲电路,可以直接与 8 位或 16 位微处理器总线相接。

AD574A 在一个芯片上集成了全部模拟和数字功能,通过有源激光微调晶片级的薄膜电阻使芯片的输出偏移,线性度和换算误差达到最小。参考电压用一个内置稳压二极管来降低噪声和漂移。在数字方面,内置连续转换寄存器,控制电路和三态输出缓冲器,可以输出 12 位数字量。

AD574A 有 6 个不同的等级,AD574AJ,K 和 L 级的工作温度在 0~+70 ℃,AD574AS,T 和 U 级的工作温度在 -55~+125 ℃。各种等级芯片都有陶瓷密封双列直插 28 脚的封装、J,K 和 L 级还有塑料双列直插 28 脚和陶瓷 PLCC 封装。

# UNIT 6　用户使用手册

## 6.1　文章

### 6.1.1　iPhone 4 介绍

　　2007 年 iPhone 的诞生彻底改变了智能手机的时代。iPhone 3GS 提供了令人难以置信的速度和性能,平均比 iPhone 3G 快了两倍。炙手可热的 4 代 iPhone,拥有超过近 100 个新功能。

　　在这里介绍几种新功能。

　　(1) 新型设计

　　iPhone 4 正反面采用玻璃镜面制作,侧面使用和新款 mac 一样的材质制作,看起来就像一台漂亮的经典莱卡相机。它要比 3 代还薄 24%,事实上,它是世界上最薄的智能手机。这里是音量控制键,这里是一个前置摄像头、这是 SIM 卡托,后面则是摄像头和 LED 闪光灯,底部,麦克风;顶部,耳机插孔,噪声消除麦克风。

　　(2) 视网膜显示

　　我们称之为视网膜显示。什么意思呢? 我们做到显示屏幕都有像素。而这个技术极大地增加了显示的像素密度,像素是原先的 4 倍。我们得到了非常清晰的文字。视网膜显示技术使得现在显示为每英寸 326 像素。

　　(3) 300 小时待机时间

　　由于我们把电池做得更大了,而且 A4 芯片很棒,所以电池寿命也有所提高。iPhone 4 能提供 7 小时的 3G 通话,6 小时 3G 上网,10 小时 Wi-Fi 上网,10 小时视频播放,40 小时音乐播放以及 300 小时待机时间。

　　(4) 四频 HSDPA,7.2 Mbit/s

　　(5) 双麦克风,支持 802.11n Wi-Fi, GPS,罗盘,加速计

　　(6) 添加了一个陀螺仪

　　我们添加了一个 3 轴陀螺仪,并将这个陀螺仪和加速计、罗盘绑到一起成 6 轴。这是游戏的完美装置。

　　(7) 万像素

　　摄像头的工作是拍摄照片和适应暗光的拍摄。所以我们把它从 300 万像素升级到了 500 万像素,并且使用了一个背照式感光元件。此外,多数人增加百万像素的方法是使像素更小,但我们则做到大小相同。拥有 5 倍数码变焦功能,配备 LED 闪光灯的 4 代 iPhone 让用户照出来的相片像素更高,更加精细。

　　(8) 高清晰视频

　　它也能拍摄每秒 30 帧 720 分辨率的高清视频。

　　(9) iPhone 4 操作系统 OS4

　　iPhone 4 操作系统 OS4 是世界上最先进的移动终端操作系统。

### 6.1.2 iPhone 用户使用手册

iPhone 概述

iPhone 4 外观如图 6.1 所示。

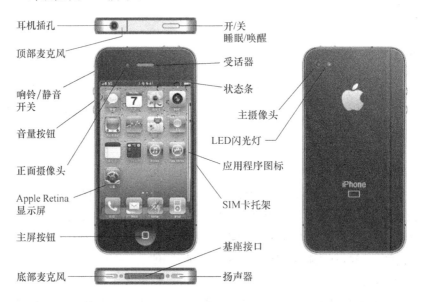

图 6.1 iPhone 4 外观

你的主屏幕可能看起来不同,取决于你拥有的 iPhone 的机型以及是否已重新排列了图标。

**1. 按钮**

**("开/关"和"睡眠/唤醒"按钮)**(图 6.2)

如果你当前没有使用 iPhone,则可以锁定它以关闭显示屏,从而节省电池电量。

锁定 iPhone:按"开/关"和"睡眠/唤醒"按钮。如果已锁定 iPhone,则触摸屏幕不起任何作用。iPhone 仍可以接听电话,接收短信以及接收其他更新。你也可以:

- 听音乐
- 当你在打电话或听音乐的时候调整 iPhone 旁边的按钮来调节音量
- 用 iPhone 耳机上的中央按钮(或 Bluetooth® 耳机上的等效按钮)来播放或暂停播放歌曲,或者接听或结束通话。

默认情况下,如果你不触摸屏幕的时间达到一分钟,则 iPhone 会锁定。

**主屏幕按钮**

随时按下主屏幕按钮以返回到主屏幕,该屏幕包含你的 iPhone 应用程序。轻按任一应用程序图标,即可开始使用。请参阅第 19 页"打开和切换应用程序"。

**音量按钮**

当你正在接听电话或欣赏歌曲、影片或其他媒体时,iPhone 侧面的按钮可以调节音量。其他情况下,这些按钮可以控制响铃、提醒和其他声音效果的音量。

若要设定 iPhone 上的音乐和视频音量限制,去设置＞音乐。

你还可以使用音量向上键,拍照或录制视频。

**响铃/静音开关**

扳动响铃/静音开关以让 iPhone 在响铃模式 🔔 或静音模式 🔕 之间切换。

【重要事项】当 iPhone 处于静音模式时,"时钟"闹钟、音频相关应用程序(如 iPod)和许多游戏仍会通过内置扬声器播放声音。

**2. 安装 SIM 卡**

如果 SIM 卡未预先安装,则必须安装它,然后才能使用 iPhone。

安装 SIM 卡:

将回形针的一端或 SIM 卡推出工具插入 SIM 卡托架上的孔中;拉出 SIM 卡托架并将 SIM 卡放入托架中;使 SIM 卡与托架平行,将 SIM 卡置于顶部,小心地装回托架。

安装 SIM 卡至 iPhone 4 中(图 6.5)。

**3. 基本功能**

**使用应用程序**

高分辨率 Multi-Touch 屏幕和简单的手指手势使得使用 iPhone 应用程序很容易。

**打开和切换应用程序**

若要在 iPhone 上打开应用程序,请在主屏幕上轻按其图标 ▢ 。

打开一个应用程序(图 6.6)。

返回到主屏幕:按下显示屏下方的主屏幕按钮 ▢ 。

切换到其他主屏幕:快速向左或向右滑动手指,或者在一行圆点的左右轻按。

双击 Home 键可以显示多任务栏,它显示了用户最近使用的应用程序(图 6.8)。点击一个应用程序来重新打开它,或轻弹,以看到更多的应用程序。

**放大或缩小**(图 6.9)

查看照片、网页、电子邮件或地图时,你可以进行放大或缩小。将您的手指合拢或张开来进行放大和缩小。查看照片和网页时,连按两次(快速轻按两次)以放大,再次连按两次以缩小。查看地图时,连按两次以放大,用两个手指轻按一次以缩小。

**以纵向或横向模式查看**(图 6.10)

许多 iPhone 应用程序都可让你以纵向或横向模式观看屏幕。转动 iPhone,显示屏也会转动显示内容,并自动调整以适合新屏幕方向。

(本文摘自 iPhone 用户使用手册)

## 6.2 阅读材料

**MiraScan 介绍**

MiraScan 是扫描仪的驱动程序,它是 TWAIN 专为用户设计的友好界面。通过它的按钮化用户界面和十分合理的任务流设计,你只要用鼠标单击几下就可以完成全部的扫描工作。

你可以用MiraScan完成下列任务:

1) 预览、扫描和输入(反射式)原件(一般的文件、不透明的文件)或透明原件(照片底片等),提供给图像编辑软件。

2) 开始用图像编辑软件编辑图像前,可以调整所扫描的图片的质量。

3) 用批扫描功能,可以让你在一幅图片上指定多个扫描区域,并开始多个扫描过程。

4) 通过反色和镜像功能可以在扫描的图片上创建特别的效果。

5) 用色彩向导可以很方便地调整图片的色彩。

**扫描不透明的原件**

第1步:把原件面朝下放在扫描仪的玻璃平板上,注意原件的方向,防止出现方向错误(图6.11),盖上扫描仪的盖板。

第2步:打开应用软件。

第3步:如果你第一次扫描,你可以在"文件"菜单中的选择扫描仪中选择TWAIN扫描仪(即本扫描仪),然后在应用软件中选择MiraScan。(这一步只需做一次,除非重新安装应用软件)。

注意根据你所使用的软件选择TWAIN扫描仪的方法可能有些不同。具体方法可以参考应用软件所附带的文件。

第4步:在你的应用软件中选择扫描新图可以打开MiraScan(这一步也会因所用的应用软件的不同而不同。)

第5步:从MiraScan主界面(图6.12)的源组合框中选择反射式(不透明),单击"预览"按钮,在预览区中会出现一幅预览的图片。

第6步:在预览区域内调整扫描面积。

第7步:用组合框中的选项指定分辨率、比例等,对扫描的图像设置扫描要求。

第8步:用工具条中的选项调整图像。

第9步:如果你需要再加上另一块扫描面积(扫描任务),按下"重复"按钮,在任务列表中加上一项新的任务(图6.13)。重复步骤6和步骤7设置扫描任务。

第10步:在完成每个扫描任务的设置以后,单击"扫描"按钮进行扫描。

第11步:几秒后,扫描的图像就输入到你的应用软件中,你可以对图像进行编辑了。

# UNIT 7 应 用

## 7.1 文章

### 7.1.1 电视

**1. 关于电视**

电视肯定是我们这个时代最有影响力的东西之一。

要了解电视,先看一下人的大脑。大脑中有两样奇妙的东西使电视成为可能,第一就是如果把一幅静止的图片切割成很多小彩色点,人的大脑会把这些彩色的点拼成一幅(有意义的)图像。在电视机和计算机显示屏上,这些点被称作像素。

人脑的第二个与电视有关的奇妙之处在于如果把一幅运动的图像分解成一连串静止画面并以很快且连续的方法显示这些静止的画面,大脑会把这些静止的画面重新组合成一个动态的场面。

### 2. 阴极射线管

现在所用的电视机有一部分是用阴极射线管(CRT)来显示图像的,我们先讨论 CRT,因为 CRT 曾经是最普通的显示器。

在一个阴极射线管中(图 7.1),"阴极"是加热的灯丝(与普通白炽灯的灯丝不同)。加热灯丝是放在一个玻璃真空管中,"射线"是一束电子束,是从加热灯丝射入真空管的。

电子是负电荷,阳极是正的,所以阳极吸引电子离开阴极。在一个电视机的阴极射线管中,电子流被聚焦阳极聚焦成一细(电子)束,加速阳极使电子束加速。这一高速电子束穿过真空撞击在真空管另一端的平面屏幕上,这个屏幕上镀了一层磷,当电子束撞击它时会发光。

在真空管中有可以产生电磁场的线圈。一组线圈产生使电子作垂直运动的电磁场,另一组线圈产生使电子作水平运动的电磁场。通过控制线圈的电压,就可以使电子束撞击到屏幕的任意位置。

在 CRT 中,屏幕的内表面镀了一层磷,当电子撞击在磷上,会使屏幕发光。黑白电视机屏幕只有一层撞击时发白光的磷,彩色电视机屏幕有排列成点状或条状的三种磷,分别发红光、绿光和蓝光,还需要三个电子光束同时使这三种不同颜色发光。

### 3. 黑白电视信号

在黑白电视机中,电子束通过每次沿着一条磷线移动电子束在屏幕上"画"出一幅图像。当电子束每次从左边扫到右边时,电子束的强度是变化的,在屏幕上显示不同的黑、灰、白点。因为这些线排列很密,人的大脑把它们组合成一幅图像。一般一个电视机屏幕从顶部到底部大约有 480 条线。

当用电视机播放电视台传送的信号或录像机中录像带上的电影时,信号要用电路划分成可以控制光束的(像点)信号,则电视机就可以正确地显示电视台或录像机送来的图像,电视台或录像机送给电视机的信号中含有以下三个部分:

- 光束扫描的强度;
- 水平返回信号即控制电视机的电子束扫描到每行的终端并返回的;
- 垂直返回信号——每秒 60 次把电子束从右下端移到左上端。

### 4. 彩色电视

一个彩色电视屏幕与黑白电视屏幕有三点不同:

- 彩色电视有三个电子束同时在屏幕上扫描,分别为红色、绿色、蓝色电子束;
- 屏幕上不是像黑白电视机只镀一层磷,而是镀了排列成点状或条状的红色、绿色和蓝色的磷。如果打开电视机或计算机显示器用放大镜凑得很近去看屏幕,可以看到这些点或条;
- 在阴极射线管的内部,在磷点附近,有一细金属屏,称为荫罩板。荫罩板上有很多细孔与屏幕上的磷光点(或条)同样排列(图 7.2)。

当彩色电视机要产生一个红点时,它射出红色电子束撞击红光磷。产生绿点和蓝点也是同样的原理。要产生一个白点,则红、绿、蓝三个电子束同时射出,三种颜色混合在一起产生白点。要产生一个黑点,所有三色电子束都在扫过这点时关掉,电视机上其他颜色是红、绿、蓝的组合。

初看起来彩色电视信号与黑白电视信号有些相似,但要在标准的黑白电视信号上多叠加一个 3.579 545 MHz 的正弦波传送一个色度信号。色度信号中相位的不同表示出要显示的颜色,色度信号的幅度决定了颜色的饱和度。表 7.1 表示颜色和相位的关系。

表 7.1　部分颜色和相位的关系

| 颜色 | 相位 |
|---|---|
| 白 | 0° |
| 黄 | 15° |
| 红 | 75° |
| 洋红(红紫色) | 135° |
| 蓝 | 195° |
| 青(蓝绿色) | 255° |
| 绿 | 315° |

黑白电视机会滤去这些色度信号。彩色电视机则取出这些信号并解调,配合一般的强度信号,去调制三个彩色电子束(显示彩色图像)。

### 7.1.2　关于冰箱

冰箱的基本原理十分简单:用液体的蒸发来吸收热量。也许你知道当皮肤上有水时会感到凉快,这是因为水蒸发时,会吸收热量,带来凉爽的感觉。如果擦酒精你会感到更凉爽,因为酒精的蒸发温度更低。

冰箱中所用的液体或称制冷剂的蒸发温度特别低,所以可以在冰箱中产生冰冻的温度。如果你把冰箱中的制冷剂放在皮肤上(绝对不是好主意,别这样做),当它蒸发时会使皮肤结冰。

冰箱由五个基本部分组成(图 7.3):
- 压缩机
- 热交换管——箱外的一组蜿蜒盘绕的管子
- 扩散阀
- 热交换管——箱内的一组蜿蜒盘绕的管子
- 制冷剂——在冰箱中蒸发以获得低温的液体,很多工业冰箱用纯氨作为

制冷剂。纯氨的蒸发温度在 $-32\ ℃$。

冰箱的基本工作原理如下:

压缩机压缩制冷剂气体,使制冷剂的压力和温度升高,冰箱外面的热交换管使制冷剂散热。

当制冷剂冷却后,收缩成液态,流过扩散阀。

流过扩散阀时,液态制冷剂从高压管中流入低压管中,制冷剂膨胀蒸发成为(淡蓝色)气体,在蒸发过程中制冷剂要吸收热量,使变成冷的气体。

冰箱内部的管子使制冷剂从冰箱中吸收热量,使冰箱内部变冷。如此反复循环。

纯氨气是有毒的,如果纯氨制冷剂泄漏对人是一种威胁,所以家用冰箱不用纯氨。你可能听说过 Freon(氟利昂),一种氨的无毒替代品,与氨有基本相同的沸点。但氟利昂对人是没有毒的,所以可以安全地在厨房中使用,但许多大的工业冰箱仍用纯氨作制冷剂。

在(20 世纪)70 年代,发现所用的氟利昂破坏臭氧层。因此,到 90 年代,所有的冰箱和空调均采用新制冷剂以减少对臭氧层的破坏作用。

## 7.2 阅读材料

### 7.2.1 数字电视

一个模拟彩电的水平分辨率约 500 点,这个分辨率在 50 年前是很高的,但今天却过时了。现在所用的计算机显示器最低分辨率为 640×480 像素,很多人用的是 800×600 像素或 1024×768 像素的显示器,计算机的显示器正在变得更加清晰和可靠,相比之下,模拟电视机就比较逊色了。

许多新的卫星(电视)系统以及 DVD,是采用可以提供十分清晰图像的数字编码机制。这种系统中,数字信息被转换成模拟格式,在模拟电视机上显示。与 VHS 式图像相比,这种图像很清晰,但如果不把这些图像转换成模拟格式,图像将会更加清晰。

现在,正开始逐渐把所有模拟电视机转换成数字电视机,这样就可以直接输出数字信号。

当提到数字电视时,指的是纯数字电视信号传输以及用数字电视机接收并播放这些数字信号。数字信号可以无线传播,也可以通过有线及卫星传播,在家中通过一个解调器以数字格式接收数字信号并直接在数字电视机上播放。

现在有一种很吸引人的数字电视,称为高清电视(HDTV)。它是高分辨率数字电视与 Dolby 格式环绕数字立体声(AC-3)的结合,这个结合创造了最好的图像和最好的声音。HDTV 要求 HDTV 电视台有新的制作和传输设备,还要求用户有新的接收设备。高分辨率图像是 HDTV 主要卖点,720 线或 1 080 线分辨率的图像与目前美国 525 线分辨率(或欧洲 625 线分辨率)的图像相比,图像绝对要清晰得多。

### 7.2.2 微波炉

微波炉由以下几部分组成(图 7.4):
- 磁电管
- 磁电管的控制电路(一般带微处理器)
- 波导管
- 加热室

微波炉是通过微波(频率一般是 2 450 MHz,波长为 12.24 cm)穿透食品来加热的。食品中的水、脂肪和糖分子吸收微波中的能量,这个过程称为电介质加热。大部分分子是电双极性的,即分子的一端是正电荷,另一端是负电荷。在微波中,分子不断前后摆动,想与微波产生的交变的电场保持一致的方向。这种分子的运动就产生了热。微波加热对液态的水最有效,对脂肪、糖、结冰的水加热效果就差一些。有种不正确的解释说,微波加热是使水分子产生共振,实际上水分子共振所需的频率要高得多,要几十吉赫兹(GHz)(1 GHz=1 000 MHz)。

加热室本身是一个法拉第笼子(即利用法拉第电磁感应屏蔽原理制成),可以防止微波外泄。炉门通常是玻璃面板,但(玻璃中)有导电网格层起屏蔽作用。因为网格的宽度小于微波波长(12 cm),所以微波不能通过炉门(造成泄漏),但可见光(其波长比微波短得多)可以(通过炉门,所以你可以看到微波炉中的东西)。

微波是无线电波,微波炉常用的频率是 2 450 MHz。这个频率的无线电波有一个有趣的性质:这个波可以被水、脂肪和糖吸收。当它们吸收微波后,就把它直接转换成原子的运动——热量。在这个频率范围的微波还有另一个有趣的性质:大部分塑料、玻璃或陶器不能吸收微波,金属会反射微波,所以在微波炉中不能用金属盘。

随着无线计算机网络日益普及,微波干扰已成为无线网络中值得关注的问题。由于微波炉会发射出大约 2 450 MHz 的无线电波,可能会对无线网络的传输造成干扰。

# UNIT 8　EDA 软件

## 8.1　文章

### 8.1.1　Quartus II

Altera Quartus II 设计软件提供完整的多平台设计环境,能够直接满足特定设计需要,为可编程芯片系统(SOPC)提供全面的设计环境。Quartus II 软件含有 FPGA 和 CPLD 设计所有阶段的解决方案。Quartus II 设计流程如图 8.1 所示。

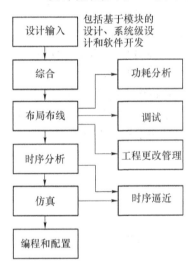

图 8.1　Quartus II 设计流程

此外,Quartus II 软件为设计流程的每个阶段提供 Quartus II 图形用户界面、EDA 工具界面以及命令行界面。可以在整个流程中只使用这些界面中的一个,也可以在设计流程的不同阶段使用不同界面。

**1. 图形用户界面**

你可以使用 Quartus II 软件完成设计流程的所有阶段;它是一个全面易用的独立解决方案。首次启动 Quartus II 软件时出现的 Quartus II 图形用户界面如图 8.2 所示。

## 2. 编译器

Quartus II 软件包括一个模块化编译器。编译器包括以下模块(标有星号的模块表示在完整编译时,可根据设置选择使用):

- 分析和综合
- 分区合并
- 适配器
- 汇编器
- 标准时序分析器和 TimeQuest 时序分析器
- 设计助手
- EDA 网表写入器
- HardCopy 网表写入器

要将所有的编译器模块作为完整编译的一部分来运行,在 Processing 菜单中单击 Start Compilation。也可以单独运行每个模块,从 Processing 菜单的 Start 子菜单中单击你希望启动的命令。你还可以逐步运行一些编译模块。

此外,还可以通过选择 Tasks window 任务窗口(图 8.3)启动编译模块。在 Tasks window 窗口中,可以改变该模块的设置文件或报告文件,还可以打开其他相关窗口。

## 3. 设计输入

Quartus II 工程包括在可编程器件中最终实现设计需要的所有设计文件,软件源文件和其他相关文件。使用 Quartus II 模块编辑器、文本编辑器、MegaWizard 插件管理器和 EDA 设计输入工具可以建立包括 Altera 宏功能模块、参数化模块库(LPM)功能和知识产权(IP)功能在内的设计。设计输入流程如图 8.4 所示。

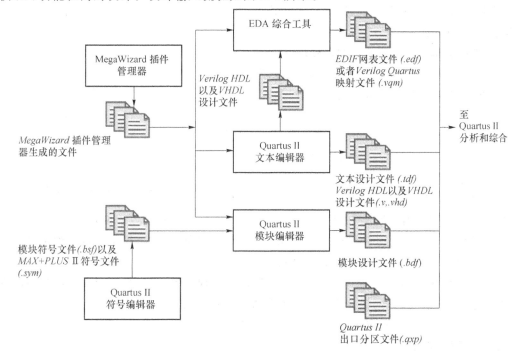

图 8.4　设计输入流程

**4. 菜单(参阅附录3)**

Quartus Ⅱ 常用的菜单命令主要有:文件、编辑、工程、配置、调试。这些菜单命令用于应用程序,是常用的处理命令。相应的菜单如图 8.5～8.9 所示。

## 8.1.2 Protel

Protel 是 Protel 公司在 80 年代末推出的 EDA 软件,在电子行业的 CAD 软件中,它当之无愧地排在众多 EDA 软件的前面,是电子设计者的首选软件。它较早在国内使用,在国内的普及率也最高,有些高校的电子专业还专门开设了课程来学习它,几乎所有的电子公司都要用到它,许多大公司在招聘电子设计人才时在其条件栏上常会写着要求会使用 Protel。

**1. Protel 的组成**

包括原理图设计系统、印刷电路板设计系统、信号模拟仿真系统、可编程逻辑设计系统、Protel 99 内置编辑器。

原理图设计系统是用于原理图设计的 Advanced Schematic 系统。这部分包括用于设计原理图的原理图编辑器 Sch 以及用于修改、生成零件的零件库编辑器 SchLib。

印刷电路板设计系统是用于电路板设计的 Advanced PCB。这部分包括用于设计电路板的电路板编辑器 PCB 以及用于修改、生成零件封装的零件封装编辑器 PCBLib。

信号模拟仿真系统是用于原理图上进行信号模拟仿真的 SPICE 3f5 系统。

可编程逻辑设计系统是集成于原理图设计系统的 PLD 设计系统。

Protel 99 内置编辑器包括用于显示、编辑文本的文本编辑器 Text 和用于显示、编辑电子表格的电子表格编辑器 Spread。

**2. 电路原理图的设计过程(图 8.10)**

(1) 设计图纸大小:首先要构思好零件图,设计好图纸大小。图纸大小是根据电路图的规模和复杂程度而定的。

(2) 设置 Protel 99/Schematic 设计环境:包括设置格点大小和类型、光标类型等,大多数参数也可以使用系统默认值。

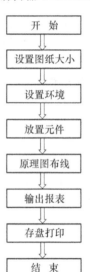

图 8.10 电路原理图的设计过程

(3) 放置零件:用户根据电路图的需要,将零件从零件库里取出放置到图纸上,并对放置零件的序号、零件封装进行定义和设定等工作。

(4) 原理图布线:利用 Protel 99/Schematic 提供的各种工具,将图纸上的元件用具有电气意义的导线、符号连接起来,构成一个完整的原理图。

(5) 报表输出:通过 Protel 99/Schematic 提供的各种报表工具生成各种报表,其中最重要的报表是网络表,通过网络表为后续的电路板设计作准备。

(6) 文件保存及打印:输出最后的步骤是文件保存及打印输出。

**3. 菜单(见附录4)**

Protel 主界面如图 8.11 所示。

在 Protel 主界面的上方有一个主菜单。Protel 常用的处理菜单命令主要有：文件、编辑、视图、放置、设计、仿真。相应的菜单如图 8.12～8.18 所示。

## 8.2 阅读材料

**MATLAB 语言**

MATLAB 是一种数字化计算环境和可编程的语言。是由数学工作室(MathWorks)开发的。MATLAB 集成计算，可视化和编程在一个极易使用的环境中，问题和解答都以人们熟悉的数学符号表示。

MATLAB 是一个交互系统，其基本数据元素是阵列，用它可以很方便地计算很多问题，尤其是含矩阵和矢量公式的问题。另外它还有一个附加 Simulink 软件包，为动态系统和嵌入式系统提供了多领域的图形仿真和基于模型的设计(方法)。

MATLAB 用起来很方便，这里举两个例子。

**1. 启动和退出**

当启动 MATLAB 时，桌面上显示一个含有管理文件、变量以及和 MATLAB 相关应用程序的工具窗口(图形化用户界面)。

图 8.19 给出常用的窗口，你可以根据你的需要调整工具和文档等窗口。

要退出 MATLAB，在菜单中选择文件→退出 MATLAB，或在命令窗口中直接输入：quit。

**2. 画图**

MATLAB 提供了很多方法显示数据图像，还有交互工具可以用来处理图像，使图像可以反映出数据的最多信息。

例如，下面的语句建立了一个变量 $x$(阵列)，它的值从 $-1$ 到 $1$，间隔为 $0.1$；第二句语句求出 $x$(阵列)的每一个值的三次方，并储存为 $y$ 阵列：

```
x = -1:.1:1;        % 定义 x 阵列
y = x.^3;           % 求出 x(阵列)的每一个值的三次方，并储存为 y 阵列
plot (x,y);         % 画 y-x 图像
```

一个简单的曲线(图)适当地显示了 $x$ 作为自变量，$y$ 作为函数的关系(图 8.20)。

你还可以在此图上加注释和打印此图，或输出图片的标准格式用以在网页浏览器或其他媒体上显示此图。

# UNIT 9　3G

## 9.1 文章

**3G 移动通信系统**

**1. IMT-2000 的移动通信网**

在世界各地第一代模拟移动通信已经有多种不同的系统被开发和使用，第二代数字通

信有3种系统共存——日本的PDC、欧洲的GSM和在美国的TIA标准。全球标准的第三代无线通信已被国际电信联盟(ITU)命名为IMT-2000。

IMT-2000实现了相当于全球标准无线电接口下的固定网络质量的移动通信系统,还可以提供广泛的服务。此外,也使在全球范围内的任何人,在任何地方和任何时候进行沟通成为可能,它也允许进行超高速、大容量数据通信和图像传输。

NTT DoCoMo公司一直在积极研究和开发有关IMT-2000的项目,而且NTT DoCoMo公司推出的W-CDMA(宽带码分多址)无线电接口也纳入到了IMT-2000内。

在2001年,NTT DoCoMo公司推出了基于IMT-2000的世界上第一个业务FOMA。FOMA实现了具有比以前更清晰和更舒适的通信环境,它提供了一种新的移动环境。在这种环境下,通过引进新技术,使得语音、静态图像与视频可以自由处理。这些措施包括使用宽频带进行大容量通信,以及使用可以根据传输信息的种类和容量来选择最优通信速率和路径的智能网络。

在21世纪,移动通信将进入一个移动多媒体服务和具有全球移动性的时代。为实现这一目标,各种技术正在不断地发展中,包括先进智能网络的发展,它将不同的通信系统融于一体,从而可建立一个完善的移动通信网络,来实现这些多媒体的服务。作为努力的一部分,NTT DoCoMo公司正在努力扩大其新的"IMN"智能移动通信网。

此外,我们的目标是在全球标准下构建我国的第三代移动通信系统(IMT-2000),使它能够处理从低速(例如,电子邮件)到高速(例如,视频点播)通信的需求。实现这个目标的技术包括用于无线电传输的W-CDMA系统,和用于有线传输的ATM系统。因为ATM模式在通信上是以固定长度的信元为单位进行数据传输,因此这种简单的传输方式可以将多种通信速度实现同步。

### 2. W-CDMA技术

W-CDMA技术支持第三代移动通信系统。CDMA能有效地利用有限的频率资源来容纳尽可能多的用户。这是通过在分配给每个用户随机码的基础上进行频率共享,而不是通过划分宽带频道的频率或时间。

在各系统中,DoCoMo公司促进了W-CDMA产品的开发,使它不但可以传输语音和传真,还可以传输高质量的活动图像,并且也允许连接到互联网上。由于它有许多优势,例如可进行高质量、低能耗的传输,所以W-CDMA是满足第三代移动通信目标的最合适技术。第三代移动通信的目标即多媒体、个人及智能系统。

### 3. TD-SCDMA技术

时分-同步码分多址,即TD-SCDMA,是由中国电信科学技术研究所(CATT)、大唐电信集团和西门子股份公司一起提出的中国3G移动通信标准。TD-SCDMA是基于扩频技术的。

TD-SCDMA系统设备有3部分:无线网络控制器(RNC)、3G系统的基站(Node B)和用户设备(UE)。在第三代合作伙伴计划(3GPP)的第五版协议(Release 5)中包含了关于基站在下行链路中将波束转换为上行链路的波束方向(DoA)的算法。基站计算专用物理控制信道(DPCCH)接收到来自所有小区的每个用户的平均上行链路信噪比值。4个最高的信噪比值和相关的小区信号发送到无线网络控制器。这种测量方法用来完成在下行链路中固定波束形成时波束转换的功能。基于指定小区的信噪比测量值,无线网络控制器会根据测量到的最高的上行链路信噪声比值专门通知基站将数据传输至相应的波束(小区)用户侧,并通过无线资源控制(RRC)信息通知用户侧使用哪个辅助公共寻呼指示信道作为相位基准。注意,波束转换只用于来自 3G 系统的基站的测量,没有来自用户侧的触发波束转换的测量方法。

## 9.2 阅读材料

### 9.2.1 手机(蜂窝)技术

(关于手机最有意思的一件事是)手机实质上是一个无线接收机。蜂窝系统是把一个城市划分成小的区域(蜂窝通常是正六边形构成的)。在美国一个典型的模拟手机蜂窝系统中,手机在穿过城市过程中可接收约 800 个频率。这些载波频率把城市分成很多区域,每个区域面积大约为 10 平方英里($26~km^2$)。这样很多频率在同一城市中(的不同区域)可以重复使用,所以数百万人可以同时打手机。

每个小区域中由一个发射塔和一幢含有无线电设备的建筑物(后来的基站有多幢建筑物),组成一个基站。

手机中有低功率的发射器,许多手机有两个信号(发射)强度:0.6 W 和 3 W,(手机)基站也是低功率发射。低功率发射(信号)有两个优点。

1) 在区域中的基站和手机的(信号)发射使信号不会超出区域范围很远,所以不相邻的区域可以重复使用同样的频率。一个城市中同样的频率可以多次复用。

2) 手机的功耗比较小,手机由电池供电,低功耗则电池也小一些,所以手机可做得比较小。

手机蜂窝技术需要在大小城市中建有大量基站,一个大城市有几百个发射塔,但因为有那么多的人用手机,所以对每个人来说使用手机的费用不高。

### 9.2.2 手机的内部结构

按"每立方英寸复杂度"准则,手机是人们日常使用的最复杂的设备。为了压缩和解压声音流,现在数字手机每秒可以进行数百万次计算处理。

如果把手机拆开,可看到其中有这样一些部件:
- 含有手机的微处理器的电路主板
- 天线
- 液晶显示器(LCD)
- 键盘(与电视遥控器有点相似)
- 话筒
- 扬声器
- 电池

在图 9.1 的图片中,可看到一些(计算机)芯片,让我们看一下其中一些芯片。模-数和数-模转换芯片把外来的声音信号从模拟转换成数字并把接收到的信号从数字转换成模拟。数字信号处理器(DSP)是专门定制的,用来高速处理信号的计算。

微处理器处理键盘输入、显示器显示,处理来自基站的命令和控制信号以及与主板上其他功能相配合等所有管理任务。

ROM和闪存芯片储存手机的操作系统和习惯设置,如电话目录。无线电频率(RF)和功率芯片处理功率管理和充电,并处理成百个调频频道,最后RF放大器芯片则处理天线接收和发送信号。

有些手机把一些信息存储在内部的闪存芯片中,而另外一些手机则用外部的类似SM卡的卡片储存信息。

手机中的扬声器和话筒非常小,很难想象它们怎么能产生这么好的声音(效果)。扬声器只有(美元)一角硬币那么大,话筒则并不比它旁边的手表电池大。说到手表电池,它是用于手机内部的时钟电路的。

所有这些功能,30年前(所有的设备)可能要占有一座办公楼的整整一层楼,现在都塞入一部手机,放在手掌中还足足有余,这是多么惊人啊。

# UNIT 10 微机

## 10.1 文章

### 10.1.1 基本型计算机

一提到计算机人们首先想到的是个人计算机,简称PC。组成一个计算机系统的基本部分是:中央处理器CPU、存储器、输入/输出端口和把它们连接在一起的总线。虽然你在编写软件程序时可以不考虑这些概念,但编写高性能的软件却需要对这些部件有一个完整的了解。

对一个计算机系统的基本设计被称为计算机的结构模型。冯·诺依曼是计算机设计的先驱,提出了今天所用的大部分计算机的结构模型。一个典型的冯·诺依曼系统有三个主要的部件:中央处理器(即CPU)、存储器及输入/输出口。一个系统中,设计这些部件的方法影响了系统的性能。在冯·诺依曼结构中,如80x86系列计算机,所有的操作都在中央处理器中执行。所有的计算都在中央处理器内部进行,数据和指令储存在存储器中,由中央处理器调用。对CPU而言,大量的输入/输出口就像存储器一样,因为CPU可以把数据存储在输出设备中,也可从输入设备中读入数据。存储器和输入/输出口主要的区别是输入/输出口通常是与(外部世界的)外部器件相连接的。

### 10.1.2 主板

主板是计算机内部的主电路板,上面有中央处理器(CPU)、存储器和扩展槽,并与计算机的各个部分直接或非直接地相连(图10.1)。

主板由芯片组(称为glue logic)、一些ROM中的代码和各种接口或总线组成。现在计算机中用各种不同的总线连接各种各样的部件。高带宽的、高速总线生产麻烦且成本高,(因)其信号的传输速度非常快,信号线只要有几厘米的传输距离就可能引起时间(延迟)问题;而电路板上的金属导线像微型无线电天线,会发射电磁噪声,从而对系统中的信号产生干扰。所以,计算机(主板)设计者要把最高速的总线限制在主板的(某块)最小的面积中,而把较慢的、较粗的总线放在其他地方。

## 10.1.3 系统总线

系统总线连接冯·诺依曼结构中的各个部件,80x86 系列计算机有三种主要的总线:地址线、数据线和控制线。总线是指一组在系统各个部件之间传递各种电信号的导线。各种处理器所需要的总线不同。但是,对所有的处理器而言,每种总线都携带相应的信息,如 80386 和 8086 有不同的数据总线(数目),但都是在处理器、输入/输出口及存储器之间传递数据信息。

**1. 数据总线**

80x86 系列处理器用数据总线在一个计算机系统的各种部分之间传递数据。在 80x86 系列中这组总线的数目是不同的,实际上,它决定了处理器的"大小"(即多少位数据的处理器)。

**2. 地址总线**

80x86 系列处理器中数据总线在中央处理器和一个特定的存储器位置或输入/输出口之间传递信息,但一个问题是,如何确定存储器或输入/输出口的位置?地址总线回答了这个问题。

对于不同的存储位置和输入/输出设备,系统的设计者指定一个唯一的存储地址。当软件想要访问一些指定的存储位置或输入/输出设备时,它把相应的地址值放在地址总线上,与存储器或输入/输出设备相连接的电路识别出这个地址,命令存储器或输入/输出设备从数据总线上读取数据或输出数据到数据总线上。

**3. 控制总线**

控制总线是一组控制处理器如何与系统的其他部分通信的信号线的集合。再来看数据总线,CPU 是通过数据总线把数据送到存储器中和从存储器中接收数据的,这就提出了一个问题,"是送数据还是接收数据?"控制总线中有两根线,读和写,就是用来指定数据流动的方向的。其他的控制线包括系统时钟线、中断线、状态线等。在 80x86 系列处理器中控制总线的数目是各不相同的,然而,有些控制线是所有的处理器都有的,值得作简短介绍。

读和写控制线:控制数据总线上数据流的方向,当这两根线都为逻辑 1 时,CPU 和存储器、输入/输出口互相之间是不通信的,如果读控制线是低电平(逻辑 0),则 CPU 从存储器中读取数据(即系统是把数据从存储器中传送到 CPU 中的)。如果写控制线是低电平,系统把数据从 CPU 传送到存储器中。

## 10.1.4 主存(内存)

主存是一个计算机系统中的中心存储单元。它是一个相当大且存取速度很快的存储器,用来储存 CPU 操作时的程序和数据。主存主要采用半导体集成电路技术。有两种可用的集成 RAM 芯片,静态 RAM 和动态 RAM。静态 RAM 本质上是用内部的触发器组成,用来储存二进制信息。只要芯片与电源相连,静态 RAM 储存的信息始终有效。动态的 RAM 以电容两极(充电)电荷的形式储存信息,芯片内的电容是由 MOS 管构成的。电容两端储存的电荷会随时间的延长而放电,要保持动态存储信息必须周期性地对电容再充电(刷新)。动态 RAM 功耗小,单一芯片的储存量大。静态 RAM 用起来方便且有较短的读和写周期(即读写速度快)。

### 10.1.5 BIOS(基本输入/输出系统)

**1. BIOS 简介**

闪存最主要的用途之一是储存计算机的基本输入/输出系统(通常称作 BIOS)(图 10.2)。BIOS 使得所有其他芯片、硬件、端口和 CPU 一起工作。

BIOS 是一种特殊的软件,是主要硬件与操作系统的接口软件,通常存储在主板的闪存芯片中,但有时也可能是存储 ROM 芯片中。

**2. BIOS 的作用是什么**

BIOS 软件有很多不同的作用,但它最重要的作用是载入操作系统。当你开机时,微处理器开始执行第一条指令,它必须从某个地方得到这条指令(就是储存在闪存中的 BIOS)。微处理器不能执行操作系统,因为操作系统存储在硬盘上,没有指令 CPU 不能从硬盘上载入操作系统,BIOS 提供了这些指令。BIOS 还提供了一些其他指令(程序),如,

电源自检(POST)用来检查系统中各个硬件是否工作正常。

激活(调用)计算机中其他不同卡上 BIOS 芯片中的程序,如 SCSI(接口卡)和图像处理卡本身自带 BIOS 芯片。

操作系统与不同硬件接口的低级处理程序,就是这些低级程序调用各种设备。尤其是计算机启动时这些程序管理键盘、显示屏、串行和并行接口等设备。

BIOS 所做的第一件事是检查储存在一微小(64 字节)RAM(一个 CMOS 芯片)中的信息,CMOS 给出了你系统的设置信息,当你系统改变时可以改变 CMOS 设置,BIOS 要根据这些信息调整或补充它的默认程序。

中断处理是一小段软件程序,就像是硬件与操作系统之间的翻译。例如,当你在键盘上按下一个键,信号就调用了键盘的中断处理程序,告诉 CPU 是什么键并送给操作系统。设备驱动是另外的软件程序,它识别基本的硬件,如键盘、鼠标、硬盘和软盘驱动器。

因为 BIOS 是不断地从硬件接收信号和输出信号给硬件的,所以为了运行更快,(计算机启动后)一般把 BIOS 复制到 RAM 中。

## 10.2 阅读材料

### 单片机(微控制器)

AT89C51 是美国 ATMEL 公司生产的低电压、高性能 CMOS 8 位单片机,片内含 4k 字节的可反复擦写的只读程序存储器(PEROM)和 128 字节的随机存取数据存储器(RAM)。器件采用 ATMEL 公司的高密度非易失性存储技术生产,兼容标准 MCS-51 指令系统。器件内置通用 8 位中央处理器(CPU)和存储单元,功能强大的 AT89C51 单片机可为你提供许多高性能的应用场合,可灵活应用于各种控制领域。

主要性能参数

- 与 MCS-51 产品指令系统完全兼容
- 4k 字节可重擦写 Flash 闪速存储器
- 1000 次控写周期
- 全静态操作:0 Hz~24 MHz

- 三级加密程序存储器
- 128×8 字节内部 RAM
- 32 个可编程 I/O 口线
- 2 个 16 位定时/计数器
- 6 个中断源
- 可编程串行 UART 通道
- 低功耗空闲和掉电模式

AT89C51 提供以下标准功能:4k 字节 Flash 闪速存储器,128 字节内部 RAM,32 个 I/O 口线,2 个 16 位定时/计数器,1 个 5 向量两级中断结构,1 个全双工串行通信口,片内振荡器及时钟电路。同时,AT89C51 可降至 0 Hz 的静态逻辑操作,并支持两种软件可选的节电工作模式。空闲方式停止 CPU 的工作,但允许 RAM,定时/计数器,串行通信口及中断系统继续工作。掉电方式保存 RAM 中的内容,但振荡器停止工作并禁止其他所有部件工作直到下一个硬件复位。

引脚功能说明

$V_{CC}$:供电电压。

GND:接地。

P0 口:P0 口为一个 8 位漏级开路双向 I/O 口,每位能以吸收电流的方式驱动 8 个 TTL 逻辑门电路。对端口写"1"时,或作为高阻抗输入端用。在访问外部数据存储器或程序存储器时,这组口线分时转换地址(低 8 位)和数据总线复用,在访问期间激活内部上拉电阻。在 FLASH 编程时,P0 接收指令字节;而在程序校验时,输出指令字节。校验时,要求外接上拉电阻。

P1 口:P1 口是一个带内部上拉电阻的 8 位双向 I/O 口,其输出缓冲器可驱动(吸收或输出电流)4 个 TTL 逻辑门电路。对 P1 口写"1",通过内部的上拉电阻把端口拉到高电平。也作为输入口,作输入口使用时,因为内部存在上拉电阻,某个引脚被外部信号拉低时会输出电流($I_{IL}$)。在 Flash 编程和程序校验期间,P1 口接收低 8 位地址。

P2 口:P2 口是一个带有内部上拉电阻的 8 位双向 I/O 口,P2 口的输出缓冲器可驱动(吸收或输出电流)4 个 TTL 逻辑门电路。对端口写"1"时,通过内部的上拉电阻把端口拉到高电平。且可作为输入口,作为输入使用时,因为内部存在上拉电阻,某个引脚被外部信号拉低时会输出一个电流($I_{IL}$)。在访问外部程序存储器或 16 位地址的外部数据存储器(例如执行 MOVX @DPTR 指令)时,P2 口送出高 8 位地址数据。在访问 8 位地址的外部数据存储器(如执行 MOVX @RI 指令)时,P2 口线上的内容(也即特殊功能寄存器(SFR)区中 P2 寄存器的内容)在整个访问期间不改变。在 Flash 编程和校验时,P2 口接收高 8 位地址信号和其他控制信号。

P3 口:P3 口是一组带内部上拉电阻的 8 位双向 I/O 口。P3 口的输出缓冲器可驱动(吸收或输出电流)4 个 TTL 逻辑门电路。对 P3 口写"1"时,通过内部的上拉电阻把端口拉到高电平。并可作为输入口,作输入使用时,被外部拉低的 P3 将用上拉电阻输出电流($I_{IL}$)。P3 口除了作为一般的 I/O 口线外,更重要的用途是它的第二功能,如表 10.1 所示。

P3 口还接收一些用于 Flash 闪速存储器编程和程序校验的控制信号。

表 10.1　AT89C51 单片机 P3 口第二功能表

| 端口引脚 | 第二功能 |
| --- | --- |
| P3.0 | RXD(串行输入口) |
| P3.1 | TXD(串行输出口) |
| P3.2 | $\overline{INT0}$(外中断 0) |
| P3.3 | $\overline{INT1}$(外中断 1) |
| P3.4 | T0(定时/计数器 0) |
| P3.5 | T1(定时/计数器 1) |
| P3.6 | $\overline{WR}$(外部数据存储器写选通) |
| P3.7 | $\overline{RD}$(外部数据存储器读选通) |

RST:复位输入。当振荡器工作时,RST 上脚出现两个机器周期以上高电平时将使单片机复位。

ALE/PROG:当访问外部程序存储器或数据存储器时,ALE 输出脉冲用于锁存地址的低 8 位字节。即使不访问外部存储器,ALE 仍以时钟振荡器频率的 1/6 输出固定的正脉冲信号,因此它可对外输出时钟或用于定时目的。需要注意的是,每当访问外部数据存储器时将跳过一个 ALE 脉冲。如有必要,可通过对特殊功能寄存器(SFR)区中的 8EH 单元的 D0 位置位,可禁止 ALE 操作。该位置位后,只有一条 MOVX 和 MOVC 指令 ALE 才会被激活。此外,该引脚会被微弱拉高,单片机执行外部程序时,设置 ALE 无效。

PSEN:外部程序存储器的选通信号。在由外部程序存储器取指令期间,每个机器周期 PSEN 两次有效,即输出两个脉冲。在此期间,当访问外部数据存储器时,这两次有效的 PSEN 信号将不出现。

EA/$V_{PP}$:外部访问允许。欲使 CPU 仅访问外部程序存储器(地址为 0000H-FFFFH),EA 端必须保持低电平(接地)。需要注意的是,如果加密位 L1 被编程,复位时内部会锁存 EA 端状态。当 EA 为高电平时,CPU 则执行内部程序存储器中的指令。Flash 编程时,该引脚加上+12 V 的编程允许电源 $V_{PP}$,当然这必须是该器件是使用 12 V 编程电压 $V_{PP}$。

XTAL1:振荡器反相放大器的输入及内部时钟发生器的输入端。

XTAL2:振荡器反相放大器的输出端。

# Appendix 2　电子类专业英语词汇

## A

| | |
|---|---|
| AC bridge | 交流电桥 |
| AC current distortion | 交流电流失真 |
| AC standard resistor | 交流标准电阻器 |
| absolute error | 绝对误差 |
| (absolute) error of measurement | 测量的(绝对)误差 |
| absolute resolution | 绝对分辨率 |
| absolute stability of a linear system | 线性系统的绝对稳定性 |
| acceleration | 加速度 |
| acceleration transducer [sensor] | 加速度传感器 |
| accelerometer | 加速度计 |
| access | 存取 |
| access time | 存取时间 |
| actual value | 实际值 |
| actual voltage ratio | 实际电压比 |
| adder | 加法器 |
| allowable load impedance | 允许的负载阻抗 |
| allowable pressure differential | 允许压差 |
| ammeter | 电流表 |
| amplitude | 幅值 |
| amplitude detector module | 振幅检测组件 |
| amplitude error | 振幅误差 |
| amplitude modulation (AM) | 幅度调制;调幅 |
| amplitude response | 幅值响应 |
| analog computer | 模拟计算机 |
| analog control | 模拟控制 |
| analog data | 模拟数据 |
| analog input | 模拟输入 |
| analog output | 模拟输出 |
| analog simulation | 模拟仿真 |
| analog system | 模拟系统 |
| analog-to-digital conversion accuracy | 模-数转换精确度 |
| analog-to-digital conversion rate | 模-数转换速度 |

| | |
|---|---|
| analog transducer [sensor] | 模拟传感器 |
| analog-to-digital converter; A/D converter | 模-数转换器; A/D 转换器 |
| analog-to-digital conversion | 模-数转[变]换 |
| analysis of simulation experiment | 仿真实验分析 |
| angle | 角度 |
| anode | 阳极 |
| artificial intelligence | 人工智能 |
| asynchronous communication interface adapter | 异步通信接口适配器 |
| asynchronous input | 异步输入 |
| asynchronous transmission | 异步传输 |
| audio monitor | 监听器 |
| automatic control | 自动控制 |
| automation | 自动化 |
| auxiliary controller bus (ACB) | 辅助控制器总线 |

# B

| | |
|---|---|
| background noise | 背景噪声 |
| background processing | 后台处理 |
| balance output | 对称输出 |
| band | 频带 |
| bandwidth | 带宽 |
| band width of video amplifier | 视频放大器频宽 |
| beat method (of measurement) | 差拍(测量)法 |
| binary coded decimal (BCD) | 二-十进制编码 |
| binary control | 二进制控制 |
| binary digital | 二进制数字 |
| binary element | 二进制元 |
| binary signal | 二进制信号 |
| bit | 比特;位 |
| bit error rate | 误码率 |
| buffer | 缓冲器 |
| bus | 总线 |
| bus line | 总线 |
| bus master | 总线主设备 |
| bus mother board | 总线母板 |
| bus network | 总线网 |
| bus slave | 总线从设备 |
| bus topology | 总线拓扑 |

| | |
|---|---|
| byte | 字节 |
| byte frame | 字节帧 |

# C

| | |
|---|---|
| cable noise | 电缆噪声 |
| cable-tension transducer | 电缆张力传感器 |
| CAMAC highway | CAMAC 信息公路 |
| CAMAC module | CAMAC 模块 |
| carrier | 载波 |
| carrier sync | 载波同步 |
| cathode | 阴极 |
| cathode of electron gun | 电子枪阴极 |
| central processing unit (CPU) | 中央处理单元 |
| central processor | 中央处理器 |
| channel | 信道;通道 |
| character | 字符 |
| character code | 字符码 |
| character recognition | 字符识别 |
| characteristic curve | 特性曲线 |
| characteristic "impulse" | "脉冲"响应特性 |
| closed loop transfer function | 闭环传递函数 |
| coefficient of chromatic aberration | 色差系数 |
| coefficient of interference | 干扰系数 |
| common mode rejection ratio (CMRR) | 共模抑制比 |
| common mode signal | 共模信号 |
| common mode voltage | 共模电压 |
| communication subnet | 通信子网 |
| communication system | 通信系统 |
| communications terminal | 通信终端 |
| comparator | 比较器 |
| compatibility | 兼容性;相容性 |
| compensation | 补偿 |
| computer aided debugging | 计算机辅助故障诊断 |
| computer aided design | 计算机辅助设计 |
| computer aided design of control system | 控制系统计算机辅助设计 |
| computer aided engineering | 计算机辅助工程 |
| computer aided manufacturing | 计算机辅助制造 |
| computer automated measurement | |

| | |
|---|---|
| and control(CAMAC) | 计算机自动测量和控制 |
| computer control | 计算机控制 |
| computer control system | 计算机控制系统 |
| computer network | 计算机网络 |
| computer simulation | 计算机仿真 |
| computer system | 计算机系统 |
| condenser microphone | 电容传声器 |
| conditional instability | 条件不稳定性 |
| conditional stability of a linear system | 线性系统的条件稳定性 |
| conductance | 电导 |
| conductivity | 传导性 |
| constant bandwidth filter | 恒定带宽滤波器 |
| constant current power supply | 恒流电源 |
| constant voltage power supply | 恒压电源 |
| contact resistance | 接触电阻 |
| contact scanning method | 接触法 |
| correlation coefficient | 相关系数 |
| coupled system | 耦合系统 |
| crest factor | 峰值因数 |
| critical damping | 临界阻尼 |
| critical stability | 临界稳定性 |
| crosstalk | 串扰 |
| CRT display device | CRT 显示器 |
| CRT display terminal | CRT 显示终端 |
| crystal | 振子;晶片;晶体 |
| current sensitivity | 电流灵敏度 |
| current stability | 电流稳定度 |
| current transformer | 电流互感器 |
| cursor | 光标 |
| cut-off frequency | 截止频率 |

# D

| | |
|---|---|
| DC bridge for measuring resistance | 测量电阻用的直流电桥 |
| damped natural frequency | 阻尼固有频率 |
| damped oscillation | 阻尼振荡 |
| damping | 阻尼 |
| damping action | 阻尼作用 |
| damping characteristic | 阻尼特性 |

| | |
|---|---|
| damping constant | 阻尼常数 |
| data acquisition | 数据采集 |
| data acquisition equipment | 数据采集设备 |
| data base | 数据库 |
| data base management system | 数据库管理系统 |
| data communication | 数据通信 |
| data processing | 数据处理 |
| data signaling rate | 数据传信率 |
| data terminal equipment (DTE) | 数据终端设备 |
| data transfer | 数据传递 |
| data transfer rate | 数据传送率;数据传输速率 |
| data transmission | 数据传输 |
| data transmission interface | 数据传输接口 |
| dead zone error | 死区误差 |
| debugging | 调试 |
| delay time | 滞后时间 |
| demodulation | 解调 |
| demodulator | 解调器 |
| diagnostic program | 诊断程序 |
| difference input | 差分输入 |
| differential amplifier | 差动放大器 |
| differential preamplifier | 差动前置放大器 |
| digital ammeter | 数字电流表 |
| digital communication | 数字通信 |
| digital compensation | 数字补偿 |
| digital computer | 数字计算机 |
| digital control | 数字控制 |
| digital control system | 数字控制系统 |
| digital controller | 数字控制器 |
| digital filter | 数字滤波器 |
| digital multimeter | 数字万用表;数字复用表 |
| digital signal | 数字信号 |
| digital signal analyzer | 数字信号分析仪 |
| digital signal processing | 数字信号处理 |
| digital simulation | 数字仿真 |
| digital voltmeter | 数字电压表 |
| digital-analog conversion | 数-模转换 |
| digital-analog converter;D/A converter | 数-模转换器;D/A 转换器 |
| discrete control system | 离散控制系统 |

| | |
|---|---|
| discrete signal | 离散信号 |
| discrete system model | 离散系统模型 |
| discrete system simulation | 离散系统仿真 |
| display device | 显示器；显示设备 |
| dynamic characteristics | 动态特性 |
| dynamic deviation | 动态偏差 |
| dynamic display image | 动态显示图像 |
| dynamic error | 动态误差 |
| dynamic error coefficient | 动态误差系数 |
| dynamic measurement | 动态测量 |
| dynamic range | 动态范围 |

## E

| | |
|---|---|
| effective emissivity | 有效发射率 |
| electromagnetic element | 电磁元件 |
| electromagnetic induction | 电磁感应 |
| electromagnetic interference | 电磁干扰 |
| electron gun | 电子枪 |
| electron microscope | 电子显微镜 |
| electron noise | 电子噪声 |
| electrostatic screen | 静电屏蔽 |
| environmental error | 环境误差 |
| equal precision measurement | 等精密度测量 |

## F

| | |
|---|---|
| fall time | 下降时间 |
| fault | 故障 |
| feasibility | 可行性 |
| feedback | 反馈 |
| feedback compensation | 反馈补偿 |
| feedback control | 反馈控制 |
| feedback controller | 反馈控制器 |
| feedback element | 反馈元件 |
| feedback gain | 反馈增益 |
| feedback loop | 反馈回路 |
| feedback path | 反馈通路 |
| feedback signal | 反馈信号 |

| | |
|---|---|
| fiber communication | 光纤通信 |
| field sweeping | 场扫描 |
| field bus | 现场总线 |
| field bus control system (FCS) | 现场总线控制系统 |
| Fourier transform | 傅里叶变换 |
| frequency | 频率 |
| frequency-amplitude characteristic | 幅频特性 |
| frequency analysis | 频率分析 |
| frequency analyzer | 频率分析仪 |
| frequency band | 频带 |
| frequency domain | 频域 |
| frequency domain analysis | 频域分析 |
| frequency domain method | 频域法 |
| frequency modulation (FM) | 频率周制,调频 |
| frequency output | 频率输出 |
| frequency-phase characteristic | 相频特性 |
| frequency response | 频率响应 |
| frequency response characteristics | 频率响应特性(图) |
| function | 功能 |
| function analysis | 功能分析 |
| function block | 功能块 |
| function key | 功能键 |
| function module | 功能模块 |
| functional simulation | 功能仿真 |
| fundamental frequency | 基本频率 |

## G

| | |
|---|---|
| gain | 增益 |
| grounded junction | 接地端 |
| grounded noise | 接地噪声 |

## H

| | |
|---|---|
| half duplex transmission | 半双工传输 |
| hardware | 硬件 |
| harmonic | 谐波 |
| harmonic analysis | 谐波分析 |
| harmonic content | 谐波含量 |

| | |
|---|---|
| harmonic content of an AC power supply | 交流电源的谐波含量 |
| harmonic wave | 谐波 |
| high value standard resistor | 高阻标准电阻器 |
| high voltage bridge | 高压电桥 |
| high-voltage cable | 高压电缆 |
| higher harmonic resonance | 高次谐波共振 |
| horizontal scanning | 行扫描 |
| hysteresis | 回差 |

# I

| | |
|---|---|
| I/O channel | 输入/输出通道;I/O 通道 |
| impulse function | 冲激函数;脉冲函数 |
| impulse response | 冲激响应;脉冲响应 |
| incremental control | 增量控制 |
| index | 指示器;指数;索引 |
| index register | 变址寄存器 |
| industrial automation | 工业自动化 |
| industrial control | 工业控制 |
| industrial control system | 工业控制系统 |
| industrial data processing | 工业数据处理 |
| industrial process | 工业过程 |
| industrial robot | 工业机器人 |
| information system for process control | 过程控制信息系统 |
| infrared radiation | 红外辐射;红外线;热辐射 |
| initialization | 初始化 |
| input device | 输入设备 |
| input impedance | 输入阻抗 |
| input matrix | 输入矩阵 |
| input/output operation | 输入/输出操作 |
| input/output port | 输入/输出端口 |
| input-output channel | 输入-输出通道 |
| input-output device | 输入-输出设备 |
| input signal | 输入信号 |
| input terminal | 输入端 |
| input unit | 输入设备 |
| input variable | 输入变量 |
| input vector | 输入向量;输入矢量 |
| instrumental error | 仪器误差 |

| | |
|---|---|
| insulating strength | 绝缘强度 |
| insulation material | 绝缘物;绝缘材料 |
| insulation resistance | 绝缘电阻 |
| intellectualized simulation software | 智能化仿真软件 |
| intelligent computer | 智能计算机 |
| intelligent control | 智能控制 |
| intelligent control system | 智能控制系统 |
| intelligent instrument | 智能仪表 |
| intelligent keyboard system | 智能键盘系统 |
| intelligent machine | 智能机器 |
| intelligent management | 智能管理 |
| intelligent management system | 智能管理系统 |
| intelligent robot | 智能机器人 |
| interface | 接口;界面 |
| international standard | 国际标准 |

## K

| | |
|---|---|
| keyboard | 键盘 |
| keyboard processor | 键盘处理器 |

## L

| | |
|---|---|
| lead capacitance | 接线电容 |
| lead compensation | 超前补偿 |
| lead inductance | 接线电感 |
| library | 程序库 |
| linear control system | 线性控制系统 |
| load | 负荷 |
| load amplitude | 负荷幅 |
| local area network (LAN) | 局域网 |
| logic control | 逻辑控制 |
| longitudinal wave | 纵波 |

## M

| | |
|---|---|
| machine code | 机器代码 |
| machine intelligence | 机器智能 |
| machine language | 机器语言 |

| | |
|---|---|
| magnification | 放大倍率 |
| magnitude-frequency characteristics | 幅频特性 |
| main storage | 主存储器 |
| man-machine communication | 人机通信 |
| man-machine interaction | 人机交互 |
| man-machine interface | 人机界面 |
| maximum output resistance | 最大输出电阻 |
| measuring amplifier | 测量放大器 |
| measuring bridge | 测量电桥 |
| memory | 存储器 |
| meter | 计；表 |
| meter electrodes | 测量电极 |
| microwave | 微波 |
| microwave detection apparatus | 微波检测仪 |
| microwave distance meter | 微波测距仪 |
| modulator | 调制器 |
| modulator-demodulator; modem | 调制解调器 |
| module | 模块 |
| multi-input multi-output control system; MIMO control system | 多输入/多输出控制系统 |
| multiplexer | 多路转换器；多路转接器 |
| multiplexing | 多路复用 |

# N

| | |
|---|---|
| natural frequency | 固有频率 |
| negative feedback | 负反馈 |
| non-line conversion | 非线性转换 |
| nonlinear characteristics | 非线性特性 |
| nonlinear control system | 非线性控制系统 |
| nonlinear control system theory | 非线性控制系统理论 |
| normal probe | 直探头 |

# O

| | |
|---|---|
| object program | 目标程序 |
| office automation (OA) | 办公自动化 |
| office automation system (OAS) | 办公自动化系统 |
| office information system (OIS) | 办公信息系统 |

| | |
|---|---|
| on-line real-time processing | 在线实时处理 |
| on-line system simulation | 在线系统仿真 |
| on-off action | 通断作用 |
| on-off controller | 通断控制器 |
| open loop | 开环 |
| open loop control | 开环控制 |
| open loop control system | 开环控制系统 |
| open loop frequency response | 开环频率响应 |
| open loop gain | 开环增益 |
| open loop gain characteristic | 开环增益特性 |
| open loop transfer function | 开环传递函数 |
| open loop voltage gain | 开环电压增益 |
| operating system (OS) | 操作系统 |
| operating temperature range | 工作温度范围 |
| operational amplifier | 运算放大器 |
| operational reliability | 运行可靠性 |
| operational unit | 运算器 |
| oscillating period | 振荡周期 |
| oscillator | 振荡器 |
| oscilloscope | 示波器 |
| output impedance | 输出阻抗 |
| output signal | 输出信号 |
| output signal "one" level | 输出信号"1"电平 |
| output signal "zero" level | 输出信号"0"电平 |
| output state | 输出状态 |
| output system | 输出系统 |
| output unit | 输出设备 |
| output variable | 输出变量 |
| output vector | 输出向量;输出矢量 |

# P

| | |
|---|---|
| parallel processing | 并行处理 |
| parallel transmission | 并行传输 |
| parameter | 参数 |
| partition coefficient | 分配系数 |
| passive transducer [sensor] | 无源传感器 |
| path | 通路 |
| peak detector | 峰值检波器 |

| | |
|---|---|
| peak-to-peak value | 峰-峰值 |
| peak value | 峰值 |
| peak voltmeter | 峰值电压表 |
| performance | 性能 |
| performance evaluation | 性能指标 |
| peripheral control unit | 外围设备控制器 |
| peripheral equipment | 外围设备 |
| phase | 相位 |
| phase analysis | 相位分析 |
| phase angle | 相角 |
| phase detection | 相位检测 |
| phase detector | 鉴相器 |
| phase difference | 相位差 |
| phase lead | 相位超前 |
| phase modulation (PM) | 相位调制;调相 |
| photo resistor | 光敏电阻器 |
| photo sensor | 光敏元件 |
| pointer | 指针;指示字 |
| port | 通信口;端口 |
| positive-negative action | 正负作用 |
| positive pressure | 正压 |
| potentiometer | 电位器 |
| power amplifier | 功率放大器 |
| power supply frequency | 电源频率 |
| power supply voltage | 电源电压 |
| power system automation | 电力系统自动化 |
| power-fail circuit | 电源故障电路 |
| preamplifier | 前置放大器 |
| probe | 探头 |
| process automation | 过程自动化 |
| process control | 过程控制 |
| process control computer | 过程控制计算机 |
| process control software | 过程控制软件 |
| process control system | 过程控制系统 |
| processor | 处理机;处理器;处理程序 |
| program run | 程序运行 |
| programmable controller | 可编程序控制器 |
| programmable logic controller (PLC) | 可编程序逻辑控制器 |
| programmer | 程序(设计)员 |

| | |
|---|---|
| programming | 程序设计 |
| programming flowchart | 程序设计流程图 |
| pulse code modulation (PCM) | 脉码调制；脉冲编码调制 |
| pulse control | 脉冲控制 |
| pulse frequency modulation control system | 脉冲调频控制系统 |
| pulse-width modulation | 脉冲宽度调制 |

## Q

| | |
|---|---|
| Q factor | Q值因数 |
| quantization | 量化 |
| quantization error | 量化误差 |
| quantized noise | 量化噪声 |

## R

| | |
|---|---|
| radiant intensity | 辐射强度 |
| radiant power | 辐射功率 |
| radiation | 辐射 |
| random access | 随机存取 |
| random error | 随机误差 |
| rated burden | 额定负载 |
| rated operating range | 额定工作范围 |
| rated output | 额定输出 |
| rating power consumption | 额定功耗 |
| read | 读 |
| read-only memory (ROM) | 只读存储器 |
| real time control | 实时控制 |
| real time control system | 实时控制系统 |
| real time date processing | 实时数据处理 |
| relative error | 相对误差 |
| relay | 继动器；继电器 |
| relay characteristics | 继电(器)特性 |
| relay control system | 继电控制系统 |
| reliability | 可靠性；可靠度 |
| remote control | 遥控 |
| resistance balance | 电阻平衡 |
| resistance thermometer detector (RTD) | 热电阻 |
| resolution | 分辨力；分辨率；分离度 |

| | |
|---|---|
| robot | 机器人 |
| robot programming language | 机器人编程语言 |
| robot system | 机器人系统 |
| robotics | 机器人学 |
| robust control | 鲁棒控制 |
| robust controller | 鲁棒控制器 |
| robustness | 鲁棒性 |

## S

| | |
|---|---|
| sampling | 采样；取样 |
| sampling action | 采样作用 |
| sampling control | 采样控制 |
| sampling control system | 采样控制系统 |
| sampling controller | 采样控制器 |
| sampling interval | 采样间隔 |
| sampling period | 采样周期 |
| sampling pulse | 采样脉冲 |
| scan rate | 扫描速率 |
| semi-automation | 半自动化 |
| serial processing | 串行处理 |
| serial transmission | 串行传输 |
| series capacitor | 串联电容器 |
| series inductor | 串联电感器 |
| series-mode rejection ratio (SMRR) | 串模抑制比 |
| series-mode signal | 串模信号 |
| series-mode voltage | 串模电压 |
| series operation | 串联工作 |
| server | 服务器 |
| signal-to-noise ratio | 信噪比 |
| simulation | 仿真；模拟 |
| simulation program | 仿真程序 |
| simulation result | 仿真结果 |
| simulation run | 仿真运行 |
| simulation software | 仿真软件 |
| simulator | 仿真器 |
| sound field | 声场 |
| sound intensity | 声强 |
| stability | 稳定性；稳定度 |

| | |
|---|---|
| standard error | 标准误差 |
| state | 状态 |
| state diagram | 状态图 |
| state equation | 状态方程 |
| statement | 语句 |
| static characteristic curve | 静态特性曲线 |
| static characteristics | 静态特性 |
| steady state | 稳态 |
| step function | 阶跃函数 |
| step motor | 步进电机 |
| storage | 存储器 |
| subroutine | 子程序 |
| subroutine call | 子程序调用 |
| supervision | 监控 |
| surface wave | 表面波 |
| synchronous transmission | 同步传输 |
| system reliability | 系统可靠性 |

# T

| | |
|---|---|
| telecommunication | 远程通信 |
| temperature compensation | 温度补偿 |
| top-down development | 自上而下开发 |
| top-down testing | 自上而下测试 |
| total harmonic distortion | 总谐波失真 |
| transfer function | 传递函数 |
| transient | 瞬态 |
| transient deviation | 瞬态偏差 |
| TV-camera system | 电视摄像系统 |

# U

| | |
|---|---|
| ultraviolet radiation | 紫外线辐射 |
| unit | 单元；单位 |
| unit step function | 单位阶跃函数 |
| utility software | 实用软件 |

# V

| | |
|---|---|
| vacuum | 真空;负压 |
| variable | 变量 |
| velocity pickup | 速度传感器 |
| vibration amplitude | 振幅 |
| voltage amplifier | 电压放大器 |
| voltage divider | 分压器 |
| voltage transducer [sensor] | 电压传感器 |
| voltmeter | 电压表 |

# W

| | |
|---|---|
| white noise | 白噪声 |
| window function | 窗口函数 |
| word | 字 |
| word length | 字长 |

# Z

| | |
|---|---|
| zener diode | 稳压二极管 |
| Z-transform | Z 变换 |
| zero | 零点;零位 |
| zero drift | 零点漂移 |
| zero-state response | 零状态响应 |

# Appendix 3　Quartus II Menu 中英文对照

**File 文件**

| | |
|---|---|
| New | 新建 |
| Open | 打开 |
| Close | 关闭 |
| New project wizard | 新建项目向导 |
| Open project | 打开项目 |
| Convert MAX+PLUS project | 转化为 MAX+PLUS 工程 |
| Save project | 保存工程 |
| Close project | 关闭工程 |
| Save | 保存 |
| Save as | 另存为 |
| Save current report section as | 保存当前部分的报告为 |
| File properties | 文件属性 |
| Create/update | 生成/更新 |
| 　　Create HDL design file for current file | 为当前文件生成 HDL 设计文件 |
| 　　Create symbol file for current file | 为当前文件生成符号文件 |
| 　　Create AHDL include file for current file | 为当前文件生成 AHDL 包含库文件 |
| 　　Create design file from selected block | 从选择的块生成设计文件 |
| 　　Update design file from selected block | 从选择的块更新设计文件 |
| 　　Create signaltap II file from design instance | 从设计实例中生成 signaltap II 文件 |
| 　　Create signaltap II list file | 生成 signaltap II 文件清单 |
| 　　Create JAM, SVF or ISC file | 生成 JAM、SVF 或 ISC 文件 |
| 　　Create/update IPS file | 生成/更新 IPS 文件 |
| Export | 输出 |
| Convert programming file | 转换编程文件 |
| Page setup | 页面设置 |
| Print preview | 打印预览 |
| Print | 打印 |
| Recent files | 最近的文档——文件路径 |
| Recent project | 最近的项目——文件路径 |
| Exit | 退出 |

**Edit 编辑**

| | |
|---|---|
| Undo | 撤销 |
| Redo | 重做 |
| Cut | 剪切 |

| | |
|---|---|
| Copy | 复制 |
| Paste | 粘贴 |
| Delete | 删除 |
| Select all | 全选 |
| Find… | 查找 |
| Find next | 查找下一个 |
| Find matching delimiter | 找到匹配的定界符 |
| Replace | 代替 |
| Go to | 转到 |
| Increase indent | 增加缩进 |
| Decrease indent | 减少缩进 |
| Insert page break | 插入分页符 |
| Insert file | 插入文件 |
| Insert template | 插入模板 |
| Set bookmark | 设置书签 |
| Delete bookmark | 删除书签 |
| Jump to bookmark | 跳转到书签 |

**View 视图**

| | |
|---|---|
| Utility windows | 实用程序窗口 |
| Project navigator | 项目领航员 |
| Node finder | 节点发现者 |
| TCL console | TCL 控制台 |
| Messages | 信息,便条 |
| Status | 地位,身份;情形,状况 |
| Change manager | 变更经理 |
| Full screen | 全屏 |

**Project 工程**

| | |
|---|---|
| Add current file to project | 将当前文件添加到工程 |
| Add\remove file in project… | 在工程中添加或删除文件 |
| Revisions | 版本信息 |
| Copy project | 复制工程 |
| Archive project | 工程档案 |
| Restore archived project | 复位工程 |
| Import database | 导入数据库 |
| Export database | 输出数据库 |
| Import design partition | 导入设计分割 |
| Export project as design partition | 输出设计分割 |
| Generate bottom-up design partition scritps | 生成底层设计分割脚本 |
| Generate TCL file for project | 生成 TCL 文件 |

| | |
|---|---|
| Generate powerplay early power estimator | 生成早期电源估测文件 |
| Organize quartus 2 setting | quartus 2 初始化设置 |
| Hardcopy utilities | 硬拷贝功用项目 |
| Hardcopy timing optimization wizard | 硬拷贝定时优化专项 |
| Hardcopy file wizard | 硬拷贝文件向导 |
| Hardcopy 2 utilities | 硬拷贝功用项目 2 |
| Create\overwrite hardcopy 2 companion revision | 创建\覆盖硬拷贝 2 同步修订 |
| Set current hardcopy 2 companion revision | 设置当前硬拷贝 2 同步修订 |
| Compare hardcopy 2 companion revision | 比较硬拷贝 2 同步修订 |
| Generate hardcopy 2 handoff report | 生成硬拷贝 2 同步报告 |
| Archive hardcopy 2 file | 文件归档硬拷贝 |
| Hardcopy 2 advisor | 硬拷贝 2 的设计器 |
| Locate | 位于 |
| Locate in assignment editor | 在任务编辑器设置 |
| Locate in pin planner | 在管脚设计器设置 |
| Set as top-level entity file | 设置为顶层文件 |
| Hierarchy | 结构组织 |

**Assignments 配置**

| | |
|---|---|
| Device | 设备 |
| Pins | 引脚 |
| Timing analysis settings | 时序分析设置 |
| EDA tool settings | EDA 工具的设置 |
| Settings | 设置 |
| Timing wizard | 时序向导 |
| Assignments editor | 分配编辑器 |
| Pin planner | 引脚规划 |
| Remove Assignments | 删除指定 |
| Demote Assignments | 降低指定 |
| Back-annotate Assignments | 反标作业 |
| Import assignment | 导入任务 |
| Export assignment | 导出任务 |
| Assignment (time) groups | 分配时间组 |
| Timing closure floorplan | 时序收敛平面布置图 |
| Logiclock region window | 逻辑锁定区域窗口 |
| Design partition window | 设计分区窗口 |

**Processing 调试**

| | |
|---|---|
| Stop process | 停止进程 |
| Start compilation | 开始编辑 |
| Analyze current file | 分析当前的文件 |

|  |  |
|---|---|
| Start | 开始 |
|     Start analysis & elaboration | 开始分析和阐述 |
|     Start analysis & synthesis | 开始分析和综合 |
|     Start fitter | 开始适配 |
|     Start assemble | 开始汇编 |
|     Start timing analyzer | 开始定时分析器 |
|     Start TimeQuest timing analyze | TimeQuest 时序分析仪启动 |
|     Start EDA netlist writer | 启动 EDA 网表文件书写器 |
|     Start design assistant | 开始辅助设计 |
|     Start PowerPlay power analyzer | 启动 PowerPlay 功耗分析仪 |
|     Start signalprobe compilation | 开始 signalprobe 编译 |
|     Start I/O assignment analysis | 启动 I/O 分配分析 |
|     Start timing analyzer(fast timing model) | 启动计时仪(快速定时模式) |
|     Start early timing estimate | 起步早的时间估计 |
|     Start timing constraint check | 开始计时约束检查 |
|     Start check & save all netlist changes | 开始检查及保存所有网表变化 |
|     Start partition merge | 启动分区合并 |
|     Start VQM writer | 启动 VQM 书写器(生成.vqm 文件) |
|     Start equation writer(post-synthesis) | 启动方程书写器(生成.eqn 文件)(后综合) |
|     Start equation writer(post-fitting) | 启动方程书写器(生成.eqn 文件)(后适配) |
|     Start test bench template writer | 启动测试台模板书写器 |
| Start EDA synthesis | 启动 EDA 综合 |
| Start EDA physical synthesis | 开始的 EDA 物理综合 |
| Update Memory Initialization File | 更新存储器初始化文件 |
| Compilation Report | 编译报告 |
| Start Compilation & Simulation | 开始编译与仿真 |
| Generate Functional Simulation Netlist | 模拟网表生成功能 |
| Start Simulation | 开始模拟 |
| Simulation Debug | 仿真调试 |
| Breakpoints | 断点 |
| Embedded Memory | 嵌入式存储器 |
| Update Simulator with Current Memory Contents | 更新模拟器与当前的内存内容 |
| Update Current Memory with Simulation Data | 更新当前的内存仿真数据 |
| Last Simulation Vector Outputs | 最后仿真矢量输出 |
| Current Vector Inputs | 输入电流矢量 |
| Overwrite Vector Inputs with Simulation Outputs | 覆盖向量与模拟输入输出 |
| Compiler Tool | 编译工具 |

| | |
|---|---|
| Simulator Tool | 仿真工具 |
| Timing Analyzer Tool | 时序分析工具 |
| Power Analyzer Tool | 功耗分析工具 |

**Tools 工具**

| | |
|---|---|
| EDA simulation tool | EDA 仿真工具 |
| Run RTL simulation | 运行 RTL 仿真 |
| Run gate level simulation | 运行门级仿真 |
| Run EDA timing analysis tool | 运行 EDA 时序分析工具 |
| Launch design space explorer | 启动工作环境管理器 |
| Advanced List Paths | 高级列表路径 |
| TimeQuest Timing Analyzer | 时序分析仪 |
| Advisors | 顾问 |
| Resource Optimization Advisor | 资源优化向导 |
| Timing Optimization Advisor | 时序优化向导 |
| Power Optimization Advisor | 电源优化向导 |
| Chip Editor | 芯片编辑器 |
| Netlist Viewers | 网络表查看器 |
| RTL Viewer | 查看器 |
| Technology Map Viewer | 技术映射查看器 |
| State Machine Viewer | 状态机查看器 |
| SignalTap II Logic Analyzer | SignalTap II 逻辑分析仪 |
| IN-System Memory Content Editor | 在系统内存内容编辑 |
| Logic Analyzer Interface Editor | 逻辑分析仪接口编辑器 |
| Signal Probe Pins | 引脚信号探头 |
| Programmer | 编程器 |
| MegaWizard Plug-In Manager | MegaWizard 插件管理器 |
| SOPC Builder | SOPC 生成器 |
| TCL Scripts | TCL 脚本 |
| Customize | 定制 |
| Options | 选项 |
| License Setup | 许可证设置 |

**Windows 窗口**

| | |
|---|---|
| New windows | 新建窗口 |
| Close All | 全部关闭 |
| Cascade | 层叠 |
| Tile Horizontally | 水平排列 |
| Tile Vertically | 垂直排列 |

**Help 帮助**

| | |
|---|---|
| Index | 索引 |

| | |
|---|---|
| Search | 查找 |
| Contents | 概述 |
| Messages | 留言板 |
| Glossary | 术语表 |
| Megafunctions/LPM | 兆函数 |
| Devices & Adapters | 器件和适配器 |
| EDA Interfaces | EDA 接口 |
| Tutorial | 教程 |
|     PDF tutorials |     PDF 教程 |
|     PDF tutorials for VHDL users |     VHDL 使用者的 PDF 教程 |
|     PDF tutorials for Verilog HDL users |     Verilog HDL 使用者的 PDF 教程 |
| MAX+PLUS II Quick Start Guide | MAX+PLUS II 快速启动向导 |
| What's New | 什么是新建 |
| Readme File | 自述文件 |
| MegaCore IP Library Readme | 大型核心 IP 库自述 |
| Release Notes | 发布通知 |
| How to Use Help | 如何使用"帮助" |
| Contacting Altera | Altera 联机 |
| Altera on the web | Altera 网络服务 |
|     Quartus II Home Page |     Quartus II 首页 |
|     Download Quartus II Updates |     下载 Quartus II 更新 |
|     Download PCB Footpints |     下载 PCB 封装 |
|     Training |     培训 |
|     Quartus II Service Request |     Quartus II 服务需求 |
|     Troubleshooters |     疑难解答 |
|     SOPC Builder Home Page |     SOPC 团队首页 |
|     Altera IP MagaStore Page |     Altera IP 在线商店 |
|     Altera Home Page |     Altera 首页 |
|     New Quartus II Information |     最新 Quartus II 消息 |
|     Quartus II Handbook |     Quartus II 手册 |
| About Quartus II | 关于 Quartus II |

# Appendix 4  Protel 部分分立元件名称及菜单中英文对照

**部分元件**

| | |
|---|---|
| AND | 与门 |
| ANTENNA | 天线 |
| BATTERY | 直流电源 |
| BELL | 铃,钟 |
| BVC | 同轴电缆接插件 |
| BRIDEG 1 | 整流桥(二极管) |
| BRIDEG 2 | 整流桥(集成块) |
| BUFFER | 缓冲器 |
| BUZZER | 蜂鸣器 |
| CAP | 电容 |
| CAPACITOR | 电容 |
| CAPACITOR POL | 有极性电容 |
| CAPVAR | 可调电容 |
| CIRCUIT BREAKER | 熔断丝 |
| COAX | 同轴电缆 |
| CON | 插口 |
| CRYSTAL | 晶体整荡器 |
| DB | 并行插口 |
| DIODE | 二极管 |
| DIODE SCHOTTKY | 稳压二极管 |
| DIODE VARACTOR | 变容二极管 |
| DPY_3-SEG | 3 段 LED |
| DPY_7-SEG | 7 段 LED |
| DPY_7-SEG_DP | 7 段 LED(带小数点) |
| ELECTRO | 电解电容 |
| FUSE | 熔断器 |
| INDUCTOR | 电感 |
| INDUCTOR IRON | 带铁心电感 |
| JFET N | N 沟道场效应管 |
| JFET P | P 沟道场效应管 |
| LAMP | 灯泡 |
| LAMP NEDN | 起辉器 |

| | |
|---|---|
| LED | 发光二极管 |
| METER | 仪表 |
| MICROPHONE | 麦克风 |
| MOSFET | MOS 管 |
| MOTOR AC | 交流电机 |
| MOTOR SERVO | 伺服电机 |
| NAND | 与非门 |
| NOR | 或非门 |
| NOT | 非门 |
| NPN NPN | 三极管 |
| NPN-PHOTO | 感光三极管 |
| OPAMP | 运放 |
| OR | 或门 |
| PHOTO | 感光二极管 |
| PNP | 三极管 |
| NPN DAR | NPN 三极管 |
| PNP DAR | PNP 三极管 |
| POT | 滑线变阻器 |
| PELAY-DPDT | 双刀双掷继电器 |
| RES1.2 | 电阻 |
| RES3.4 | 可变电阻 |
| RESISTOR BRIDGE | 桥式电阻 |
| RESPACK | 电阻 |
| SCR | 晶闸管 |
| PLUG | 插头 |
| PLUG AC FEMALE | 三相交流插头 |
| SOCKET | 插座 |
| SOURCE CURRENT | 电流源 |
| SOURCE VOLTAGE | 电压源 |
| SPEAKER | 扬声器 |
| SW | 开关 |
| SW-DPDY | 双刀双掷开关 |
| SW-SPST | 单刀单掷开关 |
| SW-PB | 按钮 |
| THERMISTOR | 电热调节器 |
| TRANS1 | 变压器 |
| TRANS2 | 可调变压器 |

| | |
|---|---|
| TRIAC | 三端双向可控硅 |
| TRIODE | 三极真空管 |
| VARISTOR | 变阻器 |
| ZENER | 齐纳二极管 |
| DPY_7-SEG_DP | 数码管 |
| SW-PB | 开关 |

# 菜单

**file 文件**

| | |
|---|---|
| New… | 新建文件 |
| New Design | 新建设计数据库文件 |
| Open… | 打开文件 |
| Open Full Project | 打开全部项目 |
| Close | 关闭 |
| Close Design | 关闭设计数据库 |
| Import | 导入 |
| Export | 导出 |
| Save | 保存 |
| Save As… | 另存为 |
| Save Copy As… | 保存复本为 |
| Save All | 全部保存 |
| Setup Printer | 设置打印机 |
| Print | 打印 |
| Exit | 退出 |

**Edit 编辑**

| | |
|---|---|
| Undo | 撤销 |
| Redo | 重做 |
| Cut | 剪切 |
| Copy | 复制 |
| Paste | 粘贴 |
| Paste Array… | 阵列粘贴 |
| Clear | 清除 |
| Find Text… | 查找字符串 |
| Replace Text… | 替换字符串 |
| Find Next | 查找下一个 |
| Select | 选择 |
|     Inside Area | 区域内 |

| | | |
|---|---|---|
| | Outside Area | 区域外 |
| | All | 全部 |
| | Net | 网络 |
| Deselect | | 撤销选择 |
| Doggleselection | | 切换选择 |
| Delete | | 删除 |
| Change | | 修改 |
| Move | | 移动 |
| | Drag | 拖拉 |
| | Move | 移动 |
| | Move Selection | 移动选择的 |
| | Drag Selection | 拖拉选择的 |
| | Move to Front | 移到前面 |
| | Bring to Front | 带到前面 |
| | Send to Back | 送到后面 |
| | Bring to Front of | 带到某个前面 |
| | Send to Back of | 送到某个后面 |
| Align | | 对齐 |
| | Align… | 对齐 |
| | Align Left | 左对齐 |
| | Align Right | 右对齐 |
| | Center Horizontal | 水平中心对齐 |
| | Distribute Horizontally | 水平均布 |
| | Align Top | 顶对齐 |
| | Align Bottom | 底对齐 |
| | Center Vertical | 垂直中心对齐 |
| | Distribute Vertically | 垂直均布 |
| Set Reference | | 设置参考点 |
| Jump | | 跳转 |
| Set Location Marks | | 设置位置标记 |
| Increment Part Number | | 增加元件号 |
| Export to Spread… | | 导出至电子表格 |

**View 视图**

| | |
|---|---|
| Fit Document | 适合文档 |
| Fit All Objects | 适合全部对象 |
| Area | 区域 |
| Around Point | 以点为中心 |

| | |
|---|---|
| 50% | 50%比例 |
| 100% | 100%比例 |
| 200% | 200%比例 |
| 400% | 400%比例 |
| Zoom In | 放大 |
| Zoom Out | 缩小 |
| Pan | 平移 |
| Refresh | 刷新 |
| Design Manager | 设计管理器 |
| Status Bar | 状态栏 |
| Command Status | 命令状态栏 |
| Toolbars | 工具栏 |
| Main Tools | 主工具栏 |
| Wiring Tools | 连线工具栏 |
| Drawing Tools | 绘图工具栏 |
| Power Objects | 电源实体 |
| Digital Objects | 数字实体 |
| Simulation Sources | 激励源 |
| PLD Toolbar | PLD工具栏 |
| Customize… | 定制 |
| Visible Grid | 可视网格 |
| Snap Grid | 捕获网格 |
| Electrical Grid | 电气网格 |

**Place 放置**

| | |
|---|---|
| Bus | 总线 |
| Bus Entry | 总线分支线 |
| Part… | 元件 |
| Junction | 节点 |
| Power Port | 电源/接地符号 |
| Wire | 导线 |
| Net Label | 网格标号 |
| Port | 输入/输出端口 |
| Sheet Symbol | 方块电路 |
| Add Sheet Entry | 图纸端口 |
| Directives | 标志 |
|     No ERC | 不做 ERC |
|     Probe | 探测点 |

| | | |
|---|---|---|
| | Test Vector Index | 测试矢量索引 |
| | Stimulus | 激励 |
| | PCB Layout | 印制电路板符号 |
| Annotation | | 注释 |
| Text Frame | | 字符串 |
| Drawing Tools | | 绘图工具 |
| | Arcs | 圆弧 |
| | Elliptical Arcs | 椭圆弧 |
| | Ellipses | 椭圆 |
| | Pie Charts | 扇形 |
| | Line | 线 |
| | Rectangle | 矩形 |
| | Round Rectangle | 圆角矩形 |
| | Polygons | 多边形 |
| | Beziers | 贝塞尔曲线 |
| | Graphic… | 图形 |
| Process Container | | 过程容器 |

**Design 设计**

| | |
|---|---|
| Update PCB… | 更新 PCB |
| Browse Library… | 选择元件库 |
| Add/Remove Library… | 添加/删除元件库 |
| Make Project Library | 生成项目元件库 |
| Update Parts In Cache | 更新缓存中元件 |
| Template | 模板 |

| | | |
|---|---|---|
| | Update | 更新 |
| | Set Template File Name… | 设置模板文件名 |
| | Remove Symbol From Sheet | 删除当前模板 |

| | |
|---|---|
| Create Netlist… | 创建网络表 |
| Create Sheet From Symbol | 从符号生成图纸 |
| Create Symbol From Sheet | 从图纸生成符号 |
| Options… | 选项 |

**Tools 工具**

| | |
|---|---|
| ERC… | 电气规则检查 |
| Find Component | 查找元件 |
| Up/Down Hierarchy | 变换层次 |
| Complex To Simple | 复杂变简单 |
| Annotate | 注释 |

| | |
|---|---|
| Back Annotate | 反向注释 |
| Database Links | 数据库连接 |
| Process Containers | 过程容器 |
|     Run | 运行 |
|     Run All | 全部执行 |
|     Configure… | 配置 |
| Cross Probe | 交叉检查 |
| Select PCB Components | 选择 PCB 成分 |
| Preferences… | 参数选择 |

**Simulate 仿真**

| | |
|---|---|
| Run | 运行 |
| Sources | 源 |
|     +5 Volts DC | 直流+5 V |
|     −5 Volts DC | 直流−5 V |
|     +12 Volts DC | 直流+12 V |
|     −12 Volts DC | 直流−12 V |
|     1 kHz Sine Wave | 1 kHz 正弦波 |
|     10 kHz Sine Wave | 10 kHz 正弦波 |
|     100 kHz Sine Wave | 100 kHz 正弦波 |
|     1 MHz Sine Wave | 1 MHz 正弦波 |
|     1 kHz Pulse | 1 kHz 脉冲 |
|     10 kHz Pulse | 10 kHz 脉冲 |
|     100 kHz Pulse | 100 kHz 脉冲 |
|     1 MHz Pulse | 1 MHz 脉冲 |
| Create SPICE Netlist | 建立 SPICE 网络表 |
| Setup | 设置 |

**PLD 可编程逻辑器件**

| | |
|---|---|
| Compile | 编译 |
| Simulate | 仿真 |
| Configure… | 配置 |
| Toggle Pin LOC | 切换管脚 |

**Reports 报告**

| | |
|---|---|
| Selected Pins… | 选择的引脚 |
| Bill of Material | 材料清单 |
| Design Hierarchy | 设计层次 |
| Cross Reference | 交叉参考 |
| Add Port References (Flat) | 增加参考端口（一层） |

Add Port References (Hierarchial)　　　增加参考端口（分层）
Remove Port References　　　删除参考端口
Netlist Compare…　　　网络表比较

**Auto route 自动布线**
all　　　全部
net　　　网络
connection　　　连接
component　　　元件
area　　　区域
stop　　　停止
pause　　　暂停
restart　　　重开始
setup　　　设置

# Appendix 5  参考答案

## UNIT 1

Ⅰ. 翻译下列短语和表达
1. electronic technology
2. wireless communications
3. computer engineering
4. combinatorial logic circuits
5. 直流电源
6. 信号放大器
7. 集成电路
8. 时序逻辑电路
9. 无线电技术
10. 交流电路

Ⅱ. 把下列句子翻译成中文
1. 你愿意去参加一个没有音响放大器、没有大屏幕或灯光效果的流行音乐会吗？
2. 这(电视的发明)应归功于英国工程师贝尔德·约翰·洛吉 (John Logic Baird)，他追随马可尼(Marconi)的足迹，想用与传送声音相同的方式传送图像。
3. 今天所说的电子技术实际上是在发现晶体管效应以后开始(发展)的。
4. 令人不可思议的是他的想法奏效了，并从此诞生了集成电路工业。
5. 这个课程模块介绍了线性应用范围中半导体器件的特征。
6. 当前，计算机及微处理器在电子工业的各个领域中应用十分广泛。
7. 这个模块中安排学生对一个简单的微处理器编程完成工业上典型的控制任务。
8. 然后通过编程利用这些器件完成控制(系统)等操作。
9. 重点放在如何运用编程技术解决工程应用的实际问题。
10. 电子技术专业将为毕业生打下一个牢固的基础，学生毕业后可以从事电气工程师的职业。

## UNIT 2

Ⅰ. 翻译下列短语和表达
1. Ohm law
2. electrical component
3. diode's behavior
4. current gain

5. 电子元器件
6. 三极管偏置电路
7. 彩色条形码(色环)
8. 电磁能
9. 半导体二极管
10. 双极型三极管

Ⅱ．把下列句子翻译成中文

1. 电阻常用作限流器,限制流过器件的电流以防止器件烧坏,电阻也可用作分压器,以减小其他电路的电压,电阻还可用在晶体管偏置电路中和作为电路的负载。

2. 电阻器一般是线性器件,它的(伏安)特性曲线形成一条直线。

3. 电容可以隔直流,但能通过充电和放电的方式通交流。

4. 有各种各样形状和尺寸的电容。

5. 当有电流流过电感器时,电感器周围就有电磁场,电感器是能以电磁场的形式暂时储存电磁能量的电子器件。

6. 这时二极管的内部电阻是很小的,将有一个较大的电流流过二极管,流过电流的大小取决于外部电路的电阻。

7. 现在用的三极管大多数是 NPN 型,因为这种类型的硅管比较容易制作。

8. 缩写词 MOS 表示 M(金属)-O(氧化物) S(半导体),过去分别用金属作门极,氧化物作绝缘层,半导体作沟道、基底等的材料。

9. 电容值与你所选取的电路有关,并与你要放大的信号频率有关。

10. 当三极管中没有电流流过时,称三极管处于截止状态(完全不通)。

# UNIT 3

Ⅰ．翻译下列短语和表达

1. digital multimeter
2. positive and negative voltage
3. peak-to-peak value
4. parallel with the component
5. 交流电压
6. 机械调节
7. 数字示波器
8. 友好的前面板
9. 外部触发
10. 自动测量

Ⅱ．把下列句子翻译成中文

1. 万用表是一种通用仪表,能用来测量直流和交流电路的电压、电流、电阻,有的还能测量分贝。

2. 一个模拟万用表可以测量正电压和负电压,只要简单地对调一下两个测试笔或拨一下极性开关。

3. 当测量电流时,电路必须断开,插入万用表表笔使之与被测电路或元件相串联。

4. 一个波形的频率可以通过在水平方向数出波形一个周期的厘米值来确定,将这厘米值乘上时间/厘米控制钮的设定值就得到它的一个周期所需的时间。

5. 一旦设定了垂直单位(电压/单位格),就确定了是用衰减器还是用放大器把输入信号转换成适当幅度的电压信号。

6. 利萨如图形可用来显示两个同频率信号之间的相位关系和根据已知频率的信号求出未知频率的信号。

7. 有两种万用表:用指针在标准刻度上的移动来指示测量值的模拟万用表和用电子数字显示器显示测量值的数字万用表。

8. 如果两个信号是同频率的,在示波器上就出现一个圆。

9. 通常,图像显示(电压)信号如何随时间变化:其垂直轴 Y 表示电压,水平轴 X 表示时间。

10. 所有的信号发生器都有一个频率范围开关,一个精调控制用来选择一个特定的频率,一个幅度控制用来改变输出电压的峰-峰值(幅值)和一些输出端口。

# UNIT 4

Ⅰ. 翻译下列短语和表达

1. semiconductor material
2. MOS technologies
3. logic building blocks
4. highest frequency logic circuits
5. 现场可编程门阵列
6. 超大规模集成电路
7. MOS 晶体管
8. 高级语言
9. 片上系统
10. 数字逻辑集成电路

Ⅱ. 把下列句子翻译成中文

1. 摩尔定律指出,在一个芯片上器件集成的数量将每两年翻一番,这些年来(集成电路的发展)是符合摩尔定律的。

2. 硅芯片的技术发展使得集成电路设计者可以在一个芯片上集成几百万个以上的晶体管,甚至现在可以在单一芯片上集成一个中等复杂的系统。

3. 但制作 PCB 板需要专用的设备,所以不推荐新手(初学者)用这个方法,除非已有现成的 PCB 板。

4. 通常(晶体管的尺寸)实际是指沟道宽度与沟道长度的比值。

5. 通过这个平台,用户可以用他们的移动电话享受原先只能由 IC 卡提供的服务。

6. 这对我们来说是一件好事,因为伽马射线、X 射线和紫外线对生物有害。

7. 这种技术的潜在应用可能包括电子票和网上信用卡业务,这些将给服务商和用户提供方便、带来增值。

8. 清零输入端在正常控制时必须保持为逻辑1。

9. 一个异步计数器中包含了若干个触发器,每个触发器的输出端与下一个触发器的输入端相连接。

10. 电子也可以在一个电视机的显像管中流动,在显像管中电子撞击显示屏,产生一个光(闪烁)点。

# UNIT 5

Ⅰ. 翻译下列短语和表达

1. bidirectional shift register
2. operating-mode-control
3. positive edge-triggered clocking
4. trigger level
5. 并行装载
6. 同步并行装载
7. 绝对最大额定值
8. 推荐工作条件
9. 非稳态(中文中也称双稳态)或单稳态输出
10. 物理尺寸

Ⅱ. 把下列句子翻译成中文

1. 这种双向移位寄存器的设计包含了系统设计师想在一个移位寄存器上实现的几乎所有的移位功能。

2. 同步并行加载:当工作方式控制端 S0、S1 均为高电平时,在时钟(CLOCK)上升沿作用下,并行数据(A—D)被送入相应的输出端 $Q_A$—$Q_D$。

3. 门槛电平和触发电平一般分别是 $V_{CC}$ 的 2/3 和 1/3。

4. 在非稳态(振荡)模式,其输出频率和占空比可分别用两个外接电阻和一个外接电容来控制。

5. 当 S0 为高电平、S1 为低电平时,在 CLOCK 上升沿作用下进行右移操作,数据由 DSR 送入。

6. NE555 是精密定时器电路,可产生精确的时间延时和振荡。

7. 如果触发输入高于触发电平且门槛端(THRES)输入也高于门槛电平,则触发器清零,输出低电平。

8. 清零(RESET)输入端可以不管任何其他端的输入情况(将输出清零),常用于定时器一个新的工作循环的初始化。

9. AD574 是一种模数转换芯片,即把模拟信号转换成数字信号的芯片,是电子技术中常用的芯片。

10. AD574 在一个芯片上集成了全部模拟和数字功能。

# UNIT 6

**Ⅰ. 翻译下列短语和表达**

1. Retina Display
2. mobile operating system
3. HD video
4. Using apps
5. 主屏幕
6. 音量按钮
7. 每英寸 326 个像素
8. 300 小时待机时间
9. 安装 SIM 卡
10. 放大或缩小

**Ⅱ. 把下列句子翻译成中文**

1. 摄像头的工作是拍摄照片和适应暗光的拍摄。

2. 当你正在接听电话或欣赏歌曲、影片或其他媒体时，iPhone 侧面的按钮可以调节音量。

3. 如果已锁定 iPhone，则触摸屏幕不起任何作用。iPhone 仍可以接听电话，接收短信以及接收其他更新。

4. 查看照片和网页时，连按两次（快速轻按两次）以放大，再次连按两次以缩小。

5. 在实际开始用图像编辑软件编辑图像前调整所扫描的图片的质量。

6. 通过它的按钮化用户接口界面和完全附合逻辑的任务流设计，你只要用鼠标单击几下就可以完成全部的扫描工作。

7. 注意根据你所使用的软件选择 TWAIN 扫描仪的方法可能有些不同。

8. MiraScan 可以把你设置的每个扫描过程记录在一个设置文件中。利用这个特点，你可以为每个设置文件中的各项扫描任务指定不同的设置。

9. 默认的单位是英寸。若要改变单位，可以用鼠标单击列表框的（箭头），在列表框中单击想要的单位。

10. 芯片中自带高精度的参考电压与时钟，电路不需要外接电路或时钟信号就能完成全部模-数转换功能。

# UNIT 7

**Ⅰ. 翻译下列短语和表达**

1. still image
2. relate to television
3. CRT or the cathode ray tube
4. create magnetic fields

5. 水平移动光束

6. 电子束

7. 发射红、绿、蓝光

8. 电信号

9. 有线电视节目

10. 选（电视节目）频道

Ⅱ. 把下列句子翻译成中文

1. 因为水蒸发时，吸收热量，带来凉爽的感觉。

2. 如果你把冰箱中的制冷剂放在皮肤上（绝对不是好主意，别这样做）当它蒸发时会使皮肤结冰。

3. 纯氨气是有毒的，如果制冷液泄漏对人是一种威胁（或译是很危险的）。

4. 氟利昂液体流过扩散阀，在这过程中蒸发成冷的低压氟利昂气体。

5. 微波加热对液态的水最有效，对脂肪、糖、结冰的水加热效果就差一些。

6. 随着无线计算机网络日益普及，微波干扰已成为无线网络工作中值得关注的问题。

7. 第一种故意用微波去加热的食品是爆玉米，第二种食品是鸡蛋（鸡蛋在一个实验者面前炸开了）。

8. 到1970年后期，技术已得到很大的改进，价格迅速下降。

9. 真空吸尘器也许看起来像一个复杂的机器，但传统的真空吸尘器实际上仅由六个基本部件组成。

10. 可以把真空吸尘器的垃圾袋放在进风口和排气口之间任何地方，只要空气流可以经过袋子。

# UNIT 8

Ⅰ. 翻译下列短语和表达

1. signal simulation system

2. system-on-a-programmable-chip

3. design flow

4. modular compiler

5. 多平台设计环境

6. 图形用户界面

7. 分析和综合

8. 完整编译

9. 原理图设计系统

10. 印刷电路板设计系统

Ⅱ. 把下列句子翻译成中文

1. Altera Quartus Ⅱ 设计软件提供完整的多平台设计环境，能够直接满足特定设计需要。

2. Quartus Ⅱ 软件含有 FPGA 和 CPLD 设计所有阶段的解决方案。

3. Quartus II 软件为设计流程的每个阶段提供 Quartus II 图形用户界面、EDA 工具界面以及命令行界面。

4. Quartus II 工程包括在可编程器件中最终实现设计需要的所有设计文件、软件源文件和其他相关文件。

5. 它当之无愧地排在众多 EDA 软件的前面,是电子设计者首选软件。

6. 印刷电路板设计系统是用于电路板设计的高级 PCB。

7. 其中最重要的报表是网络表,通过网络表为后续的电路板设计作准备。

8. MATLAB 是一种数字化计算环境和可编程的语言。

9. 它可以很方便地计算很多问题,尤其是含矩阵和矢量公式的问题。另外它还有一个附加 Simulink 软件包,为动态系统和嵌入式系统提供了多领域的图形仿真和基于模型的设计(方法)。

10. 但不幸的是,这样很容易就可以偷取有线电视台的服务(即不付钱收看),所以电视信号以一种有趣的方式编码。

# UNIT 9

Ⅰ. 翻译下列短语和表达

1. various systems
2. intelligent networks
3. image transmission
4. 在线服务
5. 数据通信
6. 全球标准

Ⅱ. 把下列句子翻译成中文

1. 在 2001 年,NTT DoCoMo 公司推出了基于 IMT-2000 的世界上第一个业务 FOMA。

2. 在世界各地第一代模拟移动通信已经有多种不同的系统被开发和使用,第二代数字通信有 3 种系统共存——日本的 PDC、欧洲的 GSM 和美国的 TIA 标准。

3. IMT-2000 实现了相当于全球标准无线电接口下的固定网络质量的移动通信系统,还可以提供广泛的服务。

4. CDMA 能有效地利用有限的频率资源来容纳尽可能多的用户。

5. 时分-同步码分多址,即 TD-SCDMA,是由中国电信科学技术研究所(CATT)、大唐电信集团和西门子股份公司一起提出的中国 3G 移动通信标准。

# UNIT 10

Ⅰ. 翻译下列短语和表达

1. dynamic RAM memory
2. high performance software

3. the input/output (or I/O) devices

4. the control bus 或 control signal lines

5. 中断线

6. 影响系统的性能

7. 通常与外部设备相连接

8. 80x86 系列微处理器（芯片）

9. 从输入设备中读取数据

10. 一个存储芯片的存储容量

Ⅱ．把下列句子翻译成中文

1. 对 CPU 而言，大量的输入/输出口就像存储器一样。因为 CPU 可以把数据存储在输出设备中，也可从输入设备中读入数据。

2. 总线是指一组在系统各个部件之间传递各种电信号的导线。

3. 信号的传输速度非常快，以至于信号线即使只有几厘米的（传输）距离都有可能导致时间（不匹配）问题。

4. 当软件想要访问一些特定的存储位置或输入/输出设备时，它把相应的地址值放在地址总线上。

5. 主存是一个相当大且存取速度很快的存储器，用来储存 CPU 操作时的程序和数据。

6. 只要芯片与电源相连接，储存的信息始终有效。

7. 在冯·诺依曼结构中，如 80x86 系列计算机，所有的操作都在中央处理器中执行。

8. 静态 RAM 用起来方便且读写周期较短（即读写速度快）。

9. 闪存最主要的用途之一是储存计算机的基本输入输出系统（通常称作 BIOS）。

10. BIOS 软件有很多不同的作用，但它最重要作用是载入操作系统。

# Appendix 6  技术词汇索引

| | | | |
|---|---|---|---|
| absorb | [əbˈsɔːb] | vt. | 吸收；吸引 |
| accelerometer | [əkˌseləˈrɒmitə] | n. | 加速计 |
| accurate | [ˈækjurət] | adj. | 精确的，准确的 |
| adapter | [əˈdæptə] | n. | 接合器；转接器 |
| address | [əˈdres] | vt. | 访问 |
| | | n. | 地址 |
| alcohol | [ˈælkəhɒlə] | n. | 酒精，乙醇；含酒精的饮料 |
| altered | [ˈɔːltəd] | vt. | 改变（alter 的过去分词） |
| aluminum | [əˈljuːminəm] | n. | 铝 |
| ammonia | [əˈməuniə] | n. | [化]氨，氨水 |
| amplifier | [ˈæmplifaiə] | n. | [电子]放大器；扩音器 |
| amplitude | [ˈæmplitjuːd] | n. | 振幅，幅值，幅度 |
| analog | [ˈænəlɔːg] | n. | 模拟 |
| anode | [ˈænəud] | n. | [电]阳极，正极 |
| antenna | [ænˈtenə] | n. | 天线 |
| approximately | [əˈprɔksimitli] | adv. | 大约，近似地；近于 |
| architecture | [ɑːkitektʃə(r)] | n. | 计算机的物理结构 |
| assemble | [əˈsembl] | vt. | 集合，召集，聚集；配装，装 |
| assembler | [əˈsemblə] | n. | 汇编程序；汇编机；装配工 |
| assign | [əˈsain] | vt. | （与 to 连用）分配；指定 |
| astable | [eiˈsteibl] | adj. | 非稳态的，非稳态多谐振荡器 |
| asterisk | [ˈæstərisk] | n. | 星号 |
| | | vt. | 注上星号 |
| axis | [ˈæksis] | n. | 轴；轴线 |
| base | [beis] | n. | 基极 |
| biased | [ˈbaiəst] | adj. | 偏压的，偏置的 |

| | | | |
|---|---|---|---|
| bidirectional | [baidiˈrekʃənəl] | adj. | 双向的;双向作用的 |
| bipolar | [baiˈpəulə(r)] | adj. | 有两极的,双极性的 |
| browsing | [ˈbrauziŋ] | n. | 浏览 |
| bus | [bʌs] | n. | (计算机)总线 |
| cable | [ˈkeib(ə)l] | n. | 电缆,此处指有线电视 |
| calibration | [kæliˈbreiʃən] | n. | 校准,定标,校正 |
| cancellation | [ˈkænsəˈleiʃən] | n. | 取消;删除 |
| capacitance | [kəˈpæsitəns] | n. | 电容量 |
| capacitor | [kəˈpæsitə(r)] | n. | (=capacitator)电容器 |
| capture | [ˈkæptʃə] | n. | 捕获 |
| capturing | [ˈkæptʃəriŋ] | v. | 捕捉(capture 的 ing 形式) |
| carbon | [ˈkɑːbən] | adj. | 碳的,碳处理的 |
| | | n. | [化学]碳 |
| cathode | [ˈkæθəud] | n. | 负极,阴极 |
| ceramic | [siˈræmik] | n. | 陶瓷;陶瓷制品 |
| chamber | [ˈtʃeimbə(r)] | n. | 室,房间;(枪)膛 |
| channel | [ˈtʃænəl] | n. | 海峡;信道,频道 |
| chip | [tʃip] | n. | 电路芯片;碎片;筹码 |
| chrominance | [ˈkrəuminəns] | n. | 色度 |
| circuit | [ˈsəːkit] | n. | 电路;回路;线路图 |
| coexist | [ˈkəuigˈzist] | vi. | 同时存在,与……共存 |
| coil | [kɔil] | n. | 线圈;卷 |
| combine | [kəmˈbain] | vt. | 使结合,混合 |
| | | vi. | 结合 |
| commercial | [kəˈməːʃəl] | adj. | 商业的,商务的 |
| communication | [kəˌmjuːniˈkeiʃən] | n. | 讯息;通信 |
| compact | [kəmˈpækt] | adj. | 紧凑的,紧密的;简洁的 |
| comparatively | [kəmˈpærətivli] | adv. | 对比地;比较地 |
| compass | [ˈkʌmpəs] | n. | 指南针 |

| compilation | [kɔmpi'leiʃən] | n. | 编辑,编译,编绘,编制 |
| compiler | [kəm'pailə] | n. | 编译器;[计]编译程序 |
| condense | [kən'dens] | vi. | (使)浓缩,精简 |
| cursor | ['kə:sə] | n. | 光标;[计]游标,指针 |
| cycle | ['saik(ə)l] | n. | 循环,周期;循环期 |
| cylinder | ['silində] | n. | 圆筒;[数]柱面;圆柱状物 |
| delay | [di'lei] | vt. vi. | 推迟;延缓;迟延 |
| density | ['densəti] | n. | 密度 |
| deservedly | [di'zə:vidli] | adv. | 理所当然地;应得报酬地 |
| dielectric | [daii'lektrik] | n. | 电介质;绝缘体 |
| differentiate | [difə'renʃieit] | vt. | 区分,区别,辨别 |
| digital | ['didʒitəl] | adj. | 数字的 |
| dissipate | ['disipeit] | vt. | 驱散,消散;浪费 |
| distinct | [dis'tiŋkt] | adj. | 明显的;独特的 |
| domestic | [dəu'mestik] | adj. | 国内的;家庭的 |
| dot | [dɔt] | n. | 点,圆点 |
| | | vt. | 在……上打点 |
| double-click | ['dʌbl,klik] | n. | 双击 |
| dual | ['dju:əl] | adj. | 二元的,双的 |
| dyadic | [dai'ædik] | adj. | 二价的;双值的;双积的;二数的 |
| dynamic | [dai'næmik] | adj. | 动力的;动态的 |
| electronics | [ilek'trɔniks] | n. | 电子学 |
| emitter | [i'mitə] | n. | 发射极,发射体 |
| entry | ['entri] | n. | 进入;入口;条目 |
| environment | [in'vaiərənmənt] | n. | 环境,周围 |
| establish | [i'stæbliʃ] | vt. | 建造,确立;认可,证实 |
| evaporation | [ivæpə'reʃ(ə)n] | n. | 蒸发,蒸发作用 |
| eventual | [i'ventʃuəl] | adj. | 最后的,可能的;终于的 |
| fabricate | ['fæbrikeit] | vt. | 制造,组装 |

| 英文 | 音标 | 词性 | 中文 |
|---|---|---|---|
| facilitate | [fə'siliteit] | vt. | 促进;帮助;使容易 |
| family | ['fæmili] | n. | 系列;家族 |
| filament | ['filəmənt] | n. | 灯丝;细丝 |
| fitter | ['fitə] | n. | 装配工 |
|  |  | adj. | 胜任的;适当的 |
| flexibly | ['fleksəbli] | adv. | 易弯曲地,柔韧地 |
| flick | ['flik] | vt. | 轻弹 |
| flip-flop | ['flipflɔp] | n. | [电子]触发器 |
| flowchart | [fləu'tʃɑ:t] | n. | 流程图,程序框图 |
| frame | [freim] | n. | 框,框架;环境;背景 |
| Freon | ['fri:ɔn] | n. | 氟利昂 |
| germanium | [dʒə:'meiniəm] | n. | [化学]锗(32号元素,符号Ge) |
| goal | [gəul] | n. | 目标 |
| graphical | ['græfikəl] | adj. | 图解的;绘画的;生动的 |
| guaranteed | ['gærən'ti:d] | adj. | 保证的 |
| gyroscope | ['dʒaiərəskəup] | n. | 陀螺仪 |
| ignorant | ['ignərənt] | adj. | (常与of,in连用)无知识的 |
| implement | ['implimənt] | n. | 工具;器具 |
|  |  | vt. | 实现;履行 |
| implementation | [implimen'teiʃən] | n. | [计]实现;履行;安装启用 |
| incorporate | [in'kɔ:pəreit] | vt. | 包含;体现 |
| inductor | [in'dʌktə] | n. | 感应器;互感,自感 |
| influential | [influ'enʃəl] | adj. | 有影响的;有势力的 |
| inhibit | [in'hibit] | vt. | 抑制;禁止 |
| innovation | [inəu'veiʃən] | n. | 革新,改革,创新 |
| innovative | ['inəuveitiv] | adj. | 创新的 |
| instrument | ['instrumənt] | n. | 仪器;器具 |
| integrate | ['intigreit] | vt. | 集成,使成整体,使一体化 |
| intensity | [in'tensiti] | n. | 强烈,剧烈;强度,亮度 |

| | | | |
|---|---|---|---|
| interchangeable | [ɪntəˈtʃeɪndʒəbl] | adj. | 可互换的；可交换的 |
| interface | [ˈɪntəfeɪs] | n. | 界面；接口；接触面 |
| interrelate | [ˌɪntərɪˈleɪt] | vt. | （使）互相联系 |
| interval | [ˈɪntəvəl] | n. | 间隔，间距；幕间休息 |
| inverter | [ɪnˈvɜːtə(r)] | n. | 反相器 |
| joule | [dʒuːl] | n. | [物]焦耳（功和能量的单位） |
| leakage | [ˈliːkɪdʒ] | n. | 漏，泄漏，渗漏 |
| linear | [ˈlɪnɪə] | adj. | 直线的，线状的，线性的 |
| liquid | [ˈlɪkwɪd] | n. | 液体，流体 |
| | | adj. | 液体的 |
| location | [ləʊˈkeɪʃ(ə)n] | n. | 地点，位置 |
| magnetron | [ˈmægnɪtrɒn] | n. | 磁电管，磁控管 |
| major | [ˈmeɪdʒə] | adj. | 主要的 |
| | | n. | 主修科目，专业 |
| measure | [ˈmeʒə(r)] | n. | 量度器，测量 |
| | | vt. | 测量 |
| measurement | [ˈmeʒəmənt] | n. | 测量，测量法 |
| merge | [mɜːdʒ] | vi. | 合并；融合 |
| meter | [ˈmiːtə(r)] | n. | 米，公尺；仪表 |
| mica | [ˈmaɪkə] | n. | [矿物]云母 |
| microprocessor | [ˌmaɪkrəʊˈprəʊsesə] | n. | 微处理机 |
| military | [ˈmɪlɪtəri] | adj. | 军事的 |
| miniaturization | [ˌmɪnɪətʃəraɪˈzeɪʃən] | n. | 小型化，微型化 |
| molecule | [ˈmɒlɪkjuːl] | n. | 分子 |
| monolithic | [ˌmɒnəˈlɪθɪk] | adj. | 整体的；庞大的 |
| monostable | [ˈmɒnəʊˌsteɪbl] | adj. | 单稳的；单稳态的 |
| motherboard | [ˈmʌðəbɔːd] | n. | （计算机）主板 |
| multilingual | [ˌmʌltɪˈlɪŋgwəl] | adj. | 使用多种语言的 |
| multimeter | [ˌmʌlˈtɪmɪtə] | n. | [电]万用表 |

| needle | [ˈniːd(ə)l] | n. | 针 |
| --- | --- | --- | --- |
| | | vt. | 刺穿 |
| optimal | [ˈɔptəməl] | adj. | 最佳的,最理想的,最适宜的 |
| optimize | [ˈɔptimaiz] | vt. | 使最优化,优化 |
| oscillation | [ɔsiˈleiʃən] | n. | 振荡,振动;摆动 |
| oscilloscope | [əˈsiləskəup] | n. | 示波器 |
| package | [ˈpækidʒ] | n. | 包,封装 |
| | | vt. | 打包,封装 |
| parameterized | [pəˈræmitəraizd] | adj. | 参数化的 |
| partition | [pɑːˈtiʃən] | n. | 划分,分开;分区 |
| period | [ˈpiərid] | n. | 时期,学时,周期 |
| periodically | [piəriˈɔdikəli] | adj. | 周期的,期刊的 |
| phosphor | [ˈfɔsfə(r)] | n. | 磷;启明星 |
| pin | [pin] | n. | 引脚,腿 |
| | | vt. | 钉住,牵制 |
| pinch | [pintʃ] | n. | 挤压,收缩 |
| pixel | [ˈpiksəl] | n. | 像素,象素,像素点 |
| plasma | [ˈplæzmə] | n. | 等离子体;等离子显示器 |
| plotted | [ˈplɔtid] | adj. | 标绘的 |
| polysilicon | [pɔliˈsilikən] | n. | 多晶硅 |
| portrait | [ˈpɔːtrit] | n. | 肖像 |
| pragmatism | [ˈprægmətizəm] | n. | 实用主义;实际观察 |
| precisely | [priˈsaisli] | adv. | 精确地;准确地 |
| precision | [priˈsiʒən] | n. | 精度 |
| | | adj. | 精确的,精密的 |
| probe | [prəub] | n. | 探针 |
| promote | [prəˈməut] | vt. | 促进;发扬;引起 |
| prompt | [prɔmpt] | vt. | (常与 to 连用)提出,提示 |
| | | n. | 提示,提词,提示符 |

|  |  |  | adj. | 迅速的;及时的 |
|---|---|---|---|---|
| reactance | [riˈæktəns] | n. | | 电抗 |
| reassemble | [riːəˈsembl] | vi. | | 重新集合 |
| recommend | [rekəˈmend] | vt. | | 推荐 |
|  |  | vi. | | 推荐;建议 |
| recruitment | [riˈkruːtmənt] | n. | | 补充;招募 |
| refresh | [riˈfreʃ] | vt. | | 刷新,消除疲劳;恢复精神 |
| refrigerant | [riˈfridʒərənt] | n. | | 致冷剂 |
|  |  | adj. | | 致冷的,冷却的 |
| refrigerator | [riˈfridʒəreitə(r)] | n. | | 冰箱 |
| reinvent | [riːinˈvent] | vt. | | 重新使用,重复发明 |
| representative | [repriˈzentətiv] | adj. | | 代表性的,典型的 |
| resistance | [riˈzistəns] | n. | | [电]电阻值,电阻 |
| resistor | [riˈzistə(r)] | n. | | [电]电阻器,电阻 |
| retina | [ˈretinə] | n. | | 视网膜,网膜,屏幕 |
| retrieval | [riˈtriːvəl] | n. | | 纠正;补偿 |
| rotate | [rəuˈteit] | vi. | | 旋转 |
| saturation | [sætʃəˈreiʃən] | n. | | 饱和;饱和状态 |
| scale | [skeil] | n. | | 标度;比率;缩尺 |
| screw | [skruː] | n. | | 螺旋;螺丝 |
| screwdriver | [ˈskruːdraivə(r)] | n. | | 螺丝刀,改锥 |
| semiconductor | [ˈsemikənˈdʌktə] | n. | | 半导体 |
| sensor | [ˈsensə] | n. | | 传感器 |
| sequence | [ˈsiːkwəns] | n. | | [数][计]序列;顺序 |
| servo | [ˈsəːvəu] | n. | | 伺服电动机 |
| shield | [ˈʃiːld] | n. | | 护罩 |
|  |  | vt. | | 保护,防护 |
| silicon | [ˈsilikən] | n. | | [化学]硅;硅元素 |
| simultaneously | [saiməlˈteinjəsli] | adv. | | 同时进行地,同步地 |

| 单词 | 音标 | 词性 | 释义 |
| --- | --- | --- | --- |
| size | ['saɪz] | n. | 计算机数据的二进制位数 |
| slab | [slæb] | n. | 厚板,平板;厚片 |
| solder | ['sɔldə(r)] | vt. | 焊接 |
| sophisticated | [sə'fɪstɪkeɪtɪd] | adj. | 精细的,高级的,精致的 |
| spreadsheet | ['spredʃiːt] | n. | 电子制表软件;电子数据表 |
| standby | ['stændbaɪ] | n. | 待机 |
| status | ['steɪtəs] | n. | 状态 |
| subcomponents | [sʌbkəm'pəʊnənt] | n. | 子部件 |
| superimposed | [sjuːpərɪm'pəʊzd] | adj. | 成阶层的,重叠的 |
| switch | [swɪtʃ] | n. | 开关,转换 |
| | | vt. | 转换,转变 |
| synchronous | ['sɪŋkrənəs] | adj. | 同步的,同时的 |
| synthesize | ['sɪnθɪsaɪz] | vt. | 综合;合成;(使)合成 |
| telegraph | ['telɪɡrɑːf] | n. | 电报,电信 |
| telemetry | [tɪ'lemɪtrɪ] | n. | 遥测技术,测距术 |
| terminal | ['tɜːmɪnəl] | n. | 终端机;终端 |
| threshold | ['θreʃhəʊld] | n. | 阈值,阈限 |
| timer | ['taɪmə] | n. | 定时器;计时器;时钟 |
| tolerance | ['tɔlərəns] | n. | 公差 |
| topology | [təʊ'pɔlədʒɪ] | n. | 拓扑数学 |
| toxic | ['tɔksɪk] | adj. | 毒的;中毒的,有毒的 |
| transistor | [træn'sɪstə] | n. | 晶体管,三极管 |
| transmit | [træns'mɪt] | vt. | 传送,传播 |
| | | vi. | 播送信号 |
| tray | [treɪ] | n. | 托盘;文件盒 |
| trigger | ['trɪɡə] | vt. | 引发,引起;触发 |
| tube | [tjuːb] | n. | 管 |
| twist | [twɪst] | n. | 扭曲 |
| | | vt. | 拧,扭曲 |

| | | | |
|---|---|---|---|
| vacuum | ['vækjuəm] | n. | 真空 |
| valve | [vælv] | n. | 阀;活门;气门 |
| vertically | ['vɜːtɪk(ə)li] | adv. | 垂直地 |
| well-informed | [welɪn'fɔːmd] | adj. | 消息灵通的,熟悉的,博识的 |
| zone | [zəun] | n. | 存储区;带,层;区域,范围 |

# 参考文献

[1] 朱一纶. 电子技术专业英语. 北京：电子工业出版社,2010.

[2] 张福强. 电子信息技术专业英语. 北京：机械工业出版社,2010.

[3] 杨志忠,卫桦林. 数字电子技术基础. 北京：高等教育出版社,2010.

[4] 孙萍. 电子技术专业英语. 北京：机械工业出版社,2005.

[5] Allan R. Hambley. 李春茂改编. 电子技术基础. 英语改编版. 北京：电子工业出版社,2005.

[6] San Jose. intro_to_quartus2. Altera Corporation101 Innovation Drive，CA 95134. http://www.altera.com.

[7] 王德年. 计算机专业英语. 北京：机械工业出版社,2006.

| | | | |
|---|---|---|---|
| vacuum | [ˈvækjuəm] | n. | 真空 |
| valve | [vælv] | n. | 阀;活门;气门 |
| vertically | [ˈvə:tik(ə)li] | adv. | 垂直地 |
| well-informed | [welinˈfɔ:md] | adj. | 消息灵通的,熟悉的,博识的 |
| zone | [zəun] | n. | 存储区;带,层;区域,范围 |

# 参考文献

[1] 朱一纶. 电子技术专业英语. 北京：电子工业出版社，2010.
[2] 张福强. 电子信息技术专业英语. 北京：机械工业出版社，2010.
[3] 杨志忠，卫桦林. 数字电子技术基础. 北京：高等教育出版社，2010.
[4] 孙萍. 电子技术专业英语. 北京：机械工业出版社，2005.
[5] Allan R. Hambley. 李春茂改编. 电子技术基础. 英语改编版. 北京：电子工业出版社，2005.
[6] San Jose. intro_to_quartus2. Altera Corporation101 Innovation Drive，CA 95134. http://www.altera.com.
[7] 王德年. 计算机专业英语. 北京：机械工业出版社，2006.